THE CONSTITUTION OF AUSTRALIA

Consistently with the aims of the series, the book canvasses the Australian constitutional system in a way that explains its form and operation, provides a critical evaluation of it and conveys a sense of the contemporary national debate. The chapters deal with the foundations of Australian constitutionalism, its history from the time of European settlement, the nature of the Australian Constitutions, the framework for judicial review, the legislative, executive and judicial branches of government, federalism and multi-level government and rights protection. Running through all chapters is the story of the gradual evolution of Australian constitutionalism within the lean but almost unchanging framework of the formal, written, national Constitution. A second theme traces the way in which the present, distinctive, constitutional arrangements in Australia emerged from creative tension between the British and United States constitutional traditions on which the Australian Constitution originally drew and which continues to manifest itself in various ways. One of these, which is likely to be of particular interest, is Australian reliance on institutional arrangements for the purpose of the protection of rights. The book is written in a clear and accessible style for readers in both Australia and countries around the world. Each chapter is followed by additional references to enable particular issues to be pursued further by readers who seek to do so.

D0024302

Constitutional Systems of the World
General Editors: Peter Leyland and Andrew Harding
Associate Editors: Benjamin L Berger and Alexander Fischer

In the era of globalisation, issues of constitutional law and good governance are being seen increasingly as vital issues in all types of society. Since the end of the Cold War, there have been dramatic developments in democratic and legal reform, and post-conflict societies are also in the throes of reconstructing their governance systems. Even societies already firmly based on constitutional governance and the rule of law have undergone constitutional change and experimentation with new forms of governance; and their constitutional systems are increasingly subjected to comparative analysis and transplantation. Constitutional texts for practically every country in the world are now easily available on the internet. However, texts which enable one to understand the true context, purposes, interpretation and incidents of a constitutional system are much harder to locate, and are often extremely detailed and descriptive. This series seeks to provide scholars and students with accessible introductions to the constitutional systems of the world, supplying both a road map for the novice and, at the same time, a deeper understanding of the key historical, political and legal events which have shaped the constitutional landscape of each country. Each book in this series deals with a single country, and each author is an expert in their field.

Published volumes

The Constitution of the United Kingdom
The Constitution of the United States
The Constitution of Vietnam
The Constitution of South Africa
The Constitution of Germany
The Constitution of Japan
The Constitution of Finland

Forthcoming titles in this series

The Constitution of France
Sophie Boyron

The Constitution of Ireland
Colm O'Cinneide

The Constitution of the Russian Federation
Jane Henderson

Link to series website
http://www.hartpub.co.uk/series/csw

The Constitution of Australia

A Contextual Analysis

Cheryl Saunders

·HART·
PUBLISHING

OXFORD AND PORTLAND, OREGON
2011

Published in the United Kingdom by Hart Publishing Ltd
16C Worcester Place, Oxford, OX1 2JW
Telephone: +44 (0)1865 517530
Fax: +44 (0)1865 510710
E-mail: mail@hartpub.co.uk
Website: http://www.hartpub.co.uk

Published in North America (US and Canada) by
Hart Publishing
c/o International Specialized Book Services
920 NE 58th Avenue, Suite 300
Portland, OR 97213-3786
USA
Tel: +1 503 287 3093 or toll-free: (1) 800 944 6190
Fax: +1 503 280 8832
E-mail: orders@isbs.com
Website: http://www.isbs.com

British Library Cataloguing in Publication Data
Data Available

ISBN: 978-1-84113-734-6

Typeset by Hope Services Ltd, Abingdon
Printed and bound in Great Britain by
TJ International Ltd, Padstow, Cornwall

For my family

Preface

This book is one of a series on Constitutions of the World. The aim of the series is to provide access to knowledge about the constitutional system of each of the countries concerned in a manner that explains its form and operation, offers a critical evaluation of it and conveys a sense of the contemporary national constitutional debate. The series as a whole is a contribution to the discipline of comparative constitutional law and is designed to capture many of its benefits. As it develops, it should become an increasingly useful indicator of international trends in constitutional law, as well as a tool for international understanding.

Two of the principal benefits of comparative constitutional law are to deepen constitutional knowledge across jurisdictional boundaries and to cast familiar domestic constitutional arrangements in a new light. In writing this book, I have attempted to capture both. To that end, I have tried to explain Australia from an insider's point of view in a way that also anticipates queries that those less familiar with the Australian constitutional system may have. At the same time, I have tried to reflect on Australia from a comparative perspective, in order to add some new dimensions to old themes for Australian readers. It is inevitable that neither purpose will be fully achieved, not only because of the constraints imposed by a relatively short book but also because the goals themselves are ambitious. Nevertheless, I hope that the book will be of interest to both audiences. I welcome comments, which will certainly be taken into account if a second edition eventuates.

Like any constitutional system, and in particular one that has developed organically over a considerable period of time, the Australian arrangements are distinctive in many respects. Two are worth noting in particular. The first is the evolutionary character of the Australian constitutional system, exemplified by reliance on incremental change, typically driven by opportunity rather than design, which attaches high priority to legal and institutional continuity and eschews an even mildly revolutionary legal break. While this characteristic is not unique to Australia, it takes an extreme form here. Most notably, the entrenched national Constitution predates independence, to which it has been gradually adapted over a period of at least 90 years by a combination of constitutional practice, highly technical mirror legislation enacted in both the United Kingdom and Australia and sometimes creative judicial interpretation. Such an approach has advantages in terms of stability and a degree of flexibility, but these are achieved at the cost of complexity and opacity. Substantive consequences to which this volume draws attention include a weak constitutional conception of citizenship; some ambiguity over the source of authority for the written constitutions and hence for the organs of state that they establish; and the retention of institutions that were imperial in origin, of which the monarchy is the most obvious example, in forms that have been moulded to better reflect contemporary realities by the same evolutionary processes.

Secondly, Australia may now be the only developed country with a liberal democratic system of government that lacks a national constitutional or legislative bill or charter of rights and that places correspondingly greater reliance on the organisation of public power for the purposes of rights protection. Australia does not provide a perfect example of political constitutionalism. The Constitutions are entrenched and the framework for the institutions established by them is protected by judicial review, offering some derivative rights protection in consequence. Given the vigour of the debate on judicial review elsewhere in the world, however, much of which is sparked by judicial interpretation of constitutional rights, the Australian experience is likely to be of some interest. As readers will see, the outcomes are mixed. Australia has a reasonable record of rights protection, although no better than might be expected of a state that enjoys such favourable economic, geographic, demographic and political circumstances. The Australian judicial system is characterised by a high degree of judicial independence, although it is too simplistic to attribute this to the absence of systemic rights protection, occasional arguments to the contrary. Rights consciousness is patchy, both in public institutions and amongst the public at large. And once again, these arrangements are complex.

The book is organised around eight chapters. The first three are scene-setting, in various ways. Chapter one outlines four foundations of the Australian constitutional system, on which the rest of the volume builds. Three of these are explained in terms of historical phases, but between them they account for many of the defining features of Australian constitutional arrangements. These features comprise, in particular, the common law origins of Australian constitutionalism, involving the adoption of typically common law constitutional institutions and principles; the federal character of the Australian polity, which infuses all aspects of the Commonwealth Constitution, however reluctant federalists Australians may be and which also accounts for the distinctive Australian combination of aspects of United States constitutional design with institutions in the British constitutional tradition; and the various constitutional consequences of the long, slow, march to independence. The fourth of the foundations with which chapter one deals concerns the relationship of Aboriginal Australians to the rest of the Australian polity, characterised in contemporary parlance in terms of reconciliation. While in one sense this represents another trajectory of the earlier historical phases it is also treated here as a foundational issue in its own right, with constitutional as well as other dimensions.

Chapters two and three elaborate these foundations in several ways, in order to assist understanding of the rest of the volume. Chapter two examines the conception of a Constitution that is the product of Australian history and constitutional tradition, in terms of status, legitimacy, and relationship with the rest of the legal order. This chapter deals separately with the constitutions of the two spheres of Australian federal government, the Commonwealth and the States, because on this issue there are significant differences between them. A similar approach is taken elsewhere in the book, where the differences between the spheres of government are sufficiently marked to warrant separate treatment. Chapter three outlines the methods and procedures of judicial review in Australia, the substantive consequences of which become apparent in the chapters that follow. While Australian judicial review is clearly in the common law tradition, it has some distinctive features, which can usefully be explained at this point. Not the least of these is the prevalence of an interpretive method still commonly known as legalism, which offers another point of contrast with many constitutional systems elsewhere.

The remaining five chapters deal with the principal substantive features of the Australian constitutional system. Chapters four to six are concerned with the legislative, executive and judicial branches of government respectively. Chapters seven and eight deal with the organising principles for federalism and rights protection. All but the last of these chapters follow a broadly similar pattern, insofar as in each the opening part canvasses the principles at stake before the manner in which they are given effect is examined in greater detail. In this way, the book explains and explores the main principles on which the Australian constitutional system rests: representative democracy; responsible government;

separation of powers, with its umbilical link to judicial independence and the rule of law; and federalism. Chapter eight necessarily is somewhat different, given the Australian approach to the protection of rights. The function of this chapter is to draw together the various threads of rights protection that have emerged from the earlier institutional chapters; to augment them with some new material, including the meaning and operation of the few entrenched constitutional rights, the contribution of the common law to rights protection and the impact of international human rights law; and to attempt an assessment of the whole. In effect, chapter eight thus serves as a conclusion to the volume.

The stability of Australian government is made possible through and nurtured by incremental change. Even as this book was being finalised a series of changes of this nature were in train. The federal election of 2010 resulted in the first minority government at the national level for 70 years; the independent Members on whom the government was forced to rely in order to continue in office demanded a degree of parliamentary reform as the price of their support; the High Court confirmed that the Commonwealth Constitution protects a right to vote, although its reasons for decision are not available at the time of writing. Continual minor but significant developments in constitutional law and practice are a hazard of any constitutional scholarship and readers should bear the potential for these in mind. Similarly, it may be expected that many of the general trends identified in this book will continue, including the insistence by the High Court that Australian constitutional law must now be traced to Australian sources, which in turn places increasing demands on the spare terms of the Commonwealth Constitution.

In the circumstances, major change is less likely. Nevertheless, as the analysis in the substantive chapters shows, many of the features of the Australian constitutional system are under a degree of pressure, which ultimately may be relieved in some way. The weight placed on electoral democracy in the Australian approach to representative and responsible government already is a target of parliamentary reformers in the wake of the 2010 elections. Whatever the future of these particular initiatives, there is enough unease about the dominance of a single governing party between elections to suggest that a somewhat more participatory and deliberative approach to government needs to be worked out. The messy compromise over the way in which the monarchy is accommodated in the Australian constitutional system makes it inevitable that the need to establish a republic will be examined seriously again at some stage although whether the opportunity will be taken to consider the broader implications of republicanism, at least to the point of rethinking monarchical forms, is far less clear. The continuing tension over Australian federalism, fuelled by the weakening of the States through a severe fiscal imbalance, demands a solution of some kind. Ideally, this would involve some rebalancing of power, coupled with revitalisation of the State sphere of government, which also would benefit democracy. As long as this remains in the too-hard basket, however, progressively deepening instalments of intergovernmental co-operation respond to particular immediate needs while exacerbating the overall problem. The introduction of legislative bills of rights in Victoria and the Australian Capital Territory raises the possibility that other States will follow suit; if this movement continues, which remains to be seen, it will throw the lack of systemic rights protection at the national level into relief eventually, perhaps, prompting more effective action than has been proposed so far. Like many other states that adhere to a form of dualism, Australia is grappling with the increasing interdependence of domestic and international law, both generally and in the constitutional context. While major rationalisation is unlikely, this phenomenon already has affected the operations of all branches of government and can be expected to continue to do so.

Many people have assisted with the writing of this book, sometimes without being aware of it. In this regard I should mention in particular my colleagues in the Centre for Comparative Constitutional Studies and at Melbourne Law School generally, who provide an intellectually challenging but collegial atmosphere in which constitutional ideas can be frankly explored and who responded generously to occasional requests to read parts of the manuscript. I am also grateful to Corpus Christi College at the University of Oxford, where I spent two peaceful terms as a Visiting Fellow in 2009, enabling writing to get underway. I have learnt a great deal from colleagues in various international constitutional networks over many years, enabling me to acquire an understanding of many other constitutional systems as well as insights into what is distinctive about the Australian experience that I almost certainly could not have gained on my own. I appreciate the support and advice of the editors of this series, Andrew Harding and Peter Leyland and I owe specific thanks to Peter for his detailed comments on successive drafts, which unerringly highlighted parts of the manuscript that required further attention. My thanks also to Putachad Leyland, who made the early stages of planning fun, as she pressed me for ideas on which she might draw in designing the splendid cover. I am particularly grateful to Richard Hart, for his uncanny knack of providing just the right amount of encouragement at critical moments. Most of all, my thanks go to my husband, Ian Baker, who was either vociferously enthusiastic or tactfully quiet at all the right times as writing progressed and was unfailingly positive throughout.

Cheryl Saunders
September 2010

Table of Contents

Table of Cases

Federal Court of Australia

Privy Council

Supreme Court of the Northern Territory

Supreme Court of Victoria

Table of Legislation

CONSTITUTION OF THE COMMONWEALTH OF AUSTRALIA

AUSTRALIA—Commonwealth Legislation

AUSTRALIA—State Legislation

CANADA

NEW ZEALAND

SOUTH AFRICA

SWITZERLAND

UNITED KINGDOM

UNITED STATES

INTERNATIONAL INSTRUMENTS

1

Foundations

———•◦•———

I. SETTLEMENT

A. Constitutional Consequences

HISTORIANS BELIEVE THAT humans first reached Australia quite early after their dispersal from Africa, around 60,000 years ago.[1] Australia's current constitutional arrangements have relatively recent origins, however. The first of four formative events that are examined in this chapter was British colonisation of the territory that now is Australia within two decades after Captain James Cook claimed possession of 'the whole eastern coast' in 1770 in the name of the British King.[2]

The first colony was a penal settlement.[3] The ships that arrived from England in 1788 under the command of Captain Arthur Phillip in order to establish a permanent settlement at Sydney Cove carried only convicts, marines, officials and their families. Unlike other British colonies to which convicts were transported, there was no civilian population, the Aboriginal peoples aside. In the circumstances, the arrangements for government were necessarily unusual; Phillip and his immediate successors as Governor held sweeping local authority which they exercised without representative institutions of any kind for 35

---

[1] C Renfrew, *Prehistory* (London, Phoenix, 2007) 102, 129.
[2] R Hough, *Captain James Cook*, (London, Hodder and Stoughton Ltd, 1994) 158.
[3] All Australian colonies except South Australia received convicts at some stage; transportation finally was abolished in 1868.

years. Nevertheless, even at this stage there was rudimentary provision for adjudication and a skeletal base on which constitutional government eventually would build. After an initial period of indecision on the part of the Imperial authorities, the Commission issued to Phillip, shortly before his departure, encouraged the development of the settlement as a colony and not merely a 'penal establishment under military government'.[4] As the character of the population changed through emancipation and an increase in the numbers of free settlers, the rule of law was gradually strengthened[5] and embryonic institutions of representative government began to emerge in response to demand.

It has sometimes been asked, only partly in jest, whether Australia's convict origins have affected its national character, with implications for attitudes to authority, including what poet Les Murray has termed Australian 'ability to laugh at venerated things'.[6] Whatever the answer, in other respects the manner of British colonisation was formative in Australian constitutional development. The pattern of British settlement determined the territorial organisation of the land mass, initially in the form of colonies and subsequently as the States and territories of the Australian federation. Settlement by the British rather than by any other European power ensured that Australian law had a foundation in English law and that the Australian legal system adopted the principles and practices of the common law tradition. At the same time, assumptions about the basis on which the common law was absorbed into Australia had disastrous consequences for the indigenous inhabitants, of whom there may have been around 500,000 when the first fleet arrived, which provide a rationale for the modern reconciliation movement.[7] British settlement also meant that the institutional structure of government that developed in Australia would be modelled broadly on the institutions, principles and practices familiar in Britain itself, adapted to suit Australian conditions and preferences including, over time, the perceived necessities of federation.

---

[4] V Windeyer, '"A Birthright and Inheritance" The Establishment of the Rule of Law in Australia' (1958–1963) 1 *Tasmania University Law Review* 639, 646.

[5] D Neal, *The Rule of Law in a Penal Colony: Law and Politics in Early New South Wales*, 2nd edn (Cambridge, CUP, 2002).

[6] L Murray, 'Some Religious Stuff I know about Australia' quoted in J Hirst, 'An Oddity from the Start: Convicts and National Character' (2008) 36 *The Monthly*.

[7] Present estimates lie between 315,000 and 750,000; the numbers may have been higher still: Australian Bureau of Statistics, *Year Book Australia, 2008*, 1301.8.

B. Territorial Organisation

With a total land mass of more than 7.5 million square kilometres Australia is only slightly smaller than the continental United States, excluding Alaska. It is much more sparsely populated, however, with a population of around 21.5 million in 2010. The relatively low population density of 2.6 people per square kilometre can be attributed in part to the terrain, two-thirds of which is arid or semi-arid. The level of its unpredictable rainfall makes Australia the driest continent in the world, apart from Antarctica.

The topography of the country also helps to explain the pattern of settlement and development. The principal original colonies were scattered around the coast in relatively hospitable locations, at considerable distances from each other. The first in time was a huge eastern colony of New South Wales, notionally covering more than half the continent, centred on the first settlement in Sydney from 1788. Over the following 40 or so years, satellite settlements were established along the east coast to the south and the north in what now are the cities of Hobart, Melbourne and Brisbane and which became the capitals of the colonies of Tasmania, Victoria and Queensland respectively. By 1859 all three had separated from New South Wales. Thereafter, for the most part, they developed independently, although under the same imperial umbrella and with a degree of intercolonial co-operation. For a brief period in 1839–40 New Zealand was governed from New South Wales as well, until the Treaty of Waitangi was signed, British sovereignty was formally proclaimed, and New Zealand was established as a colony in its own right.[8]

In 1829 another huge colony that now is Western Australia was established to lay claim to the remainder of the continent, centred on settlements in the south-west, one of which eventually became the capital city of Perth. Seven years later Adelaide was founded in the centre of the south coast, as the capital of the first fully free settlement, the Province of South Australia. For more than 40 years from 1863 the extended boundaries of this colony cut a swathe through the centre of the continent, from south to north, incorporating the Northern Territory, for which the town of Darwin was established on the north coast in

---

[8] P Joseph, *Constitutional and Administrative Law in New Zealand,* 2nd edn (Wellington, Brookers, 2001) 37–38.

1869. There was no significant change to this territorial organisation of the mainland of Australia and Tasmania after 1863 apart from the separation of the Northern Territory from South Australia in 1911 and the carving out from New South Wales of the Australian Capital Territory, in which the city of Canberra was established, as the seat of federal government in 1911.

The original colonial settlements thus became the principal cities: magnets for population, industry and government, often at the expense of development elsewhere, even where development was feasible. The Australia of the early twenty-first century is a highly urbanised and centralised society, with 65 per cent of the population living in eight cities that in turn are the capitals of the six Original States and two self-governing territories of the Australian federation. Five of the eight constituent units are huge in territorial terms and the two largest, Western Australia and Queensland, cover more than half the continent between them. The distances between State capitals vary from 883 kilometres in the case of the two most populous cities of Sydney and Melbourne, to almost 4,000 kilometres, covering three time zones, which lie between Sydney and Perth.

The territorial organisation of Australia has not gone unchallenged. There have been movements to create new States since federation.[9] None has succeeded, however, and while the Northern Territory may yet become a State, this would not fundamentally alter the territorial division of the country.[10] Proposals for the federal constitutional recognition of local government as a constituent partner in the federation also have been debated for more than 30 years and this remains a live issue despite rejection at referendum in 1988.[11] There are occasional calls for the abolition of federalism altogether, sometimes tempered by proposals to create a larger number of regions, exercising devolved power of some kind.[12] Major structural change nevertheless seems unlikely; and not only because of the innate advantage of the status quo and the difficulty of

---

[9]   A Twomey, 'Regionalism—A Cure for Federal Ills?' (2008) 31 *University of New South Wales Law Journal* 467, 483–85.

[10]   A history of the statehood movement until 2007 is provided in House of Representatives Standing Committee on Legal and Constitutional Affairs, Commonwealth Parliament, *The Long Road to Statehood*, 2007.

[11]   AJ Brown, 'In pursuit of the "Genuine Partnership": Local Government and Federal Constitutional Reform in Australia' (2008) 31 *University of New South Wales Law Journal* 435, 437–49.

[12]   Twomey, 'Regionalism' (2008), n 9 above.

constitutional amendment, outlined in chapter two. This is one of the fault lines of the Australian constitutional system, at which a range of conflicting preferences intersect, over the choices between versions of federalism and unitary government; a controlled and an uncontrolled constitution; parliamentary sovereignty and constitutional checks and balances; and the interests of Australians who live close to the centre of national power in the south-east of the country and those who live further away.

C. Common Law and Legal System

Settlement by Britain in the late eighteenth and early nineteenth centuries left the Australian colonies with a foundation of English law and with legal systems in the common law tradition.

The former incorporated into Australian law a range of English statutes of constitutional significance, including the Magna Carta, the Bill of Rights 1688, the Act of Settlement 1700 and the Habeas Corpus Act 1679, concepts of tenure and estates in property that recognised the ultimate title of the Crown and core constitutional principles derived from judicial decisions.[13] While most early English statutes have now been repealed by State Parliaments, foundational measures such as those listed above generally have been retained.[14]

The introduction of a common law legal system also influenced subsequent Australian constitutional development. The Commonwealth Constitution itself was predicated upon the principles and practices of the common law although, as chapter two shows, the precise nature of the relationship between the two is still being worked out. Until well into the twentieth century, Australian law was part of a more or less unified body of common law that applied throughout the former British Empire. Even after the emergence of distinctive national systems of common law, Australian law continued to be influenced by developments elsewhere in the common law world.[15]

[13] For example, *Case of Proclamations* [1611] 12 Co Rep 74; *Prohibitions del Roy*, [1607] 12 Co Rep 63.

[14] States have enacted Imperial Acts Application Acts for this purpose: see for example Imperial Acts Application Act 1980 (Vic). See generally PM McDermott, 'Imperial Statutes in Australia and New Zealand' (1990) 2 *Bond Law Review* 162.

[15] A Mason, 'The Break with the Privy Council and the Internationalisation of the Common Law', in P Cane (ed), *Centenary Essays for the High Court of Australia*

There is nothing unusual about the idea that colonisers take with them the law that is familiar at home. In the case of British colonies settled at the turn of the nineteenth century, this familiar colonial technique was given additional impetus by belief in the superiority of the common law and pride in the constitutional protections that it was deemed to confer. The effect of introduced law on an existing population, however, depended on the basis on which sovereignty over the territory was claimed, further complicated, in the case of Australia, by parallel changes in the conception of sovereignty over the critical period.[16] In the late eighteenth century the prevailing classification distinguished between colonies acquired by conquest or cession on the one hand and those acquired by occupation, on the other. In conquered or ceded colonies the existing law remained in place for local inhabitants unless overridden by the law of the new sovereign. In an occupied or settled colony, on the other hand, the territory was 'uninhabited', or at least 'desert and uncultivated' and English law was 'automatically there in force'.[17]

From the outset, Australia was treated largely as if it fell into the category of land acquired by occupation. For the most part there was no attempt to conclude treaties with the indigenous inhabitants; and the one attempt made, in Victoria, was repudiated by the Governor in 1835 as 'void and of no effect against the rights of the Crown'.[18] The conflict that followed settlement might well have been categorised as conquest, but there was no formal acknowledgement of the laws of the conquered peoples and of their relationship to the land.[19] English law was simply absorbed to the extent that it was applicable. In New South Wales and Tasmania, reception continued until 1828, when the circumstances of the colonies had begun to normalise and Legislative Councils had been established to make laws for the future.[20]

(Chatswood, NSW, LexisNexis Butterworths, 2004) 66, 72, noting that the emergence of the Australian common law and the internationalisation of the common law were 'virtually contemporaneous'.

[16]   B Attwood, *Possession* (Melbourne, Vic, The Miegunyah Press, 2009) 76 ff.

[17]   W Blackstone, *Commentaries on the Law of England* Book 1, (Dublin, Exshaw et al, 1766) 104–05.

[18]   Attwood, n 16, 83–84.

[19]   There was some difference in the official attitude in South Australia although not in the result: S Banner, 'Why *Terra Nullius*? Anthropology and Property Law in Early Australia' (2005) 23 *Law and History Review* 95, 120–22.

[20]   Australian Courts Act 1828 (Imp), s.24. The reception dates in the other colonies are WA (1 June 1829) and SA (28 December 1836).

The treatment of the Australian colonies was 'unusual' in this respect.[21] By contrast, colonies settled both earlier and later, in North America and New Zealand, were formally considered to be conquered or ceded or a combination of the two. The explanation may be traced in part to reports taken back to England from Cook's expedition, after claiming possession of New South Wales in 1770. According to the naturalist Sir Joseph Banks, the land was 'immense' but 'thinly inhabited' and it was possible that the interior was 'totally uninhabited'. Before he left for New South Wales in 1787, Phillips himself noted 'the general opinion' that there are 'very few Inhabitants in the Country'.[22]

Once the first fleet arrived at Sydney Cove it soon became evident that these assumptions were incorrect. Initially, however, it was unclear that the Indigenous peoples themselves were subject to the common law. But over the course of the nineteenth century, spurred by a more territorial conception of sovereignty, the present understanding of the Australian colonies as settled, with all its attendant legal consequences, gradually hardened into law, until finally confirmed by the Privy Council in 1889.[23] It was rationalised with the earlier tripartite theory by extending the notion of 'uninhabited' to include territory that was 'practically unoccupied, without settled inhabitants or settled law'.[24]

Reception of the common law on this basis profoundly affected the Aboriginal peoples as they came in contact with it, although in some cases contact was delayed for more than 100 years. It precluded legal recognition of their relationship to land and underpinned their dispossession, without process or attempt at compensation. More than 200 years later, in *Mabo (No 2)*, the understanding of the basis on which sovereignty had been claimed was revised by the High Court of Australia.[25] *Mabo* acknowledges the presence of Indigenous peoples at the time of British settlement and accepts that their pre-existing interests in the land can be recognised by the common law unless lawfully extinguished, typically by legislation. The decision does not disturb the claim of sovereignty itself, however, or the monopoly of the common law.

---

[21] P McHugh, *Aboriginal Societies and the Common Law* (Oxford, OUP, 2004) 4.

[22] Both quotations are taken from Banner, n 19, 99.

[23] *Cooper v Stuart* [1889] UKPC 1.

[24] Ibid, at [11]. See also G Simpson, '*Mabo,* International Law, *Terra Nullius* and the Stories of Settlement: an Unresolved Jurisprudence' (1993) 19 *Melbourne University Law Review* 195.

[25] *Mabo v Queensland (No 2)* (1992) 175 CLR 1.

D. Institutions

Each of the six Australian colonies achieved self-government under a Constitution of its own during the latter part of the nineteenth century. The institutions of government thus established were broadly similar to each other, to those in other comparable British colonies and to those in the United Kingdom itself. The Parliaments were bicameral, although their upper Houses, however conservative, were elected or appointed, rather than hereditary. Governments were drawn from the Parliament and depended on the support or 'confidence' of the lower, popularly elected House for continuation in office. The colonial governments in turn advised the Crown in the exercise of its powers, subject to instructions from London to the contrary, thus completing the link between Parliament and executive government that is the hallmark of a system of responsible government. Each colony also had a hierarchy of courts, culminating in a Supreme Court, from which appeal lay to the Privy Council in London.

In some respects, however, even at this early stage Australian institutions had distinctive characteristics. The development of Australian colonial government was influenced by the events and the ideas of the time: the demands of the Chartist movement in England, coinciding with revolutions in continental Europe; the struggle to extend the franchise in the United Kingdom, culminating in the Reform Acts of 1832 and 1867; the spread of utilitarianism through the work of Jeremy Bentham and JS Mill, with its pragmatism and emphasis on outcomes;[26] the rise of positivism and the command theory of law, with successive editions of John Austin's lectures, from 1832;[27] the consolidation of parliamentary sovereignty in the writings of AV Dicey towards the end of the century.[28] The Australian context was conducive to the embrace of such ideas: new systems of government, on which heavy demands were placed by the need for colonial development and a rapid influx of population following the discovery of gold in the 1850s. Famously, one consequence was substantial progress in the practice of electoral democracy over the

[26] M Warnock, 'Introduction' in M Warnock (ed), *Utilitarianism and On Liberty,* (Oxford, Blackwell, 2003).

[27] WE Rumble (ed), J Austin, *The Province of Jurisprudence Determined* (New York, CUP, 1995) comprising the text of the 5th edition of 1885.

[28] AV Dicey, *Introduction to the Study of the Law of the Constitution,* first published 1885.

course of the nineteenth century, with the introduction of universal suffrage for white males in lower Houses of Parliament; the extension of the franchise to white women in two colonies before the end of the century;[29] payment of Members; the secret ballot; shorter parliamentary terms; and Saturday voting.[30] There is debate about the extent to which the influence of some of these early attitudes continues, with results that are less benign.[31] On any view, however, electoral democracy remains a dominant focus of the Australian constitutional system.

II. FEDERATION

A. Process

i. Early Interest in Union

The possibility that some or all of the Australian colonies might form a federation of some kind was considered in both London and the colonies themselves as the huge Eastern colony of New South Wales fragmented.[32] In many ways, such a course was obvious. Most, although certainly not all, of the settlers had come from Britain or Ireland. They shared both the challenges and opportunities of living in a huge land of great economic promise with an often harsh terrain and unpredictable seasons more than 19,000 kilometres from the Imperial authorities in London. The United States and, in due course, Canada offered contemporary examples of ways in which unity and local self-government could effectively be combined in broadly similar circumstances. As the century wore on, co-operation between the colonies became increasingly frequent: 83 intercolonial

[29] South Australia (1894) and Western Australia (1899).

[30] M Sawer, 'Inventing the Nation Through the Ballot Box', Papers on Parliament 37, Australian Senate, 2001.

[31] H Collins, 'Political Ideology in Australia: The Distinctiveness of a Benthamite Society' in S Graubard (ed), *Australia: The Daedalus Symposium* (Sydney, NSW, Angus and Robertson, 1985) 147; Cf M Sawer, 'Comment: The Australian Settlement Undone' (1996) 39 *Australian Journal of Political Science* 35.

[32] Evidence for the idea is clear in the 1840s: J Quick and RR Garran, *Annotated Constitution of the Australian Commonwealth* (Sydney, NSW, Angus and Robertson, 1901) 81ff. There may be earlier signs still, dating from the separation of Van Diemen's Land, later Tasmania, in 1825: AJ Brown, 'Constitutional Schizophrenia Then and Now', Lectures in the Senate Occasional Lecture Series 2003–2004, *The Distinctive Foundations of Australian Democracy*, 14–17.

conferences were held between 1860 and 1900, over matters ranging from the overland telegraph to the collection of statistics, the maintenance of lighthouses, quarantine and defence.[33]

ii. *The Later Federation Movement Begins*

Nevertheless, no tangible steps towards federal union were taken until later in the century. In 1885, a form of confederation was established involving four Australian colonies, New Zealand and Fiji, but never New South Wales; and South Australia was a member only for a short period. The Federal Council of Australasia survived until 1900 but weakness in its structure and membership left it with only a minor role in the progression towards federation.

What with hindsight can be accepted as the beginning of the final phase was a conference of colonial leaders in Melbourne in 1890 at which all the Australian colonies and New Zealand were represented. The immediate catalyst for the meeting was colonial defence, although intercolonial tariff competition and immigration were other significant factors and federation also drew momentum from developing national sentiment, manifested in the art and literature of the time.[34] The Australasian Federation Conference agreed that 'the best interests and the present and future prosperity of the Australian colonies will be promoted by an early union under the Crown' and called for a 'National Australasian Convention . . . to consider and report upon an adequate scheme for a Federal Constitution'.[35] In the event, however, agreement on a Constitution required two Conventions and involved a decade of negotiations, characterised by perseverance, pragmatism and laborious balancing of competing interests.

iii. *The Conventions*

The first Convention met in 1891. Termed the National Australasian Convention, it comprised delegations drawn from the Parliaments of all Australian colonies and New Zealand. A draft Constitution was agreed in just over a month, but the next steps depended on the respective

---

[33] SG Foster, S Marsden, R Russell (eds), *Federation: The Guide to Records* (Canberra, NSW, National Archives of Australia, 1998) section 1.

[34] J Hirst, *The Sentimental Nation* (Melbourne, Vic, OUP, 2000) 15.

[35] Quick and Garran, n 32, 120–21.

Parliaments, and these were preoccupied with an economic depression, industrial unrest and other more immediate matters. By 1893, according to contemporary commentators John Quick and Robert Garran, 'the Parliamentary process of dealing with the Commonwealth Bill had broken down hopelessly'.[36]

In the light of this experience, the next attempt at federation had a more populist cast and left less to the vagaries of parliamentary politics. Federation Leagues were formed, initially in border areas most affected by the divisions between the colonies. At one League event, in the border town of Corowa in 1893, a proposal for a second Convention was adopted.[37] This time, however, the process was more carefully designed. The Convention would be directly elected pursuant to enabling legislation in each of the colonies, which also should require the draft Constitution to be put to the voters in the colony for approval. The draft enabling legislation approved by a majority of Premiers 18 months later was more prescriptive still. It called for ten delegates from each colony to be elected to a new Convention; provided for a compulsory adjournment of the Convention for consultation with the colonial Parliaments on the draft Constitution; set out a procedure whereby the draft would be submitted to the voters for approval within the colony; and authorised the transmission of the draft Constitution to the Imperial Parliament for enactment if at least three colonies approved.

This was, more or less, the plan that was followed, although there were setbacks along the way. Four colonies passed Enabling Acts broadly in the form that had been agreed. Ominously, however, the fifth colony, Western Australia, made no provision for a referendum and sent a delegation elected by the Parliament while the sixth, Queensland, temporarily withdrew from the entire process. Once the elections had taken place, the Federal Australasian Convention met in three sessions in 1897 and 1898. As required by the legislation, it adjourned after the first session to enable the colonial Parliaments to comment on the constitutional draft. A final version was approved by the Convention in March 1898 and submitted to referendum shortly thereafter in New South Wales, Victoria, Tasmania and South Australia. It was approved in three colonies, but deemed to be rejected in New South Wales, where

---

[36] Ibid, 150.
[37] S Macintyre, 'After Corowa' (1994) 65 *Victorian Historical Journal* 98; D Headon, 'Loading the Gun: Corowa's Role in the Federation Debate', Papers on Parliament 32, Australian Senate, 1998, 20.

local politics had caused the required number of voters in favour to be increased when the Convention did not pay sufficient regard to the concerns about the draft, raised by the Parliament during the adjournment.

iv. Enactment

Under the Enabling Acts, the Constitution could be sent to London for enactment once approved by three colonies. Federal union was impracticable, however, without New South Wales. In an effort to find a basis on which New South Wales would enter a federation, the Premiers met and made a series of changes to the draft, which included the eventual location of the capital in New South Wales, but 'not less than one hundred miles from Sydney'.[38] Queensland rejoined the process; and the Constitution as amended was put to the voters in five colonies and passed. Although no action had yet been taken in Western Australia, a delegation of colonial leaders accompanied the draft Constitution to London. A successful, last-minute, referendum in Western Australia, after the imperial legislation was passed but before proclamation of the Constitution itself, enabled Western Australia to join as an Original State,[39] but explains its exclusion from the preamble to the Constitution Act. An attempt by New Zealand to retain the option to join the federation as an Original State in the future failed, although the possibility that New Zealand might join on some basis is reflected in clause 6 of the Act.

By the standards of the times, this was a remarkably democratic process, even when allowance is made for the limited franchise, a modest voting turnout[40] and political masterminding of the popular movement behind the scenes.[41] It has left a continuing mark on the Constitution, both in the referendum requirement for constitutional change and as contested evidence of popular sovereignty as the source of constitutional legitimacy.[42] Given the imperial setting, it was also a

---

[38] Now s.125 of the Constitution.
[39] Commonwealth of Australia Constitution Act 1900 (Imp) s.6.
[40] H Irving, *To Constitute a Nation,* (Cambridge, CUP, 1997) 152–53.
[41] B de Garis, 'How Popular was the "Popular" Federation Movement?', Papers on Parliament 21, Australian Senate 1993, 101.
[42] G Winterton, 'Popular Sovereignty and Constitutional Continuity' (1998) 26 *Federal Law Review* 1, 3–5 and the authorities there cited.

notably autochthonous process.[43] It was accepted from the outset that federation required imperial legislation. Nevertheless, the Australians understandably sought enactment of the Constitution without change. The United Kingdom government, on the other hand, was determined to protect imperial interests; critically, through maintenance of appeals to the Privy Council. Once more there was compromise, before the legislation finally was passed. The Commonwealth of Australia came into existence on 1 January 1901.

B. Influences

i. *Politicians and People*

In any constitution-making exercise, process is likely to affect outcome. In Australia, the process gave three distinct groups a role that left its mark on the final Constitution.

The first comprised the governments and parliaments of the colonies. Their influence was diluted by the election of delegates to the second Convention but they provided the legal framework for the process and their support was critical to its final success. The failure of the first referendum in New South Wales in the wake of the equivocal stance of its Premier demonstrated this only too clearly.[44] In any event, almost all the elected delegates were members of colonial parliaments and while some would seek national office when the Constitution came into effect, many expected to play a continuing role in the governments and parliaments of the new States.

These competing interests dominated negotiations, as delegates sought to ensure that the Constitution established a viable national government but did not detract more than necessary from the capacities of the existing colonies; that it enabled sufficient weight to be given to the views of the national majority, likely to be concentrated for the foreseeable future in the south-eastern States of New South Wales and Victoria, while preserving the 'self-esteem' of the smaller States and

---

[43] More than 30 years earlier, in Canada, the key decisions also were locally made, but through governments and legislatures: J Ajzenstat, I Gentles, P Romney, *Canada's Founding Debates*, (Toronto, University of Toronto Press, 2003) 2–3; AF Bayefsky, *Self-determination in International Law* (Leiden, Martinus Nijhoff, 2000) 472.

[44] G Bolton, *Edmund Barton* (St Leonard's, NSW, Allen and Unwin, 2000) 171–78.

their peoples through the equality principle; that it did not favour one side or another in the struggle between free trade and protectionism, enabling the new Commonwealth Parliament to decide; and that matters deemed critical by particular, individual colonies were safeguarded. The need to balance these considerations account for the equality of State representation in a powerful Senate that nevertheless lacks full power over financial bills and is the likely loser if the deadlock mechanism is applied (ss 53, 57); an approach to the division of powers between the Commonwealth and the States that left the latter with 'all their existing powers except those surrendered to the Commonwealth';[45] and the failure of the delegates to agree on the all-important issue of the basis on which revenue would be distributed by the Commonwealth to the States after the first few years.[46]

The second group with a determinative role was the Imperial government and Parliament, whose approval was needed to bring the Constitution into effect. Their only public intervention was at the time of enactment, when they secured changes to section 74 of the draft to protect appeals to the Privy Council from Australian courts on at least some constitutional questions. British influence also was felt in other, more subtle ways, however. Detailed memoranda on the draft Constitution were prepared by the Colonial Office in 1897 and discretely fed into the deliberations of the Convention through the Premier of New South Wales. Apart from the already vexed issue of the Privy Council, these drew attention to several provisions that implied Australian authority to enter into treaties, which were duly removed in subsequent drafts.[47] More generally still, consciousness that the Constitution ultimately needed British approval affected some of the choices that the delegates made.

The final group with a determinative role were the voters in each of the colonies. The difficulty of distinguishing their voice from the rhetoric of their representatives makes it harder to pinpoint their influence reliably. Logically, however, a referendum requirement makes it necessary to try to ensure that a proposal contains nothing objectionable enough to cause

---

[45] National Australasian Convention, *Official Record of Debates* (Adelaide, SA, 1897) 12–13.
[46] C Saunders, 'The Hardest Nut to Crack' in *The Convention Debates 1891–1898: Commentaries, Indices and Guide*, G Craven (ed), (Sydney, NSW, Legal Books, 1987) 149.
[47] Bolton, n 44, 162.

popular majorities to reject the entire measure. In the circumstances of Australian federation, the influence of voters is likely to have been felt at the very least in the consensus character of the Constitution and in the concessions that were made to the interests of individual States, of which the preservation of the voting rights of women in South Australia is only one, benign, example.[48]

ii. Models

All constitutions draw on existing constitutional models, adapting them to local needs. In designing the institutions for the new Commonwealth sphere of government, the framers of the Constitution were influenced primarily by the structure and principles of British government, filtered through Australian colonial experience. Nevertheless, they initially hesitated over the adoption of responsible government, because of concern about the extent to which it was compatible with a powerful Senate in which the States were equally represented, assumed to be a concomitant of federation. The question was left open in the draft of 1891 but was resolved in favour of responsible government in the final Constitution, to the extent of requiring Ministers to be Members of Parliament (s 64).

The adoption of other features of executive government was more straightforward. Formal executive power would continue to be held by the Queen, but exercisable by a Governor-General, as her representative (s 61). The Governor-General in turn would receive formal advice through an Executive Council, of which all Ministers would be members (s 62–64). The Constitution provided only for the 'dignified' institutions of executive government. Consistently with the distinction famously drawn by Walter Bagehot thirty years earlier, the 'efficient' institutions of Cabinet and Prime Minister were left to unwritten rules and political practice.[49]

The driving purpose of the Constitution, however, was to establish a federal form of government, for which British arrangements offered no assistance. For this purpose, the Australians turned to existing federal systems of government, in the United States, Canada, Switzerland and Germany. Information about all of them was available to Convention delegates and all had some influence on the outcome: Canada and

---

[48] Commonwealth Constitution sections 41, 128.
[49] W Bagehot, *The English Constitution* (London, Chapman and Hall, 1867) 13.

Germany on the allocation of particular powers to the Commonwealth; Switzerland on the adoption of the referendum for constitutional change.

The most influential of all was the Constitution of the United States with which some of the Australian framers were personally familiar and which was accessible to all of them through the writings of James Bryce.[50] From the United States the Australians adopted a conception of a federal system of government that matches Madison's analysis in *Federalist 39* surprisingly well, given the differences in the relationship between the legislature and the executive in the two countries.[51] The manner in which the Australian Constitution was made; the composition of the institutions of national government; the operation and scope of Commonwealth powers; and the procedure for constitutional change reflect a blend of national and (con)federal elements broadly comparable with those for which Madison had argued so persuasively more than 100 years earlier. In following the United States model so closely, the Australians also adopted parts of the structure and even the text of the United States Constitution, thereby laying the foundations for the emergence of an Australian doctrine of separation of powers.

They departed from it, however, in some critical respects. The most significant was the combination of federalism and responsible government, which profoundly affected the dynamics of Australian government and also triggered a range of differences in detail, including limitation of the financial powers of the Senate and a procedure for the resolution of deadlocks (ss 53, 57). Others departures from the American prototype included provision for a minimum of six senators from each State; the direct election of Senators (s 7); and the creation of a High Court as a final court of appeal in all questions of State as well as Commonwealth jurisdiction (s 73).

Nor did the Australians adopt a bill of rights. This was less remarkable at the time than it may seem to twenty-first century eyes. In the English constitutional tradition of the nineteenth century, rights were secured through representative institutions and common law courts. The framers of the Commonwealth Constitution therefore saw neither a need for a

[50] J Bryce, *The American Commonwealth* (1888); for the influence of Bryce and other federal theorists on the Australians see N Aroney, 'Imagining a Federal Commonwealth: Australian Conceptions of Federalism, 1890–1901' (2002) 30 *Federal Law Review* 265.

[51] A Hamilton, J Madison and J Jay, *The Federalist*, WR Brock (ed), (London, JM Dent, 1992) 191.

bill of rights, nor any particular connection between rights protection and federation. On the other hand, a small amount of rights-talk did take place in the Conventions, in the context of a proposal that would have elaborated the concept of citizenship in a united Australia by combining elements of the privileges and immunities clause (Art 4, s 1) and the XIV amendment of the Constitution of the United States. It is clear from the debate on this proposal that a desire to be able to continue to enact discriminatory laws was a factor in the lack of Australian interest in constitutional rights protection, at least if it involved equality guarantees.[52]

C. Significance

The federation movement of the 1890s achieved its primary goal of bringing all six Australian colonies together under a national Constitution through a distinctively participatory process. The magnitude of the achievement appears even greater after more than a century of experience of the difficulty of constitutional change of a much less complex kind.

In at least two respects, however, the achievement was more ambiguous and contested. The first concerns the democratic credentials of the Constitution. On one view, these were impressive; a culmination of the tradition of democratic experimentation that had emerged in the colonies over the latter part of the nineteenth century. Responsible government was secured; both Houses of the Commonwealth Parliament would be directly elected; constitutional change required approval by popular vote; and the voting rights already secured by women in two colonies would be preserved in terms that made the early extension of the franchise to women in the Commonwealth sphere almost irresistible. James Bryce described it as the 'high-water mark of popular government'.[53] Writing in 1902, shortly after the Constitution came into effect, Harrison Moore claimed that its 'great underlying principle' was 'that the rights of individuals are sufficiently secured by ensuring, as far as possible, to each a share, and an equal share, in political power'.[54]

---

[52] M Lake and H Reynolds, *Drawing the Global Colour Line* (Cambridge, CUP, 2008) 139.

[53] J Bryce, *Studies in History and Jurisprudence, Vol 1* (New York, OUP, 1901) 536, cited in *McGinty v Western Australia* (1996) 186 CLR 140, 271, Gummow J.

[54] W Harrison Moore, *The Constitution of the Commonwealth of Australia*, 1st edn (London, John Murray, 1902) 329.

On the other hand, implementation of the federal principle diluted majoritarian democracy in a variety of ways. The most obvious was the equal representation of States in the Senate. The composition of the Senate could be rationalised on pragmatic grounds as the necessary price for the participation of all colonies, securing a 'nation for a continent and a continent for a nation'. In time it came to be welcomed, at least by some, as a source of checks and balances in a constitutional system that otherwise tends to concentrate power. Nevertheless, the Senate was a source of controversy from the outset, exposing underlying disagreement within Australia about how government should be structured and political decisions made.

Even if the complications of federalism are left aside, the progressive character of the Constitution from the perspective of democracy became less obvious over the course of the twentieth century as standards changed. The absence of core political rights sparked decades of litigation about the extent to which some constitutional protection can be derived from the spare provisions establishing the elected institutions. More shocking still, with hindsight, are provisions authorising discrimination on grounds of race; now tamed by constitutional change and political practice but still reflected in the Commonwealth power to make laws for 'the people of any race'(s 51(xxvi)). This feature of the Constitution may have added to its appeal to the electorate of the 1890s, on the threshold of the implementation of policies designed to preserve a white Australia. By the twenty-first century, however, its remnants are an embarrassing reminder of earlier currents of thought.

The contribution of the Constitution to what might now be called nation building was ambiguous as well. Given Australia's continuing colonial status, agreement on a federal Constitution was a remarkable and farsighted achievement, which extended Australian autonomy and laid the ground for future independence. The process by which the Constitution was made effectively confined British intervention to matters of imperial concern. Appeals to the Privy Council were limited further than the Imperial authorities preferred. The new Constitution could be altered by Australians, in contrast to the British North America Act 1867, which required change to be effected through the Imperial Parliament. The Commonwealth and the States were collectively empowered to exercise some of the powers of the Imperial Parliament in relation to Australia, in terms that ultimately would be relied upon to sever the remaining colonial restrictions on the States (s 51 (xxxviii)).

The term 'Commonwealth' was deliberately adopted as 'the noblest word ever invented to designate a free state', despite its republican connotations, which had to be explained away.[55]

On the other hand, because colonial status was taken as a given, the Constitution was written for a polity that was not yet independent. Independence was achieved well after federation by a lengthy, laborious and highly technical process. And while the Constitution was sufficiently flexible to enable this to occur without textual change, its origins have left significant traces: in the form of the Constitution and the authority for it; in the institution of the Monarchy; in the absence of an explicit constitutional conception of citizen; and in the preservation in the Constitution of procedures for imperial control, now fallen into disuse.

III. INDEPENDENCE

A. The Challenge

In most countries independence following a period of colonisation is a catalyst for a new Constitution. While this was not the case in Australia, independence was a critical event nonetheless, in constitutional terms. Quite apart from the intrinsic significance of the acquisition of statehood, independence caused the Commonwealth Constitution to be understood in new ways and its fallout continues to do so. The manner in which independence was achieved—gradual and pragmatic, without fanfare or symbolism—is characteristic of Australian constitutionalism and, indeed, has helped to form it. There are current features of the Australian constitutional system that can be understood only as products of a process of this kind.

Australia was part of the second British Empire and its first steps towards independence were shared with others in a similar situation: Canada, New Zealand and South Africa. By the time of Australian federation, Imperial policy towards what soon would be recognised as Dominions[56] reflected a willingness to concede progressive measures of self-government, replacing diminishing imperial control with voluntary ties of other kinds. Grandiose schemes for imperial federation died by

---

[55] Edmund Barton, quoted in Bolton, n 44, 79; Quick and Garran, n 33, 311–14.
[56] The term was used between (about) 1907 and 1947: KC Wheare, *The Constitutional Structure of the Commonwealth* (Oxford, Clarendon Press 1960) 6–17.

1917, if not before.[57] Instead, the empire became a commonwealth and the former colonies became independent members of it, recognising a common allegiance to the British Crown.[58]

It is important for present purposes to understand what was involved in acquiring independence in these circumstances. Internally, it required the abandonment of controls formerly exercised by the United Kingdom over the institutions of government of its colonies. These took a variety of different forms. The colonial parliaments were bound by Imperial laws directed to their colonies; the Privy Council provided a final avenue of appeal from colonial courts; the Governors-General were appointed on British advice and provided a mechanism through which the British government could intervene if imperial interests were threatened. Externally, independence meant statehood, with all the trappings of it: full capacity to conduct international relations, including the ability to act extraterritorially and to exercise authority over a territory and a people through the mutual rights and obligations of citizenship.

Steps along what became the path to independence were taken even before federation. Federation itself hastened the process by creating a larger and therefore stronger Australian voice. The independence movement gathered pace in the early years of the twentieth century, with the Imperial Conferences that were held regularly from 1897 as the principal medium. With hindsight, Dominion involvement in the First World War made change inevitable, with independence the most likely outcome. What has been characterised as 'rapid progress from autonomy to equality' culminated in the Imperial Conference of 1926, at which it was recognised that Great Britain and the Dominions were 'autonomous communities within the British Empire, equal in status, in no way subordinate to each other in any aspect of their domestic or external affairs'.[59] The resolutions of the Conference and the legislation subsequently enacted by the British Parliament as the Statute of Westminster 1931 gave effect to this statement of principle, by releasing

---

[57]　J Darwin, 'A Third British Empire? The Dominion Idea in Imperial Politics', in WR Louis (ed), *The Oxford History of the British Empire Vol. 5,* (Oxford, OUP, 1999) 64, 68.

[58]　SA de Smith, *The New Commonwealth and its Constitutions* (London, Stevens and Sons, 1964) 9–13.

[59]　Darwin, n 57, 69; key excerpts from the 'Balfour Declaration' of 1926 are reproduced in C Howard and C Saunders, *Cases and Materials on Constitutional Law* (Melbourne, Vic, Law Book Co., 1979),30.

the Dominions from colonial constraints on their actions, in ways that are described in the next section.

It has been argued that Australian independence dates from 1931, because the Statute of Westminster put Australia in a position in which it could claim independence for itself.[60] The argument is plausible and the date as good as any, if a single date must be found. It also has the advantage, from the standpoint of national pride, of locating independence earlier, rather than later in the century.

In fact, however, mopping up the residual legal constraints on power derived from colonial status took Australians another 50 years. In part this was because the Commonwealth, with New Zealand, was slow to take up the opportunities offered by the resolutions of the Imperial Conference and the Statute of Westminster.[61] But in larger part it was due to the distinctive position of the States in the Australian federation vis-à-vis the former Imperial power.[62] After federation, the States retained the direct link with the United Kingdom, through their Governors, that they had enjoyed as independent colonies. By contrast, in Canada, the Lieutenant Governors of the Provinces were appointed by the Governor-General. The somewhat unusual Australian arrangement was hard fought during the Conventions. Once settled, however, it had significant implications. It underlined the conception of federation as a system of government in which sovereignty is divided and encouraged the perception of the United Kingdom as a bulwark for the States against Commonwealth encroachment on their constitutional autonomy. In consequence, the States moved separately and much more slowly to remove the outward manifestations of their colonial status in a process that was not complete until the enactment of the Australia Acts in 1986.

---

[60] G Winterton 'The Acquisition of Independence' in R French, G Lindell and C Saunders (eds), *Reflections on the Australian Constitution* (Sydney, NSW, Federation Press, 2003) 42.

[61] Darwin, n 57, 69, noting that the Statute of Westminster was 'comprehensively ignored' in these two countries.

[62] See generally A Twomey, *The Chameleon Crown* (Sydney, NSW, Federation Press, 2006).

B. Commonwealth

i. Executive

The Commonwealth Constitution creates the position of Governor-General as the representative of the Crown in the Commonwealth sphere (s 2), able to perform the functions of Head of State locally. At the time of federation, the Governor-General was appointed by the Monarch on the advice of the British Government and acted as its representative for some purposes.[63] The Constitution confers the general executive power of the Commonwealth on the Monarch, while providing that it is 'exercisable' by the Governor-General (s 61), to whom the Monarch may also assign additional powers (s 2). The Commonwealth Parliament is defined to comprise the Monarch and while the Governor-General is empowered to assent to legislation, bills may also be reserved for the Monarch's assent or disallowed once assent has been given (ss 1, 58–60). These latter procedures were typical mechanisms for imperial control, exercised on British advice.

The effect of these provisions was dramatically changed by agreement between governments in 1926 and 1930, effectively altering the applicable constitutional conventions. The Imperial Conference of 1926 recognised that the logical consequence of the 'equality of status' of its members was that the British government should no longer intervene in decisions taken by either the Monarch or the Governor-General in relation to a Dominion and that, at least by inference, both should act on the advice of the relevant Dominion government.[64] One of several ambiguities in the way in which this was put caused King George V to baulk at Australian advice to appoint Isaac Isaacs, as the first Australian Governor-General in 1930.[65] Isaacs was appointed, however, and the Imperial Conference of 1930 made it clear that the Monarch should act on the advice of Dominion Ministers 'also in this instance', although it was expected that 'informal consultation' would take place first.[66]

---

[63] G Winterton, 'The Evolving Role of the Australian Governor-General' in M Groves (ed), *Law and Government in Australia* (Sydney, NSW, Federation Press, 2005) 44–45.

[64] Balfour Declaration, n 59.

[65] LF Crisp, 'The Appointment of Sir Isaac Isaacs as Governor-general of Australia 1930' (1964) 11 *Australian Historical Studies* 254.

[66] Imperial Conference 1930, *Summary of Proceedings*, extracted in Howard and Saunders, n 59, 33.

These developments secured independence by removing the capacity of the British government to intervene in Commonwealth decision-making while leaving the institutions of both Monarch and Governor-General in place. Subsequent developments adjusted the symbolism of this arrangement in ways that presented the Monarch as more of an Australian institution while enhancing the role of the Governor-General vis-à-vis the Monarch. Under Commonwealth legislation, in 1973, the Queen adopted the style and title of 'Queen of Australia' in relation to Australian affairs.[67] Every Governor-General since 1965 has been Australian and it is inconceivable that a non-Australian would be appointed now. Through a combination of judicial decision and political practice it has become accepted that all the executive power of the Commonwealth is 'exercisable' by the Governor-General under section 61[68] and that the Monarch retains no further power to assign to the Governor-General under section 2.[69] When asked by the Speaker to intervene in the controversy that followed the dismissal of the Commonwealth Government by the Governor-General in 1975, the Queen declined to do so, on the grounds that 'The Australian Constitution firmly places the prerogative powers of the Crown in the hands of the Governor-General'.[70] By the end of the twentieth century, there was sufficient confusion about the respective roles of the Monarch and the Governor-General for debate to occur about which of them was the de jure, as opposed to the de facto, Australian Head of State.[71]

ii. Legislative

At the time of federation, the Commonwealth Parliament was unable to legislate inconsistently with laws of paramount force of the then

[67] The current style and titles refers also to 'Her other Realms and Territories, Head of the Commonwealth': Royal Style and Titles Act 1973 (Cth). Cf the Royal Style and Titles Act 1953 (Cth), which referred to the Queen of the 'United Kingdom, Australia and Her Other Realms and Territories'.

[68] *Barton v Commonwealth* (1974) 131 CLR 477.

[69] Two assignments of power in 1954 and 1973 were revoked by the Queen in 1987 on the advice of the Prime Minister on the grounds that they had not been necessary: Constitutional Commission, *Final Report, Summary* 1988, (Canberra, NSW, AGPS, 1988) 18.

[70] Letter from the Queen's Private Secretary to the Speaker, reproduced in Howard and Saunders, n 59. 125.

[71] G Winterton, 'Who is Australia's Head of State?' (2004) 7 *Constitutional Law and Policy Review* 65.

sovereign British Parliament: a common law principle given statutory force through the Colonial Laws Validity Act 1865. This impediment to independence could be overcome only by further legislation, which was enacted by the British Parliament, with the agreement of all the Dominions, in 1931. At the Commonwealth's request, the key provisions of the Statute of Westminster would take effect in relation to Australia only when adopted by the Commonwealth Parliament.[72] A Statute of Westminster Adoption Act (Cth) finally was passed in 1942, with retrospective effect from the outbreak of the war in 1939.

The Statute released the Dominion Parliaments from restrictions on their power to legislate inconsistently with British law and authorised them to repeal or amend existing laws that applied to them. British laws establishing the Constitutions of Canada, Australia and New Zealand were excepted, to preserve their overriding effect. The constitutional continuity thus assured left its mark on the conception of a Constitution in Australia, which is explored further in the next chapter.

The Statute of Westminster kept open the possibility that a Dominion might seek British legislation in the future, for reasons of convenience. To reconcile this possibility with Dominion independence section 4 provided that such legislation would not be enacted without the request and consent of the Dominion concerned. In 1986, section 1 of the Australia Acts took the further and final step of denying that future United Kingdom legislation could 'extend, or be deemed to extend' to Australia, as part of its law. To the extent that these provisions purport to inhibit the actions of future British Parliaments, they present some difficulty from the standpoint of a theory that denies the power of a Parliament to limit its own authority, consistently with a conception of sovereignty as 'continuing'.[73] Whatever the relevance of this theory in the United Kingdom, however, it does not affect the position in Australia, where the courts would now refuse to give effect to British law, either as a straightforward application of section 1 of the Australia Act (Cth)[74] or as a corollary of the fact of Australian independence.

---

[72] A Twomey, 'Federal Parliament's Changing Role in Treaty Making and External Affairs' in G Lindell and R Bennett (eds), *Parliament—The Vision in Hindsight* (Annandale, NSW, Federation Press, 2003) 62.

[73] HLA Hart, *The Concept of Law*, 2nd edn (Oxford, OUP, 1994) ch.7; cf the distinction between 'strong' and 'weak' forms of continuing sovereignty in J Goldsworthy, 'Abdicating and Limiting Parliament's Sovereignty' (2006) 17 *King's College Law Journal* 255, 259.

[74] *Sue v Hill* (1999) 199 CLR 462, 492.

iii. Judicial

One of the lesser goals of federation had been to establish a final court of appeal within Australia on all questions of Australian law. Following the negotiations in London, the final text of the Constitution allowed appeals from the High Court to the Privy Council in all matters except constitutional questions about the respective limits of Commonwealth and State power 'inter se' and gave the Commonwealth Parliament authority to further limit appeals to the Privy Council by laws to be reserved for the Monarch's assent.[75] Section 74 did not deal with appeals from the Supreme Courts of the States, which continued as before.

On federation, therefore, appeals lay to the Privy Council from most decisions of the High Court as well as from the Supreme Courts of the States. Decisions of the Privy Council were binding in Australian law, causing decisions of the House of Lords to be treated as binding as well.[76] All this unravelled gradually in the wake of independence. Appeals from the High Court to the Privy Council effectively ceased, through exercises of the legislative power to 'limit' appeals in 1966 and 1975.[77] Until the passage of the Australia Acts in 1986, this created an unsatisfactory situation whereby appeals might be taken directly to the Privy Council from State courts, by-passing the High Court altogether. In 1978 the High Court declared that it was no longer bound by Privy Council decisions.[78] In 1986 it was provoked by a suggestion that a Supreme Court was 'constrained' by decisions of the English Court of Appeal to note that 'the precedents of other legal systems' are not binding in Australian law but are 'useful only to the degree of the persuasiveness of their reasoning'.[79]

---

[75] Under s.74, appeals in the protected category of 'inter se' questions may be taken with a certificate from the High Court itself; it is clear that no further certificates will be given, however, even if an appeal on this basis is still open: *Kirmani v Captain Cook Cruises* (1985) 159 CLR 351.

[76] Mason, n 15. 69.

[77] Privy Council (Limitation of Appeals) Act 1966 (Cth); Privy Council (Appeals from the High Court) Act 1975 (Cth). The Acts are a valid exercise of the power: *Attorney-General (Cth) v T&G Mutual Life Society Ltd* (1978) 144 CLR 161.

[78] *Viro v The Queen* (1978) 141 CLR 88.

[79] *Cook v Cook* (1986) 162 CLR 376, 390.

iv. Statehood

On independence, Australia became a state for the purposes of international law with responsibility for its own international relations. Its emergence onto the world stage was as gradual as every other aspect of its progress towards independence; it is clear, however, that for some time after federation Australia lacked this attribute of statehood and that the United Kingdom conducted international relations on its behalf. When change came, at some undefined point after the First World War, external sovereignty moved from one to the other with relative ease, through acquiescence on the part of both governments and recognition by the international community.[80] As part of the package, section 3 of the Statute of Westminster offered the Dominion Parliaments authority to make extraterritorial laws.

Internally, however, matters were more complicated, raising questions about how these new international responsibilities would be accommodated by a federal Constitution that necessarily was written without them in mind, revisionist views to the contrary.[81] The answers were found through judicial interpretation, obviating the need for constitutional change. The general executive power of the Commonwealth was held to authorise the making of treaties and other forms of international agreement[82] and the external affairs power of the Commonwealth Parliament was held to authorise their implementation, irrespective of subject-matter.[83] The Commonwealth thus filled the vacancy left by the withdrawal of the United Kingdom and became the only sphere of Australian government with international status. The justification for the conclusion, that '[t]he colonies never were and the States are not international persons'[84] has settled for Australia a question that is alive in some other federations about the extent of the capacity of constituent units to engage in external affairs. The transformation was complete when, in 1999, the High Court held that the United Kingdom is itself a 'foreign power' for the purposes of section 44(i) of the Constitution, which precludes Australians with dual citizenship from holding a seat in the Commonwealth Parliament.[85]

---

[80] Twomey, 'Federal Parliament's Changing Role', n 72 above.
[81] cf *New South Wales v Commonwealth (Seas and Submerged Lands case)* (1975) 135 CLR 337, 373.
[82] *R v Burgess; ex parte Henry* (1936) 55 CLR 608.
[83] *Victoria v Commonwealth (Industrial Relations Act case)* (1996) 187 CLR 146.
[84] *Seas and Submerged Lands case,* n 81, 373.
[85] *Sue v Hill* (1999) 199 CLR 462.

Statehood also implies a people, who owe allegiance to the state and to whom it owes protection in return. The status of Australia at the time of federation, however, left the idea of its people oddly inchoate. A proposal to recognise Australian citizenship in the Constitution was considered but rejected at the Conventions. Australian citizenship did not emerge as a distinct legal status until 1949 and then only in statutory form.[86] A purely statutory basis for citizenship, however, sits uneasily alongside a Constitution that envisages a role for 'the people', delimits a Commonwealth power by reference to 'aliens' (s 51(xix)) and provides some protection for a 'subject of the Queen' (s.117). In the course of a spate of litigation prompted by the potential mismatch of these provisions in an independent Australia it has become settled that the reference to a 'subject of the Queen' now means 'the Queen in right of Australia'[87] and that 'alien' and 'citizen' are effectively dichotomous concepts that between them exhaust the range of possibilities.[88] What remains unclear is the extent to which, in these circumstances, the Constitution provides some protection for the scope and incidents of citizenship, through the meaning attributed to the term 'alien' or as an implication from the text and structure of the Constitution as a whole.[89]

C. States

i. Lingering Colonial Ties

At the time of federation, the Australian States were subject to the same colonial restrictions on their legislative, executive and judicial capacities as the Commonwealth. They did not, however, progress towards independence in the same way or at the same pace as the Commonwealth. They were not participants in the Imperial Conferences and the declarations of 1926 and 1930 did not apply to the relationship between the Monarch, State Governors and State Ministers. Unlike the Canadian Provinces and largely of their own volition the Australian States were

---

[86] Nationality and Citizenship Act 1948 (Cth); cf H Irving, 'Still Call Australia Home: The Constitution and the Citizen's Right of Abode' (2008) 30 *Sydney Law Review* 131, 142, distinguishing British subjects and 'Australian British subjects'.

[87] *Shaw v Minister for Immigration and Multicultural Affairs* (2003) 218 CLR 28, 39, 87.

[88] *Koroitamana v Commonwealth* (2006) 227 CLR 31, 38, 46.

[89] G Ebbeck, 'A Constitutional Concept of Australian Citizen' (2004) 25 *Adelaide Law Review* 137.

not released from the colonial constraints on their legislative powers by the Statute of Westminster.

While the Commonwealth arguably was independent from 1931, therefore, the States clearly were not.[90] The Governors continued to be appointed by the Monarch on the advice of the British Government; the Monarch acted on British advice in relation to State affairs and thus as the Monarch of the United Kingdom rather than of Australia; the British Government retained some responsibility for the actions of Governors; the States were subject to British laws of paramount force and were restricted in their capacity to legislate extraterritorially; and appeals continued to lie to the Privy Council from State courts exercising State jurisdiction.

The separate paths to independence taken by the Commonwealth and the States are a remarkable demonstration of both the pragmatism of Australian constitutionalism and the depth of the institutional dualism of the Australian federation. This history also helps to explain why, in the late 1990s, it could so readily be accepted that the proposal for a republic that was put to referendum would deal only with the position of the Crown in the Commonwealth sphere, leaving the links between the States and the Crown to be sorted out later if the referendum succeeded.[91]

Whatever the outward form of the relationship between the States and the United Kingdom, it was not to be expected that the British government would continue to treat as colonies polities that were constituent parts of an independent Australia. Over the course of the twentieth century, practice adapted to this reality and both the Monarch and the Governors typically acted in accordance with the advice of the relevant State government in State affairs. As recent scholarship has shown, however, the underlying ambiguity in the position of the States was exposed by a series of events in the 1970s, some of which also involved Commonwealth interests, in which the Queen acted on British advice rather than on the advice of either the Commonwealth or the State concerned.[92] This was acceptable to neither the Commonwealth nor the States and provided new stimulus to negotiations to sever the remaining colonial ties with the United Kingdom.[93]

---

[90] See generally Twomey, *The Chameleon Crown*, n 62.
[91] Constitution Alteration (Establishment of Republic) 1999.
[92] Twomey, *The Chameleon Crown*, n 62, chs. 8–12.
[93] For the wider, British Commonwealth context in which these negotiations were conducted, see PC Oliver, *The Constitution of Independence* (Oxford, OUP, 2005).

ii. Australia Acts

The mechanism used was the Australia Acts 1986 (Cth and UK). These removed the British government as a source of advice in relation to State affairs (ss 7, 10); released State Parliaments from the overriding effect of (most) British laws of paramount force (s 3); severed appeals from State courts to the Privy Council (s 11); and authorised the States to enact legislation with extraterritorial effect, in ambiguous terms that enabled the restriction to be reinstated as a limit derived from their position as constituent units within a federation (s 2(1)).[94] The opportunity also was used to terminate the authority of the United Kingdom to legislate for Australia in the future (s 1). This in turn made it necessary to include a procedure whereby the Australian Parliaments acting collaboratively could alter both the Australia Acts and the Statute of Westminster (s 15).

The Australia Acts are important constitutional documents in their own right, with implications for the meaning and operation of the Constitution that are examined in subsequent chapters. Two features are particularly relevant for present purposes, however, and are treated here.

The first concerns their form. There are two Acts. One was enacted by the Parliament of the United Kingdom, acting pursuant to the Statute of Westminster with the request and consent of the Commonwealth, which in turn acted on the request and consent of the States pursuant to what was understood to be the requirements of convention.[95] The other, in substantially identical terms, was enacted by the Commonwealth on the request of the States in experimental use of the power in section 51(xxxviii) of the Constitution. The use of two Acts reflected disagreement between governments about whether independence should and legally could be secured by Australia acting alone. Reliance on both sources of authority enabled the question to be avoided in the short term.

With the wisdom of hindsight, however, it is obvious that legislation enacted by the Commonwealth Parliament pursuant to a power required to be exercised consistently with the rest of the Constitution might have different legal effects to an Act in the same terms passed by another Parliament under no such constraints. The question of which Act operates in Australia has now been answered in favour of

---

[94] *Union Steamship Company of Australia v King* (1988) 166 CLR 1.
[95] Australia (Request and Consent) Act 1985 (Cth); the Australia Acts (Request) Acts 1985: all States.

the Australian version, following the insistence by the High Court in 2003 that 'constitutional norms, whatever . . . their historical origins, are now to be traced to Australian sources'.[96] It is desirable that this is so, in the interests of the integrity of the Australian constitutional system, notwithstanding concerns that have been raised about the validity of parts of the Australian Act.[97]

The second feature of the Australia Acts that requires attention here concerns the source of advice to the Monarch on State affairs. Removal of the British government from Australian constitutional arrangements meant either that State advice would be channelled to the Queen through the Commonwealth or that the Queen would receive advice directly from the States. As a compromise, section 7 of the Australia Acts, enables a State Premier to advise the Monarch directly about the appointment and dismissal of a Governor but otherwise provides that, with minor exceptions, the powers of the Monarch in relation to a State are exercisable only by the Governor of the State. The section appears inadvertently to have entrenched the position of State Governor as a representative of the Queen and will need to be changed if and when Australia becomes a republic. By accepting that State Premiers can directly advise the Monarch, the outcome also threatens to bring to a head the long-suppressed question of whether there is one Australian Crown, seven Australian Crowns or a new conception of a federal Crown devised for the particular circumstances of Australia[98] in a further demonstration of the pragmatism of the Australian approach to constitutional law.

IV. RECONCILIATION

A. Causes

The relationship between Aboriginal and other Australians goes to the constitutional foundations of Australia in another way. The integrity of

---

[96]   *Attorney-General (WA) v Marquet* (2003) 217 CLR 545, 570–71.

[97]   These are explored in L Zines, *The High Court and the Constitution,* 5th edn (Annandale, NSW, Federation Press, 2008) 421–32. For an examination of how the UK version might be used to alter the Commonwealth Constitution without a referendum see G Lindell, 'Why is Australia's Constitution Binding—The Reasons in 1900 and Now, and the Effect of Independence' (1986) 16 *Federal Law Review* 29.

[98]   Twomey, *The Chameleon Crown,* n 62, ch.21; cf G Winterton, 'The Evolution of a Separate Australian Crown' (1993) 19 *Monash Law Review* 1.

the political community is a critical issue in the constitutional arrangements of any state. By contemporary standards integrity requires inclusion on terms of equality, accompanied by mutual respect. In Australia's
case integrity, understood in this way, was undermined from the outset
by assumptions about the character of the original settlement described
earlier in this chapter. The problem thus created was exacerbated by the
policies and practices of successive generations of Australians, some of
which were given effect through the Constitution and the general law. The
'collapse of faith in race thinking'[99] in the aftermath of the Second World
War led to a 'profound revolution in sensibility' in Australia as in most
other western countries by the end of the 1960s.[100] The spate of disparate changes that have since occurred can helpfully be analysed under the
rubric of reconciliation although the term was not used for this purpose
until 1991.[101] To the extent that reconciliation involves a new beginning or
at least a 'recasting of the present as a point of origin'[102] it remains a work
in progress to which the Constitution may hold a key.

British settlement of Australia from 1788 brought together two
peoples whose interests were diametrically opposed and whose
cultures, including laws, were mutually incomprehensible. The most
significant immediate consequence was that the newcomers treated
indigenous culture as irrelevant to the legal organisation of the colony.
Characterisation of the colonies as settled rather than conquered or
ceded avoided the necessity for treaties and enabled the importation of
a new, comprehensive legal system under which the dispossession of the
Aboriginal people occurred.

The profound cultural dislocation that followed has been graphically
described as 'vertigo in living'[103] and is a moving cause in the continuing
social and economic disadvantage of most Indigenous Australians.[104]

---

[99] Lake and Reynolds, n 52, 350.

[100] R Manne, 'Pearson's Gamble, Stanner's Dream' (2007) 26 *The Monthly*.

[101] Council for Aboriginal Reconciliation Act 1991 (Cth); Royal Commission into
Aboriginal Deaths in Custody, *National Report,* 1991, ch.38; G Nettheim, 'Making a
Difference: Reconciling Our Differences' (2001) 5 *Newcastle Law Review* 3, 21.

[102] EA Christodoulidis, '"Truth and Reconciliation" as Risks' (2000) 9 *Social Legal
Studies* 179, 199.

[103] WEH Stanner, *White Man Got No Dreaming* (Canberra, NSW, ANU Press,
1979) quoted in G Brennan, 'Reconciliation' (1999) 22 *University of New South Wales
Law Journal* 595, 596.

[104] For the complexity of this issue, however, see N Pearson, 'White Guilt,
Victimhood and the Quest for a Radical Centre' (2007) *Griffith Review* 16

Even after it became accepted that at the time of British settlement the Aboriginal peoples had a 'subtle and elaborate system [of law] highly adapted to the country', the official view of the status of settlement and the logic of its consequences remained.[105] Inevitably, the incomprehension and sense of superiority of the dominant majority was matched by the 'distrust, enmity and anger' of this small but significant minority.[106] The challenge of developing a shared view of national history in these circumstances is exemplified in a trivial way by the choice of the day on which the first fleet arrived in 1788 as the principal national holiday.

It is something of an irony that the majority community not only failed to recognise the distinctive interests of the Aboriginal peoples but also failed to accord them formal equality, consistently with its own philosophical tenets. Until the latter part of the twentieth century, Indigenous citizens were denied the vote federally and in the three States and Territories in which most of them lived.[107] The Commonwealth Constitution excluded them from its ambit by providing that they should 'not be counted' in calculating the numbers of people for constitutional purposes.[108] The 'aboriginal race' also was expressly excepted from the power in s 51(xxvi) to make laws for "[t]he people of any race . . . for whom it is deemed necessary to make special laws', although for reasons that seem to have been related to the perceived purpose of the power rather than with particular intent to discriminate against them.[109] In addition, over this period, Aboriginal Australians were subject to a range of other discriminatory policies. One had consequences that still reverberate: the forcible removal of part-aboriginal children from their families throughout the first half of the twentieth century, on a scale that left most families affected.[110]

---

[105]   *Milirrpum v Nabalco Pty Ltd* (1971) 17 FLR 141, 267.

[106]   Royal Commission into Deaths in Custody, n 101, 38.4.

[107]   For details, see M Goot, 'The Aboriginal Franchise and its Consequences' (2006) 52 *Australian Journal of Politics and History* 517.

[108]   s.127; see also s.25, which contemplates their continuing exclusion from voting in State elections. For the effect of s.127, see G Sawer, 'The Australian Constitution and the Australian Aborigine' (1966) 2 *Federal Law Review* 17, 25–30.

[109]   R French, 'The Race Power: A Constitutional Chimera' in HP Lee and G Winterton (eds), *Australian Constitutional Landmarks* (Cambridge, CUP, 2003) 180, 185.

[110]   Human Rights and Equal Opportunity Commission, *Bringing Them Home: Report of a National Inquiry into the Separation of Aboriginal and Torres Strait Islander Children and their Families* (1997) ch.2.

B. Progress

The relationship between Indigenous and other Australians has altered in important ways since the 1960s.

i. *Formal Equality*

One group of changes has tackled the most obvious instances of departure from formal legal equality. These have been the easiest both to conceive and implement. The federal franchise was extended to Aboriginal citizens in 1962 and remaining restrictions on their rights to vote were removed in all States by 1965.[111] The two provisions in the Constitution expressly excluding Aboriginal people from their operation were amended by referendum in 1967, with uncharacteristically huge majorities.[112] Removal of the exclusion of 'the aboriginal race in any State' from section 51(xxvi) ensured that the Commonwealth had power to make laws for Indigenous Australians, but at the questionable cost of subjecting them to a power to make laws by reference to race, which need not be used for their benefit.[113]

More generally, Australia became a party to the International Convention on the Elimination of all Forms of Racial Discrimination in 1975 and implementing legislation was enacted by the Commonwealth Parliament in the same year. The Racial Discrimination Act overrides inconsistent State law and has been a vehicle for precluding discrimination against Indigenous people under State legislation.[114] A by-product of the inevitable challenge to the validity of the Act confirmed that Commonwealth power extended to the implementation of international treaties at least where, as in this case, the subject was of 'international concern'.[115] On the other hand, the Act has the status only of ordinary legislation where the Commonwealth is concerned. It has been overridden

---

[111] Commonwealth Electoral Act 1962 (Cth). Voting was not made compulsory, as for other Australians, until 1983; R Parkinson and M Sawer, *Elections: Full, Free and Fair*, (Annandale, NSW, Federation Press, 2001) 161–2.

[112] The referendum was carried in all States and with a national majority of 90.77%.

[113] *Western Australia v Commonwealth (Native Title Act case)* (1995) 183 CLR 373, 461.

[114] *Koowarta v BjelkePetersen* (1982) 153 CLR 168; *Mabo v Queensland (No 1)* (1988) 166 CLR 186.

[115] Ibid, per Stephen J, 216–217. The qualification no longer applies: *Victoria v Commonwealth (Industrial Relations Act case)* (1996) 187 CLR 146.

by subsequent legislation in pursuit of Commonwealth policy objectives that cannot necessarily be justified as 'special . . . measures' within the meaning of Article 2 of the Convention.[116]

ii.   Land Rights

A second group of changes go beyond formal equality to recognise the distinctive interests of Aboriginal Australians in relation to land. While statutory land rights regimes began to be put in place from 1976[117] the seminal development was the decision of the High Court in *Mabo (No.2)* that the common law of Australia could recognise native title. *Mabo* was followed by the enactment of Commonwealth legislation to clarify the scope of entitlements[118] and to manage the claims process, as well as by a wave of litigation, designed to test its limits.

Mabo had symbolic importance for the relationship between Aboriginal and other Australians. It recognised the interests of the Aboriginal peoples in land at the time of British colonisation, in accordance with their own culture; it acknowledged that the basis on which the Australian colonies were characterised as settled was factually false; and it accepted that Aboriginal groups might now claim their land as a matter of right, subject to the considerable conditions that the Court had laid down.[119] On the other hand, *Mabo* left untouched the effectiveness of the claim of sovereignty in 1788, exemplified in the notion of the 'radical' title of the Crown. The characterisation of the Australian colonies as settled remained undisturbed—a messy conclusion, which also preserved the monopoly of the common law. The *Mabo* principle thus provided no springboard for future claims that other aspects of traditional law had survived British settlement.[120] Even so, the recognition of native title provoked a political storm, sourced in concern about its implications for non-indigenous property rights, which undermined its contribution to reconciliation.

---

[116]   Native Title Amendment Act 1998 (Cth) s.7(3); Hindmarsh Island Bridge Act 1997 (Cth); Northern Territory National Emergency Response Act 2007 (Cth) s.132 (2).

[117]   The details are provided in M Tehan, 'A Hope Disillusioned, An Opportunity Lost? Reflections on Common Law Native Title and Ten Years of the *Native Title Act*' (2003) 27 *Melbourne University Law Review* 523, 529–32.

[118]   Native Title Act 1993 (Cth).

[119]   *Mabo (No 2)*, n 25 above, 69–70.

[120]   *Walker v State of New South Wales* (1994) 182 CLR 45.

The practical significance of *Mabo* is similarly equivocal. Native title can be claimed only if a continuing connection to the land can be shown and there has been no supervening act of sovereignty. Given the extent of dislocation of Aboriginal groups over a period of more than 200 years, both conditions are difficult to satisfy. The claims process under the Native Title Act has proved agonisingly slow when claims are contested although agreed outcomes of various kinds have proved more successful. Subsequent decisions of the High Court have further narrowed the scope of the protection afforded to native title under both the common law and legislation.[121] On the other hand, recognition of native title in legal form provides some protection against its further erosion. Importantly, it also has given Aboriginal groups a tangible, if not necessarily equal, bargaining position in their dealings with others over the future of their traditional lands.[122]

iii. Apology

Mabo made a contribution to reconciliation through its recognition and acknowledgement of Aboriginal culture, with associated intimations of respect. The limitations on the role of a court for this purpose, however, was reflected both in the scope of the decision and in some of the reactions to it. By contrast, an Apology to Australia's Indigenous Peoples, delivered in Parliament by then Prime Minister Rudd in 2008 was sweeping in its terms and ambitious in its objectives.[123] The Apology was directed specifically to the 'Stolen Generations' of children removed from their families, many of whom were present for the occasion. More generally, however, it adopted the language and aspirations of reconciliation. The Parliament asked that the apology 'be received in the spirit in which it is offered as part of the healing of the nation'. By 'acknowledging the past' it laid 'claim to a future that embraces all Australians . . . based on mutual respect, mutual resolve and mutual responsibility'. The preamble ended with the following observation:

> There comes a time in the history of nations when their peoples must become fully reconciled to their past if they are to go forward with confidence to embrace their future. Our nation, Australia, has reached such a time. And

---

[121] N Pearson, 'Land is Susceptible of Ownership' in Cane (ed), n 15, 111.
[122] Tehan, n 117, 564 ff.
[123] Commonwealth Parliament, House of Representatives, *Hansard,* 13 February 2008.

that is why the parliament is today here assembled: to deal with this unfinished business of the nation, to remove a great stain from the nation's soul and, in a true spirit of reconciliation, to open a new chapter in the history of this great land, Australia.

The Apology received bipartisan support in the Parliament and in all Australian jurisdictions. It was widely welcomed by Aboriginal leaders. It attracted a groundswell of public support from people all over the country who had gathered in schools, workplaces and public spaces to watch, and applaud, its delivery.

iv. Follow-up

From the standpoint of reconciliation, the effectiveness of the Apology in the long term depends on steps subsequently taken to realise its promise: to build on the goodwill generated in both Aboriginal and non-indigenous communities; to bridge the gap between the life conditions of Aboriginal and other Australians; and to adopt policies that are genuinely inclusive, based on mutual respect. While some progress has been made, there is disagreement over both its speed and its direction. This has been exacerbated by continuation of a controversial federal 'intervention' in the affairs of Aboriginal people in the Northern Territory,[124] which involves suspension of the Racial Discrimination Act and discriminates against indigenous communities, triggering an adverse report from the United Nations Special Rapporteur on Indigenous Rights.[125]

In any event, however, an apology may take too insubstantial a form to provide the final basis for reconciliation. However solemn the occasion, an apology has no legal effect; and while law alone is far from sufficient as an instrument for reconciling communities the support of law may be necessary, for both practical and symbolic reasons, in the Australian context. In this regard, however, the absence of a founding treaty that can be given contemporary meaning presents a particular challenge. While there has been some discussion of a latter-day treaty or 'Makarrata',[126] the potential for political backlash against what can be portrayed as

---

[124] The Intervention was a reaction to the Report of a Board of Inquiry into the Protection of Aboriginal Children from Sexual Abuse, *Little Children are Sacred*, 2007.
[125] J Anaya, *The Situation of Indigenous Peoples in Australia*, an Addendum to a Report to the Fifteenth Session of the Human Rights Council, A/HRC/15/ 4 March 2010.
[126] S Brennan, L Behrendt, L Stelein and G Williams, *Treaty*, (Annandale, NSW, Federation Press, 2005) 14–16.

an acknowledgement of divided external sovereignty, coupled with the logistical difficulties of identifying appropriate parties, makes this a relatively unlikely option. In the circumstances, the instrument best placed to fill the gap is the Constitution, as the fundamental, national law. What it might say and what processes might be followed to decide what it should say are questions that are yet seriously to be asked.[127]

SELECTED READING

Aroney, N, *The Constitution of a Federal Commonwealth* (Cambridge, CUP, 2009)

Attwood, B, *Possession* (Melbourne, Vic, The Miegunyah Press, 2009)

Chesterman, J and Galligan, B, *Citizens Without Rights* (New York, CUP, 1997)

Cochrane, P, *Colonial Ambition* (Melbourne, Vic, MUP, 2006)

Craven, G (ed), *The Convention Debates, 1891–1898: Commentaries, Indices and Guide* (Sydney, NSW, Legal Books, 1986)

Department of the Senate, *Papers on Parliament,* Nos 30, 32 and 37

Finn, P, *Law and Government in Colonial Australia* (Melbourne, Vic, OUP, 1987)

Hirst, J, *The Sentimental Nation* (Melbourne, Vic, OUP, 2000)

Irving, H, *To Constitute a Nation* (Cambridge, CUP, 1997)

Neal, D, *The Rule of Law in a Penal Colony: Law and Politics in Early New South Wales*, 2nd edn (Cambridge, CUP, 2002)

Quick, J and Garran, RR, *Annotated Constitution of the Australian Commonwealth,* 1901 reprint (Sydney, Legal Books, 1976)

Schreuder, D and Ward, S, *Australia's Empire* (Oxford, OUP, 2008)

Twomey, A, *The Chameleon Crown* (Sydney, NSW, Federation Press, 2006)

---

[127] For a request for 'recognition' of Indigenous rights through 'serious constitutional reform' see G Yunupingu, 'Tradition, Truth and Tomorrow' (2009) 41 *The Monthly.*

2

Constitutions

—————➤◦◄—————

Form and Content – Status – Authority – Constitution and the Common Law

I. FORM AND CONTENT

A. Commonwealth Constitution

i. Purposes and Scope

O N ITS FACE, the Commonwealth Constitution has two primary purposes. One is to prescribe the legal framework for the federation. The second is to provide for the establishment of the principal institutions for the new federal sphere of government, confusingly also designated the 'Commonwealth', like the new political community that the federation created.[1] These goals are accomplished in a relatively short instrument of 128 sections divided into eight chapters of varying length.

The Constitution provides almost no protection for rights, apart from a small handful of provisions that arguably have a rights-protective effect and some limited additional protections that have been implied from institutional arrangements in recent decades. To adopt the typology of Joseph Raz, the Constitution thus is 'thin', in substance although

---

[1] J Quick and RR Garran distinguish the Commonwealth 'as a political entity and a political partnership . . . outside of and supreme over the Constitution' from the 'federal' government that the Constitution creates and that is undoubtedly subject to it: *The Annotated Constitution of the Australian Commonwealth* (Sydney, NSW, Angus and Robertson, 1901) 366, 927–28, also acknowledging some 'confusion of meaning' in the Constitution itself.

not in form.[2] It represents what now is a relatively rare approach to constitutional design, which empowers but does not constrain other than through the organisation of power. Persistence with this approach typically is justified on the ground that rights are adequately protected by the traditional combination of representative and responsible government and independent courts administering the common law, with consequences that are examined in chapter eight. From this perspective it is possible to understand Australian constitutional arrangements as only partly codified, leaving important questions as to general law and political practice, which elsewhere are covered by written constitutions. But a written constitution exerts a strong pull on the legal and political imagination, whatever its contents.[3] There is little sign of recognition in Australia that principles of a constitutional kind may be at stake outside the formal constitutional framework.[4]

The remainder of this part provides an overview of the subject-matter and legal form of the Constitution, as a basis for the discussion of the status of the Constitution and the authority for it that follows in parts two and three. The final part examines the nature of the Constitution from the different perspective of its relationship with the common law.

ii. Institutions

The institutions of government are established and empowered in the first three chapters of the Constitution, dealing respectively with the Parliament, the Executive Government and the Judicature. The similarity with the layout of the first three Articles of the Constitution of the United States contributed to what now is settled doctrine that the Constitution embodies a three-way separation of powers in the Commonwealth

---

[2] J Raz, 'On the Authority and Interpretation of Constitutions: Some Preliminaries' in J Raz, *Between Authority and Interpretation* (Oxford, OUP, 2009) 323, 324–25.

[3] W Gummow, 'The Constitution: Ultimate Foundation of Australian Law?' (2005) 79 *Australian Law Journal* 167.

[4] Whether such principles control the power of legislatures is a different question: on which see eg MD Walters, 'Written Constitutions and Unwritten Constitutionalism' in G Huscroft (ed), *Expounding the Constitution: Essays in Constitutional Theory* (Cambridge, CUP, 2008) 245; cf the critique in J Goldsworthy, 'The Myth of the Common Law Constitution' in DE Edlin, *Common Law Theory* (Cambridge, CUP, 2007) 204.

sphere.[5] Unlike in the United States, however, in Australia the government is required to be drawn from the Parliament in accordance with the principles of responsible government (s 64). The result is an asymmetrical separation of powers: weak as between the legislature and the executive, in institutional and functional terms, but pronounced as far as the judiciary is concerned.

iii. Federalism

Most of the rest of the Constitution puts the federal system in place. Legislative, executive and judicial power is divided between the Commonwealth and the States under chapters I, II and III. Chapter IV, on finance and trade, protects the freedom of internal trade that the framers of the Constitution sought, prescribes the limited federal financial settlement on which they were able to agree and requires parliamentary approval of expenditure, in provisions that also have played a role in the development of the federal spending power. Chapter V draws together a range of sections dealing with the place of the States in the Australian federation including, crucially, sections 106–8 preserving the Constitutions, powers and laws of the former colonies, now established as States and the provision in section 109 for paramountcy of Commonwealth law. Chapter VI deals with new States and territories; chapter VII with the 'miscellaneous' but highly sensitive issue of the location of the federal capital; and chapter VIII with the procedure for formal constitutional change.

Federation transformed the former colonies into States and necessarily deprived them of some power. Otherwise, however, the scheme of the Constitution is to impose remarkably few constraints on the structure and operation of State government. The State Constitutions, which are described in the next part, provide parallel institutions for State government and in this respect lie almost wholly within the control of the respective States. There are exceptions, however, and the list may not be closed. The establishment of the High Court as a court of appeal from the Supreme Courts of the States (s 73) has consequences for State authority over State court systems, which are examined in chapter six. Similarly, the implied constitutional freedom of political communication, originally

---

[5] *Victorian Stevedoring General Contracting Company Pty Ltd v Dignan* (1931) 46 CLR 73, 78.

justified as necessary to the operation of Commonwealth representative institutions, also inhibits State institutions, in an even more telling illustration of the difficulty of constitutionally disentangling the spheres of government from each other.[6]

iv. Form

For the reasons described in chapter one, in legal form the Commonwealth Constitution is section 9 of an Act of the Parliament of the United Kingdom, the Commonwealth of Australia Constitution Act 1900. The remainder of the Act comprises a preamble that recites the agreement of the people of the several colonies to unite in 'an indissoluble Federal Commonwealth under the Crown', some transitional provisions and a few sections with continuing substantive effect. From their historical vantage point in 1901, Quick and Garran regarded these provisions as dealing with the 'establishment of the new community', as opposed to the Constitution proper, which dealt 'only' with its 'governing organization'.[7] To avoid confusion with sections of the Constitution, these eight sections of the Act now are referred to as the 'covering clauses'.

How to repeal the covering clauses to enable the Constitution to stand alone is one of the minor puzzles of Australian constitutional law.[8] The problem was not confronted by the 1999 republican proposal, characterised by a former Chief Justice as a 'veritable constitutional camel' for this reason.[9] Removal of the Constitution from its casing in a British Act of Parliament will almost certainly be part of any future proposal to break the links between Australia and the Crown.

B. State Constitutions

Each of the Australian States has a constitution of its own. Self-government legislation also has been enacted by the Commonwealth Parliament for the

---

[6] *Lange v Australian Broadcasting Corporation* (1997) 189 CLR 520, 567.

[7] Note 1, 366.

[8] A Twomey, *The Constitution of New South Wales* (Annandale, NSW, Federation Press, 2004) 780–86.

[9] A Mason, 'Constitutional Issues Relating to the Republic as they Affect the States' (1998) 21 *University of New South Wales Law Journal* 750, 753, quoted in Twomey, n 8, 781, who also notes a proposal to deal with the problem simply by not reprinting the preamble and covering clauses in the future.

two mainland territories and for Norfolk Island.[10] These function as constitutions but, unlike the constitutions of the States, cannot be changed by
the territories themselves.

The original colonial Constitutions were enacted by colonial
Parliaments pursuant to British authority. Most have since been re-
enacted by the Parliaments of the States. Unlike the Commonwealth
Constitution, none is a direct enactment by the British Parliament. Since
federation, moreover, section 106 of the Constitution offers an alternative foundation of some kind, through its requirement that:

> The Constitution of each State of the Commonwealth shall, subject to this
> Constitution, continue as at the establishment of the Commonwealth . . . until
> altered in accordance with the Constitution of the State.

A parallel provision, in section 107, continues the power of State
Parliaments unless withdrawn in some way by the Commonwealth
Constitution.

In their commentary on section 106, Quick and Garran suggested
that section 106 'confirmed and continued' the State Constitutions but
that they are not 'created thereby'.[11] Intriguingly, they also observed that
'it may be argued that the Constitutions of the States are incorporated
into the new Constitution' so that '[t]he whole of the details of State
Government and Federal Government may be considered as constituting one grand scheme . . . in which the new national elements are
blended harmoniously with the old provincial elements . . . producing
a national plan of government having a federal structure'. This vision
has not materialised and the meaning of section 106 remains unsettled.

Like the Commonwealth Constitution, the State Constitutions deal
almost exclusively with the institutions of government and the allocation
of power amongst them.[12] As a generalisation they are longer, less structured and more diffuse, mixing matters of relatively minor detail with the
establishment of the principal organs of the State. In some States what
is conceived as the 'Constitution' is spread over more than one written
instrument, for reasons that are linked to the mechanism for constitutional
entrenchment, which is described below. This mechanism also helps to

---

[10] See generally, G Carney, *The Constitutional Systems of the Australian States and Territories* (Cambridge, CUP, 2006) ch.12.

[11] See Quick and Garran, fn 1, 928.

[12] Cf the recognition (without legal effect) of the Aboriginal people as the 'original custodians' of the land in the Constitution Act 1975 (Vic) s 1A.

explain why only parts of the principal constitutional instrument are protected by special alteration procedures in each State.

II. STATUS

A. Concept

The status of a constitution might be determined by a number of factors: an indication of its making by the *pouvoir constituant*; the significance of its function and content; the manner in which it can be changed; its position in the hierarchy of legal norms; and measures to effectuate its supremacy. In twenty-first century Australia, a constitution typically is distinguished from ordinary law by special alteration procedures, which underpin its status as supreme law. Typically also, constitutional supremacy is enforceable through judicial review, although this is not invariably so.[13]

When the Commonwealth Constitution first came into effect, the manner of its making was determinative. This had two dimensions: design and approval within Australia and enactment by the Imperial Parliament. The latter gave the Constitution the status of supreme law within Australia. This status was carefully maintained by the terms of the Statute of Westminster and the Australia Acts as independence was achieved and British authority to legislate for Australia was repudiated. While constitutional supremacy was thus placed beyond question, however, enactment of the Constitution by the British Parliament was no longer a satisfactory explanation for it, stimulating new interest in the significance of the events that took place in Australia, before the Constitution became law. The result has been 20 years of still inconclusive debate on the authority for the Constitution, which is examined in the next part.

Imperial legislation hovered in the background of the State Constitutions as well, as authority not only for their enactment but also for the obligation of colonial Parliaments to comply with what were described as 'manner and form' requirements in enacting legislation 'respecting the constitution, powers and procedures' of the legislature.[14] Legislation that did not

---

[13] Some sections of the Commonwealth Constitution are not 'justiciable': ss 53 and 54, dealing with the relations between the Houses of Parliament over money bills are examples.
[14] Colonial Laws Validity Act 1865 (Imp) s 5.

comply with such requirements was invalid, effectively giving these parts of State Constitutions effect as superior law. This approach to the problem of constitutional status is the product of a legal tradition that drew no distinction between constitutional and ordinary law and in which a Parliament, as ordinarily constituted, was assumed to be unable to bind its successors. If this is the default position, any authority to depart from it assumes disproportionate significance. Accordingly, when the final legal links with the United Kingdom were broken in 1986, the authority for State Parliaments to impose manner and form requirements was transferred from imperial legislation to the Australia Acts (s 6). The focus on State capacity to prescribe special procedures for the enactment of particular laws has given rise to a byzantine jurisprudence. As will be seen, there presently is real doubt about State authority to protect a wider range of constitutional provisions, including human rights provisions, even against implied repeal. At the same time, there appears to be no doubt about the power of a simple majority in a State Parliament to prescribe high hurdles to alteration of those parts of the State Constitution that fall within the former imperial remit.

Uncertainty about both the source of authority for the Commonwealth Constitution and the scope of effective entrenchment of State Constitutions, is attributable to the absence of a developed conception of constituent power that acknowledges the role of the people as a collective entity in the 'founding act'.[15] Martin Loughlin has shown how the concept was lost to the British constitutional tradition as the Crown in Parliament not only achieved legal supremacy but 'usurped the role of "the people" in the constitutional imagination'.[16] In Australia's case, the relevance of constituent power has been obscured further still by the original constitutive role of the British Parliament: since displaced, but not yet definitively replaced.

B. Commonwealth Constitution

i. *Supremacy*

However its authority is explained, the Commonwealth Constitution is supreme law in Australia. Covering clause 5 specifically makes the

---

[15] M Loughlin and N Walker, *The Paradox of Constitutionalism* (Oxford, OUP, 2007) 3.
[16] M Loughlin, 'English Constitutional Argument' in Loughlin and Walker, ibid, 28–29.

Constitution and Commonwealth laws enacted pursuant to it binding on the States, which in any event are subject to the paramountcy of Commonwealth law under section 109 of the Constitution itself. The Constitution applies directly to the Commonwealth, by establishing and conferring power on its institutions. The text of the Constitution can be changed only by a procedure involving both passage by Parliament and acceptance at referendum; the law and practice of section 128 is examined in greater detail below. Despite the absence of express authority for it, judicial review of legislation on grounds of constitutionality has never seriously been doubted. Courts can and do hold statutes of either the Commonwealth or State Parliaments invalid on the grounds of inconsistency with the Commonwealth Constitution. The status of the Constitution is assumed and accepted by officials and the public alike.

The supremacy of the Commonwealth Constitution over the Constitutions of the States follows from the design of the federation. It is made explicit by the insistence in section 106 that 'The Constitution of each State . . . shall, *subject to this Constitution*, continue'.[17] Section 106 thus ensures that provisions of the Commonwealth Constitution that impact on the Constitutions of the States are given full effect. But its implications for the relationship between the State Constitutions and an exercise of Commonwealth legislative power pursuant to section 51, itself expressed to be 'subject to this Constitution' are less obvious. The issue is further complicated by restrictions on Commonwealth legislative power to burden the States 'in the exercise of their constitutional functions', which have been implied from the federal character of the Constitution.[18]

Nevertheless, it appears now to be settled that a Commonwealth law enacted under section 51(xxxviii) of the Constitution, at least, can affect the Constitution of a State. In *Port Macdonnell* the legislation in issue sought to ensure the power of the States to make extraterritorial laws with respect to fisheries beyond the limits of their coastal waters.[19] It thus either confirmed or extended the legislative powers conferred on the States by their Constitutions. While the High Court held that the challenged fisheries regime fell within State legislative power, in any event, it proceeded also to 'express a view' on the validity of the Commonwealth

---

[17]   Emphasis supplied.
[18]   *Austin v Commonwealth* (2003) 215 CLR 185, 258; see further, ch 7.
[19]   *Port Macdonnell Professional Fishermen's Association Inc v South Australia* (1989) 168 CLR 340; the legislation was the Coastal Waters (State Powers) Act 1980 (Cth).

legislation. In a short passage, it concluded that the continuation of State Constitutions in section 106 'until altered in accordance with the Constitution of the State' is subject to an exercise of power under section 51(xxxviii). The reasoning of the Court is based in part on the character of section 51(xxxviii), including the requirement for State co-operation. The decision thus does not necessarily apply to the exercise of any other head of power, although it is likely to do so.

As explained in chapter one, reliance subsequently was placed on section 51(xxxviii) to enact the Australian version of the Australia Act. Section 6 of that Act authorises the States to impose 'manner and form' requirements for the alteration of parts of their Constitutions. In *Marquet*, the Court characterised this section as restricting State power, but confirmed the conclusion in *Port Macdonell* that a Commonwealth Act under section 51(xxxviii) prevails over the protection of State Constitutions in section 106.[20] Some even more complex issues raised by the relationship between the Australia Acts and section 106 are examined below in the context of the extent of State power to entrench State Constitutions.

ii. Constitution Alteration

The effects of the Commonwealth Constitution can be altered in a variety of ways; judicial interpretation; intergovernmental co-operation; the extension of Commonwealth legislative powers through a reference from State Parliaments; the enactment of legislation to supplant transitional arrangements put in place by the Constitution. There are limits to the usefulness of constitutional development through evolution, however. Deliberate textual change to the Commonwealth Constitution can be achieved only through the procedures laid down in section 128.

Section 128 leaves the initiative for proposing change with the Commonwealth Parliament. A Constitution Alteration bill must be passed by each House with an absolute majority, or by one House twice in accordance with a prescribed deadlock procedure. Approval of a proposal for change requires passage at referendum by double majorities: a national majority and a majority of voters in a majority of States. In exceptional cases, diminishing constitutionally guaranteed State representation in the Parliament, altering State boundaries or affecting the constitutional provisions relating to State boundaries including, presumably, section 128 itself,

---

[20] *Attorney-General (WA) v Marquet* (2003) 217 CLR 545, 571; but cf Kirby J at 614, describing section 106 as 'one of the fundamental postulates of the Constitution'.

a majority is required in the States affected, which in practice may mean a majority in all States. The final step is assent by the Governor-General, which unlike the rest of the procedure, is a formality.

The design of the Constitution alteration procedure is consistent with the federal structure of the Constitution, the manner in which it was made and the generally progressive aspirations for it in 1901. There is both a national and a federal element in each of the procedures for initiation and approval of change. The requirement for a referendum complements the way in which the constitutional draft was approved in Australia in the first place. The referendum was viewed by some delegates as the next stage in the evolution of democracy, whatever its theoretical and practical difficulties in a system of government that otherwise relied on representation,[21] which were partly accommodated in any event by leaving the Parliament with sole responsibility for the initiative. After a flirtation in 1891 with the use of constitutional conventions along United States lines, the Australians also turned to the referendum in the expectation that it would strike a better balance between constitutional protection and constitutional change.[22]

The expectation has not been realised. It has proved very difficult to persuade voters to support the proposals that the government and Parliament are prepared to put forward. Only eight out of 44 referendum bills have been accepted in the more than 100 years since federation. At least two of these were minor;[23] three made useful but limited changes to institutional arrangements;[24] and another three dealt with the organisation of power in ways that have been reasonably significant.[25] Almost three-quarters of all proposals have failed to attract national majorities and only five have failed on the requirement for a majority of States alone.[26] No referendum has passed since 1977 and the last two

[21] For example, Isaac Isaacs, noting a 'sure shifting of power from the Parliament to the people' since the enactment of the Reform Act 1832: Australasian Federal Convention, Melbourne, *Debates*, 758–59; cf Patrick Glynn, arguing that the referendum involved repudiation of the 'wisdom of centuries', at 738.

[22] Thus in *Wollaston's case* (1902) 28 VLR 357, 383 Madden CJ referred to s 128 as 'a very easy method of amending the Constitution' in comparison to the 'much more ponderous' American requirements.

[23] Constitution Alteration (Senate Elections) 1906; (State Debts) 1910.

[24] Constitution Alteration (Casual Vacancies) 1977; (Retirement of Judges) 1977; (Referendums) 1977.

[25] Constitution Alteration (State Debts) 1928; (Social Services) 1946; (Aborigines) 1967.

[26] Of these, two attracted majorities in two States and three attracted majorities

proposals put to referendum, in 1999, attracted national support from only 45.13 per cent and 39.34 per cent of the voters respectively.[27] The record of constitutional change discourages it from being attempted when it is needed and places additional pressure on judicial review.

The difficulties of the referendum as a mechanism for the approval of constitutional change are notorious. A negative vote may be caused by a range of factors: disapproval of other aspects of a government's policy or performance; lack of understanding of the proposals; disagreement with part of a larger constitutional package. In Australia, additional features of the way in which the referendum works in practice may affect the outcome as well. One is the obligation to vote in referendums; or at least to turn up to the polling booth.[28] Another is the highly adversarial character of most referendum campaigns, which often become an extension of the contest between the parties in Parliament. The problem is exacerbated by the fact that the only official information made available to the public about the meaning and purpose of a referendum proposal is a short case for and against it, prepared by the supporters and opponents of the proposal in Parliament and distributed by the Electoral Commission. In 2009 a parliamentary inquiry recommended that while the 'yes/no' case should be retained it should be supplemented by additional material approved by a Referendum Panel.[29] Significantly, this recommendation was opposed by three of the four non-government members of the relevant committee.

The referendum requirement in the Commonwealth Constitution is similar to its counterpart in the Swiss Constitution and undoubtedly was adapted from it. In Switzerland, however, the outcomes are strikingly different, with 152 of 205 mandatory referenda approved between 1848 and 2005.[30] This might be explained in a number of ways: the absence of a mechanism in Australia for popular initiative;[31] the more adversarial

in three States; Australian Electoral Commission *Referendum Dates and Results* (http://www.aec.gov.au/Elections/referendums/Referendum_Dates_and_Results.htm (viewed 25 July 2010).

[27] Constitution Alteration (Republic) 1999; Constitution Alteration (Preamble) 1999.

[28] Commonwealth Electoral Act 1918, s 128A.

[29] House of Representatives Standing Committee on Legal and Constitutional Affairs, *A Time for Change: Yes/No?* December 2009.

[30] J Reich, 'An Interactional Model of Direct Democracy: Lessons from the Swiss Experience' (June 2008), http://ssrn.com/abstract=1154019 (viewed 27 August 2010).

[31] Cf Swiss Federal Constitution, Articles 138, 139.

Australian political system and culture; the relatively more frequent use of the referendum in Switzerland. For those with an interest in the consequences of constitutional borrowing, the use of the referendum in Australia offers an interesting case.

C. State Constitutions

i. *Legal Framework*

By contrast, the starting assumption for examination of the status of the Constitutions of the States has been that a State Parliament has plenary authority to enact and change the Constitution, subject to any constraints in a higher source of law. On this basis, the default status of State Constitutions is that of ordinary law and the organising principle is parliamentary sovereignty, presumed to be of the continuing variety, reflecting the intellectual genesis of these Constitutions in the British constitutional tradition of the latter part of the nineteenth century.

The colonies were self-governing rather than sovereign, however and the constituent authority of their Parliaments depended on the authority they were given under imperial law. The initial grant of constituent authority authorised the Legislative Council of a colony to enact a Constitution providing for a bicameral legislature. Typically, however, this grant of authority and most of the Constitutions made in reliance on it prescribed special procedures to be followed in altering particular provisions.[32] In the 1860s, in South Australia, uncertainty about the precise legal border between self-government and imperial control came to a head in a series of incidents, some of which questioned the power of the South Australian Parliament to alter the colonial Constitution.[33] To overcome the 'doubts' thus raised, the Imperial Parliament enacted the Colonial Laws Validity Act 1865 (Imp) (CLVA), section 5 of which provided that 'every representative legislature shall . . . have, and be deemed at all times to have had, full power to make laws respecting [its] . . . constitution, powers, and procedure'. This was, however, subject to a proviso that 'such laws shall have been passed in such manner and form as shall from time to time be required'.

---

[32] Australian Constitutions Act (No.2) 1850 (Imp), s 32, imposing procedures for reservation and disallowance.

[33] Carney, n 10, 180–81.

It may be accepted that, historically, the primary purpose of the CLVA was to confirm, rather than to limit plenary power; that preservation of the status of colonial constitutions by reference to 'manner and form' requirements reflected the type of constraints then imposed by imperial law; and that the limitation of the proviso to matters respecting the 'constitution, powers, and procedure of the legislature' similarly can be explained in terms of the scope of the constraints imposed at the time, in relation to which doubts had arisen.[34] Nevertheless, the CLVA offered explicit authority, from a higher power, for State entrenchment of at least parts of their Constitutions and became the centrepiece around which understanding of the status of State Constitutions evolved.

By the time the Australia Acts were negotiated, manner and form procedures were a familiar feature of State constitutional design. In several cases they had been used to protect parts of a constitution that at some stage or another had been regarded as politically sensitive in the State concerned: unicameralism in Queensland; bicameralism in New South Wales; the office of Governor in Queensland and Western Australia. Double entrenchment, so as to prevent evasion of the manner and form requirement itself by a two-step procedure had become the norm, highlighting the extent to which observance of the Constitution depended on the legal requirements for constitutional change, rather than on respect for constitutional procedures.

And while there was considerable legal uncertainty about the scope of State power to give their Constitutions higher legal status in this or any other way, two ends of a spectrum of possibilities had been settled by judicial decision. One was that, if no manner and form provision applied, a State Constitution could be altered by implication by a later, inconsistent Act.[35] The other was that a law respecting the 'constitution, powers and procedure of the legislature' within the meaning of CLVA section 5 was invalid if it failed to comply with a specified procedure for law- making, including a requirement for approval at referendum.[36]

With hindsight it is unfortunate that by 1986 no more rounded conception had emerged of the place of a State Constitution in the legal order of both the State and the Australian federation and that the significance of section 106 was relatively unexplored. In any event, the

---

[34] Twomey, *The Constitution of New South Wales*, n 8, 273–75.
[35] *McCawley v The King* [1920] AC 691.
[36] *Attorney-General (NSW) v Trethowan* (1931) 44 CLR 394.

prospect that even the limited facility for entrenchment offered by CLVA section 5 might be a casualty of the removal of the authority of laws of paramount force under the Australia Acts caused the latter to be designed to preserve the effects of section 5. In the Australia Acts, however, the section 5 proviso is enacted in a section of its own. Under section 6 of the Australia Acts, a State law 'respecting the constitution, powers or procedure of the State Parliament shall be of no force or effect unless it is made in such manner and form as may from time be required'.

On one view, section 2(2) of the Australia Acts performs the task of the rest of section 5 by declaring that State legislative power includes 'all . . . powers that the Parliament of the United Kingdom might have exercised before the commencement of this Act for the peace, order and good government' of the State. There are two differences, however, which may yet prove significant. One is that the purpose of section 2(2) was to overcome doubts about the capacity of the States to legislate in ways that affected the powers previously exercised by the United Kingdom in relation to the States, rather than generally to confirm their plenary power.[37] The second is that, unlike CLVA section 5, the Australia Acts make no specific reference to the constituent power of the Parliaments of the States.

ii. The Price of Path-Dependency

The continuing dependence of State constitutional law on rules laid down in the context of transition to colonial self-government that have long since lost their point has come at a cost.

Arguably, two competing principles are at stake in determining the status of any constitution. One is the right of each generation to make decisions about its own affairs, including arrangements for government, untrammelled by constraints from the past. The other is the value of protecting the framework of principle within which a polity operates from hasty change by 'transient majorities'.[38] The current law and practice in relation to the status of State Constitutions satisfies neither. Laws that fall within the ambit of section 6 of the Australia Acts can be

---

[37] Twomey, *The Constitution of New South Wales,* n 8, 96.
[38] J Goldsworthy, 'Manner and Form in the Australian States' (1987) 16 *Melbourne University Law Review* 403, 421–22, also canvassing some of the literature on each of these positions.

heavily burdened by procedural requirements that effectively qualify the authority of a current majority.[39] Entrenchment under section 6 affects any law that can be characterised as one 'respecting the constitution, powers, or procedure of the legislature' and is not necessarily confined to alteration of a State Constitution.[40] Entrenching provisions can be put in place by simple parliamentary majorities, in the course of the ordinary legislative process.

The crowning anomaly is the doubt that exists under the current regime about the capacity of States to provide protection for their constitutional rules outside the ambit of section 6. Always a problem, this has become increasingly significant as individual States have moved to entrench constitutional provisions dealing with a wide range of matters: local government; the Supreme Court; independent organs of State such as the Ombudsman; even the public delivery of water services.[41] A growing interest in mechanisms for rights protection has begun to focus attention on the potential to entrench rights as well. On the law as it presently stands, it is unlikely that legislation to amend provisions of this kind would fall within the ambit of section 6 of the Australia Acts, although this is not finally settled.[42] A question thus arises about whether and on what basis a State can confer the status of superior law on parts of the State Constitution that are not covered by section 6.

iii. Theoretical Possibilities

At one level, the Australian States share this problem with other polities in the British constitutional tradition, including New Zealand and

---

[39] Although not so heavily that they amount to an abdication of power. In *West Lakes Ltd v South Australia* (1980) 25 SASR 389, 397, King CJ explained approval by referendum as a requirement going to the 'manner' of enacting legislation rather than an abdication of legislative power, on the grounds that it involves the 'direct approval of the people whom the "representative legislature" represents'.

[40] On the scope of these categories see *Trethowan*, n 36, 429–30; *Marquet*, n 20, 572–73; Carney, n 10, 164–170.

[41] These examples are taken from the Constitution Act 1975 (Vic) s 18.

[42] For the difficulties of an expanded view of a law respecting the 'powers' of the Parliament see Carney, n 10, 164–66; Goldsworthy, 'Manner and Form', n 38, 415–17. But, as Carney notes, intermediate courts have assumed the effectiveness of the entrenchment of the Supreme Court and local government in the Victorian Constitution; see further, in relation to the Supreme Court, *Smith v R* (1994) 181 CLR 338, 352–53, per Deane J. The question was left open by the High Court in *Marquet*, at 572.

the United Kingdom itself, that historically have accepted the Diceyan understanding of parliamentary sovereignty. As the idea of a constitution as a legal norm distinct from and superior to ordinary statute law gained hold over the course of the twentieth century, the challenge in all these jurisdictions was to identify ways in which rules of a constitutional kind might receive some protection against amendment while maintaining, at least nominally, a parliamentary sovereignty framework.

Two broad sets of possibilities emerge from the case law and scholarship. One is to conclude that parliamentary sovereignty is self-embracing after all, so that a Parliament, presumably acting as a constituent assembly, might establish a constitution with the status of supreme law. HLA Hart described this as representing 'an even larger sphere of legislative competence' that 'might equally well, perhaps even better, deserve the name of "sovereignty"'.[43] Another, prompted by the technique of manner and form, argues that Parliament can be 'reconstituted' for certain law-making purposes without affecting its continuing sovereignty.[44] There are several variations on the latter approach, designed either to maintain the representative character of the reconstituted legislature or to overcome the obvious objection that extensive procedural constraints on law-making, under the guise of reconstitution of the legislature, could be virtually undistinguishable from substantive constraints.[45] A less sweeping but nevertheless significant modification of the view that a Parliament is unable to bind its successors would accept the effectiveness of constraints on the 'form' of legislation, so as to preclude implied repeal of statutes of a constitutional kind.

The idea that Parliament can be constrained, at least procedurally, in altering constitutional arrangements that fall outside the bounds of the CLVA has gained some purchase in the reasoning of courts in other common law jurisdictions.[46] An example to which it will be necessary

---

[43]   HLA Hart, *The Concept of Law*, 2nd edn (Oxford, OUP, 1994) 149.

[44]   Ibid, 150–51.

[45]   See for example Goldsworthy, 'Manner and Form Revisited', n 38, 34–35, accepting that the imposition of 'pure' procedures, comprising absolute majorities, but not super majority or referendum requirements, would not affect continuing sovereignty.

[46]   On acceptance of 'form' requirements in the UK see *Factortame Ltd v Secretary of State (No 2)* [1991] 1 All ER 102; and more recently *Thoburn v Sunderland City Council* [2003] QB 151. On the 'manner' of legislation, see *Jackson v Attorney-General* [2006] 1 AC 262, [81], [161–63], cf [113].

to return is the observation of the Privy Council in *Ranasinghe* that a 'legislature has no power to ignore the conditions of law-making that are imposed by the instrument that itself regulates its power to make law. The restriction exists independently of the question whether the legislature is sovereign'.[47] In a parallel development, confidence has grown that, should a Parliament attempt to impose a special manner of law-making for constitutional arrangements, its effectiveness would be accepted by the courts as long, at least, as the procedure is not unduly constraining and that there is a 'general consensus among the public' on proceeding in this way.[48]

iv. Impact of the Australian Constitutional Framework

In Australia these possibilities also have been explored and occasionally accepted, although not by a majority of the High Court. But in any event, in Australia, such ideas must give way to provision to the contrary in superior law. There are two possible sources of superior law for this purpose: the Commonwealth Constitution and the Australia Acts. To complicate the matter further, the relationship between them is unclear, as far as the entrenchment of State Constitutions is concerned.

In principle, the Commonwealth Constitution should be the starting point for determining whether superior law affects the entrenchment of State Constitutions outside the procedures of section 6 of the Australia Acts. It will be remembered that section 106 continues the Constitution of each State 'until altered in accordance with the Constitution of the State'. This may be read either as requiring compliance with constitution alteration procedures as prescribed in State Constitutions from time to time or as merely preserving whatever constitution alteration procedures exist independently of section 106. Scholarly opinion favours the latter, encouraged by the language of continuity in the text of section 106.[49] On the other hand, this view places no weight on the possible significance of independence, including the effective withdrawal of the United

---

[47] *The Bribery Commissioner v Pedrick Ranasinghe* [1965] AC 172, 197.

[48] M Chen and Sir G Palmer, *Public Law in New Zealand*, 2nd edn (Oxford, OUP, 1993) 140–48.

[49] See for example, Carney, n 10, 190–91; Goldsworthy, 'Manner and Form', n 38, 427, both of whom also point to the potential ambiguity of the concept of a State Constitution in section 106. Cf the possible view to the contrary in *Western Australia v Wilsmore* [1981] WAR 179, 184; R French, 'Manner and Form in Western Australia: An Historical Note' (1993) 23 *University of Western Australia Law Review* 335.

Kingdom as the source of State constituent power.[50] From the stand-point of the coherence of the Australian constitutional system, there would be considerable advantage in grounding State Constitutions in section 106, as a framework for the exercise of State constituent power, subject to the Constitution as a whole.

If section 106 of the Constitution does not provide the answer, the Australia Act 1986 (Cth) might be understood to affect State capacity to entrench State Constitutions in a variety of ways. The retention of the limited 'manner and form' procedures in section 6 alone may raise a pre-sumption that manner and form requirements cannot affect other cate-gories of constitutional laws. Potentially more serious is section 2(2), if it is understood as conferring continuing sovereignty on State Parliaments or even confirming its existence, rather than merely overcoming the residual consequences of colonial status. This wider view of section 2(2) would preclude acceptance of any form of 'self-embracing' State legislative power including, presumably, the application to the States of a suitably tailored version of the principle in *Ranasinghe* that 'a legislature has no power to ignore the conditions of law-making that are imposed by the instrument which itself regulates its power to make law.[51] Because section 2(2) confers power on the 'Parliament' of each State, which must be taken to refer to the Parliament as defined in the State Constitution, the section also creates an additional hurdle for the argument that in imposing a referendum requirement for the purposes of constitutional change the Parliament is merely 'reconstituting' itself unless, at least, the constitutional definition of 'Parliament' itself is altered.[52]

If the Australia Act is the controlling instrument and if any of these arguments are sustained, the release of the States from colonial restric-tions on their power will have had the bizarre consequence of freezing the constituent power of State Parliaments along colonial lines, with all their faults, with no other supporting rationale.[53] By contrast, section 106

---

[50] By way of contrast, the fact of independence has caused the High Court to revise the understanding of other parts of the Constitution: see for example *Sue v Hill* (1999) 199 CLR 462.

[51] [1965] AC 172, 197.

[52] Carney, n 10, 186; Goldsworthy 'Manner and Form' n 38, 412–14. See also the further complication identified by Goldsworthy of identifying democratic limits on the extent to which a Parliament might be redefined for section 2(2): at 423–25.

[53] Cf the maintenance of some extraterritorial constraints on State power through s 2(1) of the Australia Acts, which has a modern day rationale in the

has the potential to develop as the framework for a conception of the Constitutions of the States in an independent Australia, free from the accidents of imperial history.

v. What Next?

There is no shortage of criticism of this aspect of Australian constitutional law, from the standpoint of both majoritarian democracy and constitutionalism. In *Marquet*, Justice Kirby favoured a limited interpretation of section 6 of the Australia Acts in terms that could be interpreted as opposition to any form of entrenchment, although it is equally possible that he was reacting against the way in which entrenchment is used, to 'impose the dead hand of past political notions and factional interests' by means of a simple majority in a State Parliament.[54] Others have proposed widening the scope of provisions that might be subject to entrenchment.[55] Even in the absence of formal change the widespread use of entrenchment by governments and parliaments and its acceptance by State courts suggests a shift in the rule of recognition. Proposals to formally extend the potential for entrenchment often also suggest reform of the procedures by which decisions to entrench are given effect by a Parliament. In effect, this is a plea for Parliaments to distinguish their constituent from their ordinary law-making role.

It is generally suggested that these changes could best be made by alteration of section 2 of the Australia Acts by the Parliament of the Commonwealth at the request of the Parliaments of the States, pursuant to section 15(1). This would be easy enough to achieve, granted the political will. In other respects, however, it would be unfortunate. It would perpetuate the focus on 'manner and form' procedures at the expense of the nature and significance of State Constitutions. It would reinforce the role of the Australia Acts vis-à-vis the Commonwealth Constitution on a central aspect of constitutional law.

---

avoidance of inconsistency between State laws: *Union Steamship Company of Australia Pty Ltd v King* (1988) 166 CLR 1.

[54] See Marquet, n 20 at 610.

[55] Including J Goldsworthy, 'Manner and Form Revisited: Reflections on *Marquet's* case', in M Groves (ed), *Law and Government in Australia* (Annandale, NSW, Federation Press, 2005) 18, 38–39; he would exclude the use of super-majority requirements, however, as 'unnecessary and undemocratic': at 39.

It is not impossible that the current unsatisfactory state of the law could be ameliorated by judicial decision. The role that section 106 of the Constitution plays in relation to State Constitutions has not finally been decided. Strands of Australian authority that appear to support a self-embracing view of State sovereignty, not the least of which are the extrajudicial remarks of Sir Owen Dixon that the principle of parliamentary sovereignty accepted at Westminster was 'not otherwise a necessary part of the conception of a unitary system of government' and that 'to suppose otherwise is to mistake what may be and often is for what must be'.[56]

More recent pronouncements of the High Court are not encouraging, however. There are observations of the majority in *Marquet* that generally are taken to deny that the States can entrench provisions of their Constitutions otherwise than pursuant to section 6 of the Australia Acts.[57] Admittedly, the *Marquet* majority qualified its statement that the 'express provisions of s 6 can leave no room for the operation of any other principle' by adding 'at the very least in the field in which s 6 operates' which on its face leaves the question undecided outside that field.[58] On the other hand, an observation of Gummow J in *McGinty,* on which the joint reasons in *Marquet* build, assumes that State Parliaments otherwise have 'plenary . . . power', as a result of section 2(2).[59]

One final observation is prompted by a query raised by the majority of the High Court in *Marquet* about whether the principle derived from *Ranasinghe* 'can be applied in a federation'.[60] The query may presume that in a federation an overriding federal constitution makes provision for such matters, leaving no room for the *Ranasinghe* principle. But whether the Commonwealth Constitution does so provide, and to what effect, are the very questions in issue. The understanding of the nature of a constitution that informs *Ranasinghe* could assist in answering these questions too.

---

[56] O Dixon, 'The Common Law as the Ultimate Constitutional Foundation' (1957) 31 *Australian Law Journal* 240, 241–42.
[57] (2003) 217 CR 545, 574. See also Gummow J in *McGinty* (1996) 186 CLR 140, 297 and extrajudicially in W Gummow, 'The Constitution: The Ultimate Foundation of Australian Law', n 3, 170.
[58] (2003) 217 CR 545, 574.
[59] (1986) 186 CLR 140, 297.
[60] (2003) 217 CLR 545, 574.

III. AUTHORITY

A. The Nature of the Difficulty

The special status of a constitution requires an explanation of some kind, by way of justification. Usually this points to the authority on which a constitution draws and which distinguishes it from ordinary law. The authority may be legal, in the sense that the constitution derives its status from a higher legal source. Typically, however, where the constitution is an 'originating' constitution,[61] the authority for it will not lie in 'a norm of positive law'.[62]

There are many accounts of how constitutions of this kind acquire and retain their legitimacy. The one most frequently invoked, however, is that they draw their authority from the people of the state to which the constitution applies. The 'original and supreme will' of the people was the explanation offered by Chief Justice Marshall in *Marbury v Madison*[63] for the 'superior' status of the constitution of the United States as 'paramount' law. The 'Nation alone', according to Sieyès during the heady days of the French revolution, had the right to make a constitution.[64] Of course, there are innumerable objections to such explanations, ranging from the typically virtual way in which the 'people' are involved in any constitution-making exercise; the limited conception of the relevant 'people' when the older constitutions, at least, came into effect; and the increasing awkwardness of reliance on the authority of a founding generation over time. Nevertheless, recourse to the authority of the people has symbolic attraction and serves to distinguish a constitution from ordinary law in a way that is readily understood. Increasingly, the way in which constitutions are made gives such claims a degree of verisimilitude, at least in the early years.

It is not unusual for the question of the authority for the constitution of a state to provoke disagreement and debate. As the issue presents itself in Australia, however, it is distinctive; and although at one level

---

[61] Raz, n 2, 330, noting an exception for the initial constitutions of countries emerging from colonialism.

[62] H Kelsen, 'Professor Stone and the Pure Theory of Law' (1965) 17 *Stanford Law Review* 1128, 1141.

[63] 5 US 137, 177 (1803).

[64] EJ Sieyès, *Qu'est-ce que le tiers-état?* (Paris, Éditions du Boucher, 1789) 50, 53.

the Australian dilemma is shared with other post-colonial States in the British constitutional tradition, in some respects it also is unique. The critical components are as follows. First, Australia has a federal constitution that is deeply entrenched and that undoubtedly represents supreme law. Secondly, when the Constitution came into effect in 1901 the explanation for its supremacy lay in its enactment by the British Parliament, which at the time was accepted in Australia as a higher law-making authority. Admittedly, the degree of popular involvement in the design and approval of the draft in Australia before enactment was significant at the time and has become increasingly significant with hindsight; nevertheless, imperial enactment was the *sine qua non*. Thirdly, at some point the British Parliament lost its authority in Australia and while this may have happened as a matter of convention well before the enactment of the Australia Acts, it was confirmed in unmistakeable terms in 1986. Finally, throughout the long procession to independence, Australia was concerned to avoid a break in legal continuity.

From the standpoint of constitutional theory, the implications for the Constitution of the repudiation of British authority to legislate for Australia could simply be ignored. By 1986, the supremacy of the Constitution had been accepted without question for 85 years.[65] All relevant officials assumed that the section 128 procedure must be followed to change the constitutional text, which until then was binding;[66] there was a 'presupposition' on the part of jurists and others that 'one ought to act as the constitution prescribes';[67] it was clearly arguable that Australians had an 'active belief' that the Constitution deserved 'respect or obedience';[68] as an older Constitution, it had become 'self-validating' over time.[69]

If it matters whether citizens understand their own constitutional arrangements, such theoretical explanations are not entirely satisfactory, however.[70] The story of Australian independence is already complicated

---

[65] Although cf *Joosse v Australian Securities and Investment Commission* (1998) 159 ALR 260, in which the plaintiff argued that a 'break in sovereignty' in Australia had implications for the validity of the Constitution and legislation dependent on it. The argument was dismissed.

[66] Hart, n 43, 105–07.

[67] H Kelsen, 'What is a Legal Act?' (1984) 29 *American Journal of Jurisprudence* 199, 201. For Kelsen's purposes, the Constitution also was 'efficacious'.

[68] R Fallon, 'Legitimacy and the Constitution' (2005) 118 *Harvard Law Review* 1787, 1795, developing a notion of 'sociological legitimacy', drawing on Max Weber.

[69] Raz, n 2, 348–49.

[70] G Lindell, 'Why is the Constitution Binding? The Reasons in 1900 and Now, and the Effect of Independence' (1986) 16 *Federal Law Review* 29, 30.

enough. It would be convenient to be able to identify a less abstract replacement for the authority of the British Parliament to explain the continuing supremacy of the Commonwealth Constitution.

B. Options

The most obvious alternative source of authority for the Commonwealth Constitution is the Australian people themselves. This is a familiar explanation for the authority of constitutions elsewhere. It has a grounding in Australian experience, through the way in which the Constitution was made and the continuing requirement of a referendum for constitutional change. The dual approval processes for the Constitution in the 1890s, in both Australia and in London, simplify the task of historical reconstruction that is involved in lowering the significance of one and elevating that of the other.

On the other hand, reliance on the authority of the Australian people is subject to all the usual objections once the explanation is probed. In addition, in Australia, some further difficulties arise. The first is familiar in other federations: are the 'people' to be understood as organised nationally or in States in order to endow the Constitution with authority? The second is shared by other countries with an indigenous population whose status is the subject of ongoing dispute. What are the implications of the collective 'sovereignty' of the Australian people for the original claims of the Aboriginal peoples and for their status in contemporary Australia?[71] The third is entirely practical. If the explanation for the authority of the Commonwealth Constitution changed in 1986, there was no official acknowledgement of it; no fanfare of the kind that might be expected to mark a shift in authority not just from Britain to Australia but from Parliament to people. If change had happened how, in these circumstances, was it to be recognised at all?

In 1986, a perceptive Australian constitutional scholar wrote an article to explore why, in the wake of independence, the Constitution was now 'binding'.[72] He concluded that 'an additional, although not necessarily alternative' explanation for the status of the Constitution lay in the 'will and authority' of the people and argued that the High Court might

---

[71] F Brennan, 'The Indigenous People' in PD Finn (ed), *Essays on Law and Government, Vol I, Principles and Values* (Sydney, NSW, Law Book Co, 1995) 33, 33–39.

[72] Lindell, n 70 above.

adopt such an explanation, consistently with its approach to constitutional interpretation. What followed may not have been cause and effect; even before the article was written there had been suggestions from within the Court that the 'traditional' theory of the authority for the Constitution might require reconsideration.[73] In 1992, however, Chief Justice Mason observed, citing Lindell, that the Australia Acts 'marked the end of the legal sovereignty of the Imperial Parliament and recognized that ultimate sovereignty resided in the Australian people'.[74] The observation has since been repeated by others.[75]

The view that the people of Australia provide the authority for the Constitution is now widely accepted. It is not uncontested, however; and the points at which issue is joined shed some light on the *mentalité* of Australian constitutional arrangements.[76] Leaving aside the complication of colonial status, had a Constitution been made and approved in most countries in the way in which the draft Constitution was agreed within Australia in the 1890s it would have been accepted as an exercise of constituent power in some form, whether or not the term actually was used. It is a mark of the continuing influence of parliamentary sovereignty—as well as, perhaps, the essentially pragmatic character of Australian constitutional discourse—that much of the commentary on the authority for the Constitution in twenty-first century Australia worries about the distinction between legal and political sovereignty, rather than accepting that the two might 'coalesce' in an entrenched Constitution for an independent state.[77] It is a mark of Australia's attachment to evolution and continuity that commentators also distinguish the goal of autonomy, undoubtedly secured by the Australia Acts, from autochthony, which on this line of reasoning may never be attained.[78]

---

[73] *Kirmani v Captain Cook Cruises* (1985) 159 CLR 461; *University of Wollongong v Metwally* (1984) 158 CLR 447, 477, Deane J (referring to the 'people from whom the artificial entities called Commonwealth and States derive their authority').

[74] *Australian Capital Television v Commonwealth* (1992) 177 CLR 106, 137–38.

[75] S Evans, 'Why is the Constitution Binding? Authority, Obligation and the Role of the People' (2004) 25 *Adelaide Law Review* 103, citing such references prior to 2003.

[76] P Legrand, 'Comparative Legal Studies and the Matter of Authenticity' (2006) 1 *Journal of Comparative Law* 365, 376.

[77] P Finn, 'A Sovereign People, A Public Trust' in Finn, n 71, 1,4. As Evans notes, some of the judges reconcile the two through a concept of 'ultimate' sovereignty, drawing on the work of James Bryce: n 75, 107–108.

[78] The terms are drawn from A Dillon, 'A Turtle by Any Other Name: The Legal Basis of the Australian Constitution' (2001) 29 *Federal Law Review* 241, 253.

C. Significance

In 1935 the distinguished Australian jurist Owen Dixon drew a distinction between the Constitutions of Australia and the United States in the following terms:

> [T]he Constitution of our Commonwealth . . . is not a supreme law purporting to obtain its force from the direct expression of a people's inherent authority to constitute a government. It is a statute of the British Parliament . . . In the interpretations of our Constitution this distinction has many important consequences. We treat our organs of government simply as institutions established by law, and we interpret their powers simply as authorities belonging to them by law. American doctrine treats them as agents for the people who are the source of power.[79]

If the effect of the Australia Acts is to substitute the Australian people as the source of continuing authority for the Commonwealth Constitution, Dixon's analysis prompts the question of what, if any, substantive implications this might have.

One possibility emerges, at least by implication, from Dixon's own description. The change might be regarded as altering the relationship between the people and the organs of government in a way that Paul Finn has described as government as a 'trust'. For Finn, 'all who exercise the devolved power of the public do so as servants of the public', and must meet standards of integrity, open government and public accountability.[80] This is a somewhat elusive implication of the change, however. To the extent that effectuation of a doctrine of public trust requires attitudinal change on the part of the organs of state themselves, it is unlikely to be secured so late in the evolution of Australian government through an acknowledgement of popular sovereignty by the courts alone, even if the new perception flowed through consistently to other judicial doctrine. It is also difficult to attribute an improvement in standards along the lines identified by Finn to the acknowledgement of the people as the authority for the Constitution rather than to the more familiar dynamics of a competitive essentially two party democracy.

Secondly, recognition that the authority for the Constitution derives from the people might have implications for the rights of individuals

---

[79] Sir O Dixon, 'The Law and the Constitution' (1935) 51 *Law Quarterly Review* 590, 597.
[80] Finn, n 71, 22.

vis-à-vis the state. Such implications are not inevitable; it can equally be argued that the authority of the people is given effect collectively through decisions of the majority in Parliament. Nevertheless, this is the context in which the new perception of authority for the Constitution has had most substantive effect. In 1993, Chief Justice Mason described an 'evolving concept of a modern democracy' that 'goes beyond simple majoritarian government and parliamentary sovereignty' and 'extends to a new notion of responsible government which respects the fundamental rights and dignity of the individual'.[81] Many of the early observations about the people as authority for the Constitution are found in cases in which the Court found some protection for individual rights and freedoms in provisions of the Constitution establishing the institutions of government.[82] For a time, at least, a new focus on rights could be seen also in other aspects of the jurisprudence of the Court, dealing with native title,[83] the criminal law[84] and the interpretation of statutes that override fundamental rights.[85]

A final possibility is that a change in the understanding of the authority for the Constitution might affect the approach of the Court to constitutional interpretation, insofar as it had previously been influenced by the character of the Constitution as a British statute. Here again, however, the analysis of both cause and effect is complex. The Court does not consistently interpret the Constitution as a statute; or at least, not as an ordinary statute. And in any event, interpretation of a constitution inevitably employs techniques that are also in use in the interpretation of other legal texts, of which legislation is the nearest in kind. The approaches that are taken in Australia to the interpretation of the Constitution are examined more closely in the next chapter. First, however, the final part of this chapter makes a necessary digression, to examine the relationship between the Constitution and the common law, which in Australia has had a formative effect on each.

---

[81] A Mason, 'Opening Address', New South Wales Supreme Court Judges Conference, quoted in Finn, n 71, 7.

[82] Including *Australian Capital Television v Commonwealth* (1992) 177 CLR 106.

[83] *Mabo v Queensland (No.2)* (1992) 175 CLR 1; *Wik Peoples v Queensland* (1996) 187 CLR 1.

[84] *Dietrich v R* (1992) 177 CLR 292.

[85] *Coco v R* (1994) 179 CLR 427.

IV. CONSTITUTION AND THE COMMON LAW

A. The Foundation of the Common Law

Every constitution depends on assumptions about its meaning and operation that draw on the legal and political background against which it was
made and in which it will take effect. In the Australian case, however,
the relationship between the Constitution and the surrounding law was
deepened by the unbroken continuity of the legal system, itself founded
on a body of imperial common law, from colonial settlement, through
federation, to independence.[86] What has been described as a 'symbiotic'
relationship between the Constitution and the common law has had at
least three distinct sets of continuing consequences for the Australian constitutional system.[87] One, which is the subject of this section, concerns the
significance of the foundation of the Constitution in the common law in
the sense that 'the general law . . . is the source of the legal conceptions
that govern us' for the contemporary meaning of the Constitution.[88] The
second, the notion that there is a single Australian common law, also follows at least in part from the foundation of the Constitution in the common law but has had a significant impact on the system of government in
its own right. The third concerns the indirect effect of the Constitution
on the common law, in the interests of maintaining consistency between
them. These last two issues are dealt with in the two succeeding sections.

The common law most obviously feeds into the Constitution through
constitutional terms that originate in the common law and draw some
meaning from it. The guarantee of 'trial by jury' for trials on indictment
in section 80 is one of many examples, which is examined more closely
in chapter eight.

Even in this apparently straightforward context, however, some difficulties arise. To what extent is the meaning of a constitutional term
fixed by reference to the state of the common law in 1901? To what

---

[86] As long as only the Australian version of the Australia Acts is regarded as
operative in Australia, there is a break in continuity in 1986: for an assumption to
this effect, see W Gummow, 'The Constitution: Ultimate Foundation of Australian
Law?' n 3, 170.

[87] *Theophanous v Herald & Weekly Times Ltd* (1994) 182 CLR 104, 141.

[88] O Dixon, 'The Common Law as an Ultimate Constitutional Foundation',
n 56, 241.

extent do subsequent developments in the common law, in Australia or (now less probably) elsewhere, affect the meaning of a constitutional term? These questions have not finally been answered and the answers may in any event vary between parts of the Constitution. It is clear that, however, notwithstanding their provenance, the meaning of a 'constitutional expression' is developed over time in accordance with the prevailing rules of constitutional interpretation, in the context of the Constitution as a whole.

Somewhat less obviously, but no less certainly, the Constitution assumes certain rules of common law origin. The principle that taxation can be imposed only with the authority of Parliament is nowhere stated but nevertheless is a constitutional rule.[89] An exercise of legislative power under section 1 of the Constitution can control the executive power derived from section 61, in accordance with the common law understanding of the relationship between legislative and executive power, notwithstanding the constitutional separation of powers and at the price of further asymmetry with the separation of judicial power.[90] Consistently with the assumptions of the common law, the power to enter into treaties has been held to fall within the executive power in section 61, but treaties require implementing legislation in order to change legal rights and duties under Australian law.[91]

These relatively uncontroversial examples encourage speculation about whether there are other common law principles that might affect the meaning and operation of the Constitution. One particular, much more controversial context in which this thought has been pursued is in relation to the protection of rights, on which the constitutional text is largely, although not entirely, silent. Two aspects of the common law might be relevant for this purpose. First, insofar as common law doctrine acknowledges particular rights, some or all of these might be implied into the Constitution. Secondly, common law principles of statutory interpretation that minimise the impact of statute on common law rights might be adapted to constitutional purposes.

This was never a project with a chance of much success in the Australian constitutional context. The common law's own record on

---

[89] *The Commonwealth v Colonial Combing, Spinning and Weaving Co Ltd* (1922) 31 CLR 421, 433, per Isaacs J, describing it as 'forbidden ground'.

[90] L Zines, *The High Court and the Constitution,* 5th edn (Annandale, NSW: Federation Press, 2008), 368–9.

[91] *Victoria v Commonwealth* (1996) 187 CLR 416, 480.

rights protection is not sufficiently consistent; common law principles typically can be overridden by legislation; the Constitution offers limited purchase for the implication of most common law rights; there is historical evidence that the framers consciously decided against the inclusion of particular rights. While there was a flurry of interest in this aspect of the relationship between the Constitution and the common law in the 1990s, in the end it produced little substantive change.

The reasoning of two Justices in *Leeth*[92] is generally regarded as the high water mark of the attempt to give common law rights a base in the Constitution. In *Leeth* Deane and Toohey JJ relied on 'the equality of all persons under the law and before the courts' as a 'fundamental . . . doctrine of the common law' that was necessarily implied into the Constitution to invalidate legislation that applied State sentencing legislation to federal prisoners at the price of an 'extraordinary degree of disproportionality' in the non-parole periods served by federal prisoners in different States.[93] Theirs was only a minority view,[94] however, and it was expressly disapproved five years later by a majority of the Court, in rejecting a claim that the laws under which Indigenous children were removed from their parents were inconsistent with a constitutional guarantee of legal equality.[95]

Shortly after *Leeth* was handed down, an extrajudicial suggestion by one of the Justices involved noted that it might have been possible to adapt common law principles of statutory interpretation to require an 'unambiguous . . . expression of . . . will' in the Constitution before the Commonwealth heads of legislative power were interpreted to allow legislation that infringed 'fundamental liberties'.[96] The argument was clearly speculative and at odds with a recent observation by the Chief Justice that 'it is difficult if not impossible to establish a foundation for the implication of general guarantees of fundamental rights and freedoms' into the Constitution.[97] The possibility that rights might be constitutionalised by implication in this way nevertheless created a minor furore. It

---

[92] *Leeth v Commonwealth* (1992) 174 CLR 455.

[93] Ibid, 486, 490.

[94] Although the reasons of two other Justices also drew on implied principles of equality or non-discrimination: Brennan J at 475, Gaudron J at 502.

[95] *Kruger v Commonwealth* (1997) 190 CLR 1, 14, 45, 63–68, 154.

[96] J Toohey, 'A Government of Laws and Not of Men' (1993) 4 *Public Law Review* 158, 170.

[97] *Australian Capital Television v Commonwealth* (1992) 177 CLR 106, 136.

has since been made clear by the Court that laws will not be invalidated for inconsistency with common law rights.[98]

This catalogue of failures may give a somewhat misleading impression of the impact of common law principles on the understanding of the Constitution. While attempts to incorporate rights as a direct limitation on power generally have been unsuccessful, common law principles have infused much of the reasoning on the meaning of the institutional provisions of the Constitution with some rights-protecting effect, as subsequent chapters show.

B. A Single Common Law

Since the abolition of appeals to the Privy Council, if not before, it has been settled that there is an Australian common law,[99] in the sense of a common law the principles of which may (but need not) diverge from other national bodies of common law. More significantly for present purposes, however, it appears also to be settled that the Australian common law is a single body of law[100] that does not differ between States and perhaps, depending on its rationale, cannot differ between States.

At one level, the perception that Australia has a single body of common law follows from the institutional reality that the High Court is a final court of appeal in all matters of State as well as federal law. If this were the only basis for the doctrine, however, it might have been possible to conceive of distinct bodies of State common law, at least until a matter reached the High Court on appeal. It might even have been possible to conceive of a system in which the High Court determined the common law differently in relation to different States in response to, for example, the derivative application of State legislation. But there is an additional suggested basis for the doctrine as well that, if correct, precludes these possibilities. On this account, the Australian common

---

[98] *Durham Holdings v New South Wales* (2001) 205 CLR 399, 408–9. *Durham Holdings* concerns State laws; for an assumption that the same principle applies to Commonwealth laws see W Gummow, 'The Constitution: Ultimate Foundation of Australian Law', n 3, 169.

[99] A Mason, 'Future Directions in Australian Law' (1987) 13 *Monash University Law Review* 149, attributing the emergence of 'indigenous solutions adapted to Australian conditions and circumstances' to 'the past twenty years at least': 149.

[100] *Lange v Australian Broadcasting Corporation* (1997) 189 CLR 520, 563; *Kable v Director of Public Prosecutions* (1996) 189 CLR 51, 112.

law was united from the time of settlement as part of a wider body of imperial common law and national unity was undisturbed by independence so that the doctrine is, in a sense, assumed by the Constitution.[101]

An earlier version of the doctrine of a single common law received substantial support from Owen Dixon.[102] As revived after the enactment of the Australia Acts, however, the doctrine has assumed a more aggressive form. Initially, it encountered scepticism.[103] And while the general thrust of the doctrine is now settled, it remains difficult to pinpoint a more convincing basis for it than as a practical corollary of the position of the High Court as a final court of appeal. Nor has the occasion arisen to force a determination of whether the common law is essentially State law or a more free-floating national law,[104] akin to what Justice Holmes memorably characterised as the 'brooding omnipresence in the sky'.[105] The problem of the law to be applied in federal jurisdiction, which might have done so, has been met by section 80 of the Judiciary Act 1903 (Cth), which applies the 'common law in Australia' where Commonwealth laws are insufficient.[106] The difficulty about choice of law that might otherwise have arisen in cases involving parties from two or more States is diminished by the unity of the common law.

Whatever its advantages in terms of efficiency, the doctrine has a homogenising effect. Two examples illustrate the point. First, the perceived imperatives of a single common law lie behind the recent insistence by the High Court that 'intermediate appellate courts . . . should not . . . depart from decisions . . . in another jurisdiction' unless they are 'convinced' that the decision is 'plainly wrong' and that an intermediate court should not depart from 'seriously considered dicta' of a majority

---

[101]   McHugh J describes the Constitution as having 'intended' the courts to administer a 'single body of common law' in *Kable v Director of Public Prosecutions* (1996) 189 CLR 51, 112; cf I Clark, *Studies in Australian Constitutional Law* (Melbourne, Vic, Charles F Maxwell, 1901) 192.

[102]   O Dixon, 'Address to the section of the American Bar Association for International and Comparative Law' (1943) 17 *Australian Law Journal* 138; O Dixon, 'The Common Law as an Ultimate Constitutional Foundation', n 56.

[103]   LJ Priestley, 'A Federal Common Law in Australia?' (1995) 6 *Public Law Review* 221.

[104]   The latter has considerable implicit support in case law: see for example *John Pfeiffer Pty Ltd v Rogerson* (2000) 203 CLR 503 [1].

[105]   *Southern Pacific Co v Jensen* 244 US 205, 222 (1917).

[106]   An earlier reference to the 'common law of England' was replaced by the Law and Justice Legislation Amendment Act 1988 (Cth) s 41.

of the High Court.[107] Secondly, the doctrine appears to preclude a State legislative bill of rights from applying to State courts so as to encourage the courts to develop the common law in a way that is consistent with the protected rights.[108] In both respects, the single common law discourages the diversity and competition between ideas that are potential by-products of a federal system of government.

C. Consistency

The single common law has also proved useful in maintaining consistency between the Constitution and the common law; indeed, this was a large part of the impetus for its revival.

The supremacy of the Constitution ensures that no difficulty arises where the Constitution overrides a common law rule. By way of example: the conferral of original jurisdiction on the High Court in section 75(iii) in relation to matters 'in which the Commonwealth . . . is a party' has been held to preclude the application of common law doctrines conferring procedural immunity on the executive government in actions in contract or tort.[109] Even where the Constitution does not directly contradict the common law, however, questions of consistency may arise. In such cases, the position of the High Court as the final court of appeal on both constitutional questions and questions involving the application of common law rules that operate Australia-wide enables it to adapt the common law to what it perceives to be the requirements of the Constitution. The technique is relatively new however and the parameters within which the Court is acting are not always clear, as the following examples show.

One example concerns the common law rules about choice of law, as they operate between jurisdictions within Australia, with particular reference to the law of torts. The question to be resolved in *Pfeiffer*[110] was whether the 'traditional' choice of law rules that tend to favour the law of the forum but that require the matter also to be actionable

---

[107] *Farah Constructions v Say-Dee Pty Ltd* (2007) 230 CLR 89, 151–52.

[108] Charter of Human Rights and Responsibilities Act 2006 (Vic) s 4(1)(j) (excluding courts from the definition of 'public authority'); cf Human Rights Act 1998 (UK) s 6(3)(a).

[109] *British American Tobacco Australia Ltd v Western Australia* (2003) 217 CLR 30.

[110] *John Pfeiffer v Rogerson* (2000) 203 CLR 503.

in the jurisdiction where the wrong occurred are consistent with the Constitution. There is nothing in the Constitution that deals directly and comprehensively with this issue, although section 118 requires 'full faith and credit' to be given to 'throughout the Commonwealth to the laws . . . of every State'. The Court nevertheless found that, in effect, the existing rules were inconsistent with the constitutional scheme. In doing so it drew attention to the nature of Australian federalism, in which 'sovereignty is shared' between the Commonwealth and the States; to the 'indication' to be derived from section 118 that 'the States are not foreign powers as are nation states for the purposes of international law'; and to the fact that questions of choice of law might arise in either State or federal jurisdiction, prompting the Court to reflect that the rules should provide 'certainty and uniformity of outcome' whether a matter is 'litigated in federal or non-federal jurisdiction'. It consequently 'developed' the common law rules by discarding the double actionability requirement, requiring courts to apply the substantive law of the place where the wrong occurred and narrowing the scope of the procedural laws to be applied as the law of the forum. It put aside the possibility that aspects of the new choice of law rules were 'dictated' by the Constitution, noting that in this case legislative power to alter the rules would be restricted as well.[111]

In a second example, of a different kind, the Court resorted to the technique of adapting the common law to reconcile divisions within its own ranks over whether the implied constitutional freedom of political communication could be claimed as a defence to an action in defamation where the defamatory material involved governmental and political matters.[112] In *Lange* a unanimous Court held that the existing common law defences were inconsistent with the constitutional freedom but that the Constitution itself only precluded 'curtailment of the . . . freedom by the exercise of legislative or executive power'.[113] The solution to this dilemma of the Court's own making was to adapt the common law defences to comply with constitutional norms.

---

[111] For elaboration of the extent to which some choice of law rules are now constitutionalised see G Hill and A Stone, 'The Constitutionalisation of the Common Law' (2004) 25 *Adelaide Law Review* 72.

[112] *Theophanous v Herald & Weekly Times Ltd* (1994) 182 CLR 104; *Stephens v Western Australian Newspapers* (1994) 182 CLR 211.

[113] *Lange v Australian Broadcasting Corporation* (1997) 189 CLR 520; see further, ch 4.

Lange provided a precedent for the adaptation of the common law to constitutional norms in future cases, on which *Pfeiffer* built. But exactly what the Court did in *Lange* remains unclear. Unlike in *Pfeiffer* the Court appears to have regarded itself as bound to act, in the face of 'constitutional imperatives'. It did not, however, identify whether the source of the obligation lay in recognition that adjudication is merely another form of State action that does not imperil the essentially vertical operation of constitutional norms[114] or in the Court's perception that the Constitution, all legislation and the common law form 'one system of jurisprudence', thus giving the Constitution an indirect horizontal effect on the development of the common law. Like so much else in the evolving understanding of the relationship between the Constitution and the common law, this question remains for future decision.[115]

SELECTED READING

Carney, G, *The Constitutional Systems of the Australian States and Territories* (Cambridge, CUP, 2006)

Dixon, O, 'The Law and the Constitution' (1935) 51 *Law Quarterly Review* 590

——, 'The Common Law as the Ultimate Constitutional Foundation' (1957) 31 *Australian Law Journal* 240

Finn, PD, 'A Sovereign People, A Public Trust' in Finn, PD (ed), *Essays on Law and Government, Vol I, Principles and Values* (Sydney, NSW, Law Book Co, 1995) 22

Goldsworthy, J, *Sovereignty of Parliament* (Oxford, OUP, 1999)

Gummow, W, 'The Constitution: Ultimate Foundation of Australian Law?' (2005) 79 *Australian Law Journal* 167

Lindell, G, 'Why is the Constitution Binding? The Reasons in 1900 and Now, and the Effect of Independence' (1986) 16 *Federal Law Review* 29

Loughlin, M and Walker, N (eds), *The Paradox of Constitutionalism* (Oxford, OUP, 2007)

Mason, A, 'Future Directions in Australian Law' (1987) 13 *Monash University Law Review* 149

---

[114] See Hill and Stone, n 111, 84 ff.
[115] C Saunders 'Constitutional Rights and the Common Law' in A Sajo and R Uitz (eds), *The Constitution in Private Relations* (The Hague, Eleven International Publishing, 2005) 183.

Quick, J and Garran, RR, *Annotated Constitution of the Australian Commonwealth* (1901, repr Sydney, NSW, Legal Books 1976)

Saunders, C, 'The Parliament as Partner: A Century of Constitutional Review' in Lindell, G and Bennett, R (eds), *Parliament, The Vision in Hindsight* (Annandale, NSW, Federation Press, 2001) 454

Twomey, A, *The Constitution of New South Wales* (Annandale, NSW, Federation Press, 2004)

3

Constitutional Review

Framework – Approach – Sources – Representative Democracy

I. FRAMEWORK

A. Authority for Review

THE CONSTITUTION HAS been shaped by more than a century of interpretation and application by courts and, in particular, by the High Court of Australia. The consquences are explored in the chapters that follow. The purpose of this chapter is to place the process of constitutional review in context: to outline how and when it occurs, the procedures that are followed and the interpretive methods on which courts primarily rely.

Constitutional review is an established feature of Australian constitutional arrangements. Review was assumed by the framers of the Constitution, either as a consequence of the status of the Constitution as an Act of the Imperial Parliament or as a necessary incident of federation or both.[1] It was accepted with equanimity by the first Commonwealth Attorney-General on introducing the legislation to establish the High Court.[2] That Court heard significant constitutional cases in the first year of its establishment and within five years had invalidated some laws of both spheres of government.[3] This was consistent with Quick

---

[1] JA Thomson, 'Constitutional Authority for Judicial Review: A Contribution from the Framers of the Constitution' in G Craven (ed), *The Convention Debates 1890–1898, Commentaries, Indices and Guide* (Sydney, NSW, Legal Books Pty Ltd, 1986) 173,186.

[2] Commonwealth, House of Representatives, *Parliamentary Debates*, 18 March 10965.

[3] For example, *Deakin v Webb* (1904) 1 CLR 585 (State); *R v Barger* (1908) 6 CLR 41 (Commonwealth).

and Garran's expectation that the Court would be a 'guardian of the Constitution' against 'encroachments' from either the Commonwealth or the States.[4] In 1951, a Justice of the High Court described 'the principle of *Marbury v Madison*' as 'axiomatic' in Australia.[5] The description has become *de rigeur* and unquestionably reflects the Australian position.

It is sometimes noted, nevertheless, that the Constitution does not explicitly provide for review. While review of legislation on grounds of constitutionality is entirely consistent with federalism, moreover, it is less compatible with the assumptions on which that other strand of the Australian constitutional inheritance, responsible government, is based. Neither of these points should be overstated. There is ample evidence in the text of the Constitution, as well as in extrinsic sources, that constitutional review was intended.[6] The tension between responsible government and constitutional review is a somewhat more complex point, drawing on a symbiotic mix of the tradition of parliamentary sovereignty and what often is claimed to be a greater degree of public confidence in the institutions of elected government in a system of this kind.[7] But parliamentary sovereignty was never a feature of Australian constitutional arrangements and arguments that elected institutions in a unitary system can be trusted to respect constitutional principles adequately cannot automatically be transferred to a federal constitutional setting.

Ironically, the view that federal constitutional compliance can be left to elected central institutions is more persuasive in the United States, with its system of checks and balances, including the more effective institutional representation of the States in central organs of government.[8] It has relatively little influence on the institution of constitutional review in Australia, where the High Court is recognised as the ultimate interpreter of the Constitution, there is no developed doctrine of deference and compliance with the orders of a Court is regarded as integral to the rule of law.[9] Nevertheless, the perceived tension between

---

[4] J Quick and RR Garran, *Annotated Constitution of the Australian Commonwealth* (Sydney, NSW, Angus and Robertson, 1901) 725.

[5] *Australian Communist Party v Commonwealth* (1951) 83 CLR 1, 262, Fullagar J.

[6] Covering clause 5; sections 74 and 76(i).

[7] S Gageler, 'Foundations of Australian Federalism and the Role of Judicial Review' (1987) 17 *Federal Law Review* 162, 169.

[8] H Wechsler, 'The Political Safeguards of Federalism' (1954) 54 *Columbia Law Review* 543; and see discussion in Gageler, ibid at 193 ff.

[9] M Gleeson, 'Courts and the Rule of Law' in C Saunders and K Leroy, *The Rule of Law* (Annandale, NSW, Federation Press, 2003).

responsible government and constitutional review helps to explain the Australian approach to constitutional interpretation, which is examined more closely in the next part.

B. Jurisdiction

As in most common law legal systems that accept constitutional review the form of review in Australia is diffuse, in the sense that the review function is not assigned to a specialist constitutional court. Diffuse review has two consequences that are relevant for present purposes. The first is that a court that interprets and applies the Constitution typically has jurisdiction to apply other legal norms as well. In particular, the Australian High Court can apply any rule of Australian law, whether found in Commonwealth or State legislation or the common law, giving it maximum flexibility to avoid unnecessary application of constitutional norms, if it is minded to do so.[10] The second is that constitutional review is not the province of a single court, but may be carried out by other courts when a constitutional question is raised.

The Commonwealth Constitution draws a distinction between federal and State jurisdiction. There are nine 'heads' of federal jurisdiction, five of which are conferred directly on the High Court in its original jurisdiction (s 75), leaving the remaining four to be conferred on the Court at the Parliament's discretion (s 76). While the constitutional review jurisdiction is, oddly, in the latter group, several of the heads of jurisdiction in section 75 may involve constitutional review and effectively entrench it. All the heads of jurisdiction in sections 75 and 76 can be conferred as federal jurisdiction on State courts or on other federal courts (s 77(i),(iii)).

Even in the absence of federal jurisdiction, State courts originally had State jurisdiction to apply the Constitution. On this basis, the Supreme Court of Victoria dealt with a constitutional dispute in 1902, before the High Court was established.[11] After the establishment of the High Court, however, Commonwealth legislation removed State jurisdiction in areas also covered by federal jurisdiction and replaced it with federal jurisdiction, thus controlling appeals to the Privy Council from State courts in

---

[10] For a classic illustration of such an approach, see the reasons of Gleeson CJ in *Al-Kateb v Godwin* (2004) 219 CLR 562, 571ff.

[11] *In Re the Income Tax Acts (No 4) Wollaston's Case* (1902) 28 VLR 357.

these matters.[12] There is now no extant State jurisdiction 'arising under' the Commonwealth Constitution or 'involving its interpretation',[13] but the Federal Court and State courts at all levels have express federal jurisdiction to carry out constitutional review.

Under section 73 of the Constitution the High Court also has broad appellate jurisdiction from both federal and State courts, which it now exercises only when it grants special leave.[14] Constitutional disputes thus can go directly to the High Court, or reach it in its capacity as the final court of appeal. Supporting legislation adds further flexibility to these arrangements. The High Court may deal with a matter lodged in its original jurisdiction if it considers it appropriate to do so; if not, it may remit the matter to an appropriate lower court.[15] Alternatively, a constitutional question that begins in a lower court must be removed into the High Court on the application of an Attorney-General and may be so removed, in the discretion of the Court, on the application of another party.[16] A legislative requirement for notice to be given to all Attorneys-General when a constitutional question is raised in any court is effective in alerting governments to the need to intervene or seek removal, but is also a cause of delay, prompting recommendations from the Australian Law Reform Commission to streamline the procedure.[17]

C. Concrete Review

Constitutional review in Australia is concrete, rather than abstract, consistently with the common law preference for determining legal questions in a factual setting, typically involving two or more parties in an adversarial relationship to each other. In addition, in Australia, concrete review effectively is mandated by the constitutional separation of judicial power, understood to preclude federal courts from exercising any power

---

[12] Judiciary Act 1903 s 39 is an exercise of power under s 77(ii); *Minister of State for the Army v Parbury Henty & Co Pty Ltd* (1945) 70 CLR 459, 505.

[13] *Felton v Mulligan* (1971) 124 CLR 367, 373.

[14] Judiciary Act 1903 (Cth) ss 35 and 35AA (for appeals from State and Territory courts), s 35A (for special leave criteria).

[15] Judiciary Act 1903 (Cth) s 44.

[16] Judiciary Act 1903 (Cth) s 40.

[17] Australian Law Reform Commission *The Judicial Power of the Commonwealth: A Review of the Judiciary Act 1903 and Related Legislation,* Report No 92, 2001, Recommendation 13-1.

that is not 'federal judicial power' within the meaning of the Constitution. There is a complex case law on the meaning of judicial power, which is examined more closely in chapter six. The concept of 'federal' judicial power is further constrained, however improbably, by the word 'matter' that prefaces all the heads of federal jurisdiction.[18] As defined, federal judicial power in turn has largely subsumed the requirements of justiciability.[19] The justiciability of an issue is occasionally queried, although rarely, and there is no developed political question doctrine.

i. Advisory Opinions

Because federal courts can exercise only federal judicial power, they cannot be asked to give advisory opinions. This was first made clear in 1921, when the High Court invalidated a law that purported to confer advisory jurisdiction on it. The power arguably was judicial in character: the Court was authorised to give opinions on the validity only of enacted legislation and its determination would be 'final and conclusive'.[20] The law was invalid nevertheless because there was no 'matter' within the meaning of the Constitution. In the absence of an 'immediate right, duty or liability to be established', the Court was left to make a 'declaration of the law divorced from any attempt to administer' it.[21] There have since been occasional proposals to amend the Constitution to enable the High Court to give advice on constitutional questions, but none has advanced to the referendum stage[22] and formal change now seems unlikely.

The principal argument in favour of allowing such opinions is the convenience of being able to determine the constitutional validity of legislation before action is taken pursuant to it. One reason why change has come to be regarded as less pressing is that other forms of legal

---

[18] A decision from which an appeal is taken under s 73 also must 'finally determine the parties rights and obligations': *Mellifont v Attorney-General (Qld)* (1991) 173 CLR 289, 300.

[19] *Thomas v Mowbray* (2007) 233 CLR 307, 354; there is a distinct but limited category of issues that are not justiciable because they are held to be entrusted by the Constitution to one of the other branches of government.

[20] The court construed this to require 'an authoritative declaration of the law': *In Re Judiciary and Navigation Acts (Advisory Opinions* case) (1921) 29 CLR 257, 264.

[21] Ibid, 265–66.

[22] Constitution Alteration (Advisory Jurisdiction of the High Court) 1983; for details of all proposals see H Burmester, 'Limitations on Federal Adjudication' in B Opeskin and F Wheeler (eds), *The Australian Federal Judicial System* (Melbourne, Vic, MUP, 2000) 227, 242–44.

action have been used to bring questions about the validity of new legislation before the Court in the absence of a full-blown dispute, without contravening the requirement for a 'matter'. The most important of these is a challenge to the validity of Commonwealth legislation after it is enacted but before proclamation, brought on behalf of one or more plaintiff States. Questions about the validity of Commonwealth legislation dealing with pharmaceutical benefits, marriage and corporations were resolved early in this way.[23] A declaration of invalidity of an Act of the Commonwealth or a State Parliament also can be sought by an individual plaintiff whose legal interests are 'or in the immediate future probably will be' affected by the legislation in question.[24]

ii. Declarations of Incompatibility

Nevertheless, the narrowness of the distinctions drawn between actions that are sufficiently concrete and those that are not, coupled with some disagreement within the Court about exactly what constitutes a 'matter', makes it difficult to predict with any certainty on which side of the line some actions may fall.[25] The uncertainty has practical significance for any attempt on the part of the Commonwealth to introduce a legislative bill of rights in a form that preserves the final supremacy of the Parliament on human rights questions but enables a court to make a 'declaration of incompatibility' where it finds that legislation infringes protected rights, thus promoting 'dialogue' between courts and the elected branches.[26] This issue was much debated in Australia in 2009, when the Commonwealth government seemed to be prepared to sponsor such a measure. In the event, however, as chapter eight shows, the government decided against proceeding with a bill of rights at all and the question remains unresolved.

---

[23] *Attorney-General (Vict); ex rel Dale v Commonwealth (Pharmaceutical Benefits* case) (1945) 71 CLR 237; *Attorney-General (Vic) v Commonwealth (Marriage Act* case) (1962) 107 CLR 529; *New South Wales v Commonwealth (Incorporation* case) (1990) 160 CLR 482.

[24] *Croome v Tasmania* (1997) 191 CLR 119; cf *Bass v Permanent Trustee* (1999) 198 CLR 334, 356, requiring the action to be 'based on facts, found or agreed'.

[25] Compare *Mellifont v Attorney-General (Queensland)* (1991) 173 CLR 289 with *Director of Public Prosecutions (SA) v B* (1998) 194 CLR 566 and *North Ganalanja Aboriginal Corporation v Queensland* (1996) 185 CLR 595; see generally Burmester, n 22, 238–42.

[26] The prototype is the Human Rights Act 1998 (UK) s 4.

D. Standing

The Australian rules of standing reflect tension between two views. One, which historically has been dominant, is that the primary role of courts is to protect the 'legal rights of individuals' at the instance of the individuals concerned, leaving public rights to be enforced by representatives of the public.[27] The second is that everyone has an interest in the observance of the law generally and compliance with the Constitution in particular, which justifies the standing of any willing party who can prosecute an action effectively and responsibly.

Consistently with the former view, Australian law is generous in its recognition of the standing of the Attorneys-General of the Commonwealth and the States. To this end, it has adapted the traditional common law right of an Attorney-General to take legal action in the public interest to the more demanding conditions of a federal political system. Attorneys-General may initiate action to uphold the Commonwealth Constitution against a law of any jurisdiction, including their own.[28] Their statutory rights to intervene in constitutional cases and to require removal of constitutional proceedings into the High Court complement this general rule.[29]

The standing of individuals is more restrictive. Standing to seek a declaration or an injunction to enforce public rights requires a 'special interest in the subject matter of the action'.[30] The test is liberally applied, but must be satisfied if the point is raised. It presently is unclear whether a taxpayer has standing to challenge unconstitutional expenditure[31] or a voter to challenge unconstitutional electoral laws[32] although Members

---

[27] *Bateman's Bay Local Aboriginal Council v Aboriginal Community Benefit Fund Pty Ltd* (1998) 914 CLR 247, 275–77.

[28] But cf *Re McBain; Ex parte Australian Catholic Bishops' Conference* (2002) 209 CLR 372, 410: 'the Attorney-General . . . cannot have a roving commission to initiate litigation to disrupt settled outcomes in earlier cases, so as to rid the law reports of what are considered unsatisfactory decisions respecting constitutional law'.

[29] Judiciary Act 1903 (Cth) ss 78A, 40(1); see also s 78B. Intervention rates are high: E Campbell, 'Intervention in Constitutional Cases' (1998) 9 *Public Law Review* 255, 256.

[30] *Australian Conservation Foundation v Commonwealth* (1980) 146 CLR 493, 530.

[31] *Victoria v Commonwealth and Hayden (AAP* case) (1975) 134 CLR, 387–88; the point is raised, but not settled, in *Pape v Federal Commissioner of Taxation* (2009) 238 CLR 1.

[32] *Attorney-General (Cth); ex rel McKinlay v Commonwealth* (1975) 135 CLR 1, 26.

of Parliament have been accorded standing for the former purpose.[33] The basis on which the Court is prepared to grant individuals leave to intervene or to appear as amici curiae parallels the standing requirements. The former must show a sufficient interest. Amici must show that they will 'assist the Court in a way that the Court would not otherwise have been assisted'.[34] A would-be complainant who lacks standing may seek a fiat from an Attorney-General to mount a relator action in reliance on the Attorney's authority, but the grant lies entirely within the Attorney's discretion.[35]

There are signs of change, driven in part by evolving attitudes towards the role of citizens in a democracy but also by scepticism about the efficacy of leaving the enforcement of public rights to the office of Attorney-General, which in Australia is filled by an elected Member of Parliament who also is a Minister and typically a member of the Cabinet. Restrictive standing rules also sit uneasily with some heads of the entrenched jurisdiction of the High Court in section 75. And so it is possible to detect a degree of relaxation of the special interest test;[36] some greater willingness to accept the submissions of amici;[37] and a tendency on the part of individual Justices to question the history and logic of the standing rules.[38] It is accepted that the Parliament may broaden the right to take legal action in relation to the enforcement of its own legislation.[39] On the other hand, recommendations by the Australian Law Reform Commission to formally relax the rules of standing have not been implemented[40] and the linkage of both justiciability and standing with the constitutional requirement for a 'matter' suggests that there are limits to the extent to which the rules of standing can constitutionally expand.[41]

---

[33] *Combet v Commonwealth* (2005) 224 CLR 494, 557.

[34] *Levy v Victoria* (1997) 189 CLR 579, 604; cf 650.

[35] C Maxwell, 'In the Line of Fire: *Re McBain* and the Role of the Attorney-General as a Party' (2002) 13 *Public Law Review* 283, 287.

[36] *Bateman's Bay* (1998) 914 CLR 247, 265–67 and the cases cited there.

[37] *Wurridjal v Commonwealth of Australia* (2009) 237 CLR 309, 408 ff.

[38] *Bodruddaza v MIMA* (2007) 228 CLR 651, 668; *Combet v Commonwealth* (2005) 224 CLR 494, 557.

[39] *Truth About Motorways v Macquarie* (2000) 200 CLR 591.

[40] Australian Law Reform Commission, *Beyond the Door-keeper: Standing to Sue for Public Remedies* (Report No 78 1996).

[41] *Croome v Tasmania* (1997) 191 CLR 119, 133. In this respect, however, a 'matter' is wider than the requirement for 'cases' and 'controversies' under Article III of the Constitution of the United States; see *Truth About Motorways v Macquarie* (2000) 200 CLR 591, 632–37.

II. APPROACH

The interpretive approach of the High Court exhibits tensions that are familiar in other constitutional systems: between constitutional development through judicial review as opposed to formal textual change; between principles used to interpret other legal texts and recognition of the distinctive demands of a Constitution; between the intentions of the makers of the Constitution and the concerns of later generations; between the responsibility of courts to uphold the Constitution and of elected institutions to take action in the public interest. In Australia's case, these tensions are exacerbated by cultural differences between the two constitutional traditions on which the Australian constitutional system draws, requiring a delicate balancing act on the part of the courts.

Famously, the product of these tensions in Australia is an approach to constitutional interpretation generally described as 'legalism'. Legalism has no precise limits, however and its application often is a matter of degree.[42] This part begins by sketching five phases of constitutional interpretation during which Australian legalism has waxed and waned. The following section examines more closely the techniques of legalism and its principal Australian competitor, sometimes identified as a weak form of realism. The final section outlines the extent to which the Australian interpretive approach enables the meaning of the Constitution to evolve over time.

A. Phases

Any attempt to divide the interpretive history of a constitution into phases must necessarily be rough. Phases are dictated by a combination of circumstances and people. It is rare for either to signal a sharp change from one interpretive style to another. In any phase, moreover, there are likely to be outliers on the court who complicate generalisations. These caveats should be born in mind for the purposes of the following account.

---

[42] For a perceptive analysis see L Zines, *The High Court and the Constitution*, 5th edn (Annandale, NSW, Federation Press, 2008) ch.17.

i. 1903–1920

The first decade or so after the establishment of the High Court was dominated by two federalism-related problems for which the Constitution made no specific provision.[43] The first was the extent to which laws of one sphere of government could apply to institutions of the others, a question that first arose in the context of State taxation of Commonwealth officers, only to appear shortly after in reciprocal form, in relation to the application of Commonwealth industrial relations legislation to State employees.[44] The second problem concerned the dividing line between listed Commonwealth powers and the unexpressed residue of power left to the States, particularly when the scope of the former was ambiguous and a wider interpretation interfered with a settled area of State activity.[45]

The first High Court comprised three justices, all of whom had been framers of the Constitution and two of whom had been leaders of the Conventions of 1891 and 1897–8 respectively.[46] Their answer to these problems was that, in general, each sphere of government is immune from legislation of the other, and Commonwealth powers should be interpreted where possible so as not to affect powers deemed to be reserved by the Constitution to the States. In developing both doctrines the Court relied on conceptions of the type of federation established by the Constitution. It drew also on decisions of the Supreme Court of the United States on 'analogous questions', pointing to the similarity between the two Constitutions.[47] In 1906, two additional Justices were added to the Court,[48] both of whom had been elected members of the second Convention and Attorneys-General of the new Commonwealth. They took a different view of both implications doctrines and in 1920, their views prevailed.

---

[43] For other important constitutional questions raised in this period: see G Sawer, *Australian Federal Politics and Law 1901–1929* (Melbourne, Vic, MUP, 1956).

[44] *D'Emden v Pedder* (1904) 1 CLR 91; *Federated Amalgamated Government Railway and Tramway Service Association v New South Wales Railway Traffic Employees Association (Railway Servants'* case) (1906) 4 CLR 488.

[45] As in *Huddart, Parker & Co Pty Ltd v Moorehead* (1909) 8 CLR 330.

[46] Samuel Griffith (CJ; Convention of 1891; also previously Chief Justice of Queensland); Edmund Barton (Convention of 1897–8; also first Prime Minister); Richard O'Connor (Convention of 1897–8; also Senator for New South Wales).

[47] Eg *D'Emden v Pedder* (1904) 1 CLR 91, 111–13 per Griffith CJ. Influential cases included *McCulloch v Maryland* (1819) 4 Wheat 316 and *Collector v Day* (1871) 11 Wall 113.

[48] Isaac Isaacs and Henry Bournes Higgins.

ii. 1920–1944

A second, distinct interpretive phase began in 1920, shortly after the end of the First World War. The movement towards Australian independence was underway. A sense of Australian nationhood had been encouraged by the experience of the war and in particular by the disaster of the Gallipoli campaign, which remains a symbol for Australian national sentiment. Looking back at this time 50 years later, admittedly with the benefit of hindsight, Windeyer J remarked on the 'growing realization that Australians were now one people and Australia one country'.[49]

The event that marks the beginning of this period with such certainty was the decision in the *Engineers'* case, which repudiated the immunities doctrines and instituted a new approach to constitutional interpretation generally and to the treatment of Commonwealth legislative powers in particular.[50] The Constitution was to be interpreted 'naturally in the light of the circumstances in which it was made, with knowledge of the combined fabric of the common law, and the statute law which preceded it'.[51] Implications not referable to constitutional text or common law principle were precluded. The interpretive approach of the Privy Council was to be preferred to that of the Supreme Court of the United States. The latter was distinguishable by reference to responsible government and the indivisibility of the Crown, as 'two cardinal features' of the Australian political system. The potential for 'extravagant use of granted powers' was a matter for the political process and not relevant to the deliberations of a court. It followed that Commonwealth powers should be given full effect, according to their terms; that in most cases Commonwealth law could bind State institutions; but that State law normally would not bind the Commonwealth because Commonwealth law was supreme.

There is room for argument about when this period ends. 1944 marks the approach of the end of the Second World War, during which the Court upheld the validity of a scheme whereby the Commonwealth unilaterally took over State powers to impose income tax, in a classic application of *Engineers'* case methodology.[52] More importantly, how-

---

[49]   *Victoria v Commonwealth* (1971) 122 CLR 353, 396.
[50]   *Amalgamated Society of Engineers v Adelaide Steamship Co Ltd* (1920) 28 CLR 129.
[51]   Ibid, 152.
[52]   *South Australia v Commonwealth* (*First Uniform Tax* case) (1942) 65 CLR 373. Cases decided in this period also laid down the ground rules for the paramountcy of

ever, Owen Dixon returned to active service on the High Court in 1944, beginning a largely unbroken period of 20 years of his intellectual domination of the Court.[53]

iii. 1944–1981

Dixon was a puisne Justice of the High Court for the first eight years of this period and Chief Justice from 1952 to 1964. Under his influence, a form of Australian legalism that most closely approached what he described as the 'strict logic and the high technique of the common law' reached its zenith.[54] Dixon's form of legalism required judges to make their 'best endeavour to apply an external standard . . . found in a body of positive knowledge' and not 'deliberately to abandon' a legal principle 'in the name of justice or of . . . social convenience'. On the other hand, it also assumed that the law would be 'developed . . . adapted . . . and . . . improved' by the 'enlightened application of modes of reasoning traditionally respected in the courts'.[55]

In a telling demonstration of the use to which high technique could be put, Dixon had earlier noted, with apparent ingenuousness, that '[s]ince *Engineers'* . . . a notion seems to have gained currency that . . . no implications can be made' adding that 'of all instruments a written Constitution seems the last to which' such a 'method of construction' can be applied.[56] On his watch, implications returned, not only to justify limitations on the power of the Commonwealth to enact a law 'which discriminates against States, or . . . which places a particular disability or burden' on them[57] but also in the form of an inference from chapter III of the Constitution that sharpened the separation of judicial power.[58]

Commonwealth law and for a broad understanding of how the States grant power: see *Clyde Engineering v Cowburn* (1926) 37 CLR 466; *Hume v Palmer* (1926) 38 CLR 441; *Victoria v Commonwealth* (1926) 38 CLR 399.

[53]   Dixon had been a leader of the Victorian Bar. He was appointed to the High Court in 1929 but held a range of other positions during the war and from 1942–44 was Australian Minister in Washington. Early signs of his interpretive approach can be seen in, for example, *West v Commissioner of Taxation (NSW)* (1937) 56 CLR 657.

[54]   O Dixon, 'Concerning Judicial Method' (1956) 29 *Australian Law Journal* 468, 469.

[55]   Ibid, 471–72.

[56]   *West v Commissioner of Taxation (NSW)* (1937) 56 CLR 657,681.

[57]   *Melbourne Corporation v Commonwealth (State Banking* case) (1947) 74 CLR 31, 79.

[58]   *R v Kirby; ex parte Boilermakers' Society of Australia (Boilermakers'* case) (1956) 94 CLR 254.

Both doctrines rely on foundational principles of the Constitution which would now be explained in terms of 'structure' but that also inevitably rely on ideas about the organisation of public power that lie outside the instrument altogether.

Legalism continued as the dominant interpretive mode after Garfield Barwick succeeded Dixon as Chief Justice in 1964. Its application was more stylised, however, and in key areas the legal tests by which it was claimed validity could objectively be determined became increasingly less convincing, producing some arbitrary results.[59] The election of a Labour government in 1972, after more than 20 years in opposition, also produced three years of turbulent politics during which the Court was faced with a range of novel constitutional questions about the institutions of government, including the electoral rules, which were not so readily resolved by old formulae and which assisted in laying the ground for the next phase.

iv. 1981–1998

This period was influenced by two changes in the context in which the Court operates.[60] The first was the countdown to formal independence, finally given effect by the Australia Acts in 1986, leaving the High Court as the final court of appeal in all questions of Australian law. Coupled with a new discretion to choose the cases that it would hear following the introduction of a special leave requirement in 1984, this gave the Court the opportunity to exercise what one of Australia's most senior advocates described as 'the traditional functions of an ultimate appellate court . . . to declare the law on particular matters, and to remedy significant miscarriages of justice'.[61] The second was the phenomenon of internationalisation and globalisation, accelerated by the collapse of communism in Europe in 1989. One manifestation in Australia was a dramatic increase in the international arrangements to which Australia

---

[59] The areas most affected were the meaning of duties of excise under s 90 and the scope of the 'absolute' freedom of trade, commerce and intercourse among the States in s 92: see A Mason, 'Future Directions in Australian Law' 13 *Monash University Law Review* 149, 156–57.

[60] For a full treatment of this period see R Gray, *The Constitutional Jurisprudence and Judicial Method of the High Court of Australia* (Adelaide, SA, Presidian Legal Publications, 2008).

[61] D Jackson, 'The Role of the Chief Justice: A View from the Bar' in C Saunders (ed), *Courts of Final Jurisdiction* (Annandale, NSW, Federation Press, 1996) 21, 22.

was a party, many of which had implications for Australian law whether they were formally incorporated or not.[62]

There was a discernible shift in the interpretive method of the High Court during this period. In part this was marked by changes in tone and style, which were evident under all three of the Chief Justices who held office in these years, but which are particularly associated with the Chief Justiceship of Anthony Mason, from 1987 to 1995.[63] In a major speech made shortly after taking office as Chief Justice, Mason noted that the Court had departed from 'strict formalism'; acknowledged its law-making role; and argued that courts had a responsibility to develop the law with 'an eye to the justice of a rule and 'to the fairness and practical efficacy of its operation'. As a corollary, the style of judicial reasoning should assist the understanding of judgments so that law is not 'an esoteric mystery, administered by a priestly class'.[64]

More explicit acknowledgement of the creative role of a final appellate court was paralleled by substantive changes in the methodology of the Court. Most obviously, during this phase, the Court was prepared to look at substance rather than form; to supplement textual analysis with consideration of purpose; to sacrifice sometimes illusory objectivity to the more subjective demands of proportionality; and to rely on policy considerations in choosing between courses of judicial action.[65] Some of the touchstones for validity developed in the previous phase were abandoned and the meaning of a group of constitutional provisions dealing with 'legal and social unity' was reconceived.[66] Secondly, the Court displayed greater boldness in what Dixon had described as 'reasoning from the more fundamental of settled legal principles to new conclusions', in ways that also placed new emphasis on the role of people in a democratic society. The most controversial cases in this category found some protection for liberty and due process in the constitutional

---

[62] The Senate Legal and Constitutional Affairs Committee estimated in 1995 that more than 300 treaties had been concluded in the previous decade: *Trick or Treaty? Commonwealth Power to Make and Implement Treaties* (November 1995) para 2.6; significantly also, Australia accepted the competence of the Human Rights Committee pursuant to the First Protocol of the ICCPR from January 1993.

[63] The others were William Gibbs (1981–1987) and Gerard Brennan (1995–1998).

[64] Mason, n 59, 158.

[65] Respectively, *Hematite Petroleum Pty Ltd v Victoria* (1983) 151 CLR 599; *Cole v Whitfield* (1988) 165 CLR 360; *Castlemaine Tooheys Ltd v South Australia* (1990) 169 CLR 436; *Commonwealth v Tasmania (Tasmanian Dam* case) (1983) 158 CLR 1.

[66] Sections 92 and 117 in particular; to a lesser extent, s 90. The quotation is from *Street v Queensland Bar Association* (1989) 168 CLR 461, 512.

separation of judicial power[67] and, in a more novel development still, implied a guarantee of freedom of political communication from the third pillar of principle on which the Constitution rests: representative and responsible government.[68] Thirdly, in at least one case, *Mabo (No 2)*, the Court abandoned settled legal principle for reasons that were primarily connected with justice and contemporary standards of decency in Australia and elsewhere.[69]

How far the substantive changes to the methodology of the Court during this phase departed from the Australian interpretive norm is a matter for consideration in the next part. In any event, both the methodological shift and some of the more high profile cases caused considerable controversy and greater than usual friction with the elected branches of government. In a notable softening of new doctrine towards the end of this phase, the constitutional guarantee of freedom of political communication was tied more closely to the 'text and structure' of the Constitution,[70] heralding a return to a form of reasoning more readily identified as legalism over the final decade.

v. 1998–

The first part of this phase was marked by continuing tension between the courts and executive government over judicial decisions on indigenous rights. Other sources of tension emerged later, over legislation that attempted to limit the jurisdiction of the courts in refugee cases and restricted civil liberties in the interests of security following the attacks in New York in November 2001 and the bomb attacks in Bali in 2002. To the extent that inter-branch tension is a theme of this period, it might be deemed to begin a year or so earlier, following the decision in *Wik* that native title can co-exist with pastoral leases.[71] But the appointment in 1998 of a new Chief Justice, Murray Gleeson, who from the outset identified both judicial independence and judicial restraint as attributes of the rule of law, makes this an equally convenient starting point.[72] Gleeson retired in 2008 and was succeeded by Robert French. It is too

[67] *Chu Kheng Lim v Minister for Immigration, Local Government and Ethnic Affairs* (1992) 176 CLR 1; *Kable v Director of Public Prosecutions* (1996) 189 CLR 51.
[68] *Australian Capital Television Pty Ltd v Commonwealth* (1992) 177 CLR 106.
[69] *Mabo v Queensland (No 2)* (1992) 175 CLR 1.
[70] *Lange v Australian Broadcasting Corporation* (1997) 189 CLR 520.
[71] *Wik Peoples v Queensland* (1996) 187 CLR 1.
[72] M Gleeson, 'The Judiciary' in M Gleeson, *The Rule of Law,* Boyer Lecture 6, 2000.

early to tell whether this and other changes in the membership of the court will mark transition to a new phase.

As a generalisation, the characteristics of the court's interpretive method during this phase have been greater recourse to sometimes highly technical legal argument; reliance on legal criteria for decision-making, supported by historical analysis; a consequential repudiation of the relevance of other considerations; and a corresponding tendency to downplay the extent of judicial choice. Legalism has been reaffirmed as the Court's guiding methodology.[73]

On closer examination, however, it is clear that the clock has not entirely been turned back to the legalism of phase three; itself a compound of different approaches.[74] The 'high technique' of the earlier phase is less evident. On the other hand, many of the developments in constitutional doctrine in the wake of 1986 remain in place, although sometimes in modified form. The Court in this phase also has had creative moments of its own, which make repudiation of extra-legal considerations implausible. Some of these have been prompted by the continuing need to adapt the Constitution to Australian independence, as novel issues arise.[75] The conclusion that all Australian law is derived from Australian sources, which has become a leitmotif of this phase, has been productive of considerable 'doctrinal development'.[76]

B. Legalism and its Alternatives

i. Legalism

On the occasion of his swearing in as Chief Justice in 1952, Owen Dixon affirmed his commitment to 'strict and complete legalism'.[77] That commitment was echoed by two of his predecessors, whose periods as Chief Justice spanned most of the following 55 years.[78] Legalism is widely accepted as the orthodox methodology for constitutional adjudication in Australia.

---

[73] AM Gleeson, 'Judicial Legitimacy' (2000) 12 *Judicial Officers Bulletin* 41.

[74] M McHugh, 'The Constitutional Jurisprudence of the High Court: 1989–2004' (2008) 30 *Sydney Law Review* 5.

[75] *Sue v Hill* (1999) 199 CLR 462; *Singh v Commonwealth* (2004) 222 CLR 322; *Joosse v Australian Securities and Investment Commission* (1998) 159 ALR 260.

[76] W Gummow, *Change and Continuity* (Oxford, OUP, 1999) 77.

[77] *Swearing in of Sir Owen Dixon as Chief Justice* (1952) 85 CLR xi, xiv.

[78] Garfield Barwick (1964–1981), Murray Gleeson (1998–2008).

It is difficult to pinpoint the outer parameters of Australian legalism, however. This is partly because it is not applied consistently, so that exceptions to most generalisations can readily be found. More importantly, however, it is because it has been applied by different judges in different contexts over time. At its core is insistence that courts resolve questions before them by reference to standards drawn from a body of existing law and not on standards that are 'subjective or personal' to a judge. Appropriate 'external' standards most obviously are found in constitutional and statutory text and precedent, but at least for the most famous advocate of legalism, the sources from which the court might properly derive assistance are somewhat wider, including 'fundamental . . . settled legal principles'.[79]

Beyond this core requirement, itself somewhat fluid, methodological approaches with claims to the mantle of legalism can be ranged along a spectrum. At one end the spectrum shades into formalism and textualism. Approaches at the other end draw on the very considerable variety of analytical options authorised by the 'strict logic' and 'high technique' of the common law, understood also as including the embellishments of equity, with its preference of 'substance to form'.[80] In this mode, legalism lends itself to some development of the law to achieve just and workable outcomes, although without acknowledgement of choices consciously or unconsciously made. At least in its application to constitutional questions, legalism also can accept that considerations on the basis of which a court acts are susceptible to characterisation as political and that implications are necessary to constitutional construction.[81] 'High technique' often enables an inconvenient line of authority to be circumvented,[82] but a precedent may also be expressly repudiated, at least where it involves a 'fundamental error in constitutional principle' with significance that spreads beyond the immediate case.[83]

ii. Realism

By contrast, the approach of the Court in the period immediately before and for a decade after the enactment of the Australia Acts has

---

[79] Dixon, 'Concerning Judicial Method', n 54, 471–72.
[80] Gummow, *Change and Continuity*, n 76, 74.
[81] *Melbourne Corporation v Commonwealth*, (1947) 74 CLR 31, 82.
[82] The *Boilermakers'* case is an example: (1956) 94 CLR 254.
[83] *Commonwealth v Cigamatic Pty Ltd (In Liq)* (1962) 108 CLR 372, 377.

occasionally been characterised as 'realism'.[84] The term draws attention to the fact that, during this phase, the Court did not accept that 'distinctively *legal* rules and reasons . . . justify a unique result in most cases' and was prepared to identify the considerations by reference to which choices were made.[85] These considerations ranged beyond legal and constitutional principle to aspects of contemporary context and, cautiously, 'community' values.[86] Perception of a qualitative difference in the methodology of the Court during this period is further encouraged by extrajudicial observations of some of its leading members, including the deliberate rejection of 'legal formalism' by Chief Justice Mason himself.[87]

On the other hand, the distinctiveness of this phase in the interpretive method of the High Court should not be overstated. Consideration of external factors that are not legal in character, involving at least implicit acknowledgement of judicial discretion, is not unknown in other phases of the history of the Court although it occurred more regularly during this time.[88] More importantly perhaps, the Court of the latter part of the twentieth century was too much the heir to the Australian tradition of constitutional interpretation to stray so far from the influence of constitutional text, structure and authority to deserve classification as realist in the sense of an approach to adjudication in which 'judges respond primarily to the stimulus of the facts of the case, rather than to legal rules and reasons'.[89] At best, this is a species of Australian realism under which the options for a court are restricted but not

---

[84]   Gray, n 60, 57, 64 ff, drawing on the extensive literature generated at the time.

[85]   B Leiter, 'American Legal Realism' in W Edmundson and M. Golding (eds), *The Blackwell Guide to Philosophy of Law and Legal Theory* (Oxford, Blackwell, 2003), referring to the formalist approach to adjudication, which was repudiated by the American realists.

[86]   Zines, n 42, 631–42.

[87]   Mason, 'Future Directions in Australian Law', n 59, 155 ff; cf, more cautiously A Mason, 'The Role of a Constitutional Court in a Federation: A Comparison of the Australian and United States Experience' (1986) 16 *Federal Law Review* 1, 28.

[88]   Zines, n 42, 618–28; see also *New South Wales v Commonwealth* (*Workchoices* case) (2006) 229 CLR, 1, 79: '. . . it is essential to recognise the fundamental and far-reaching legal, social, and economic changes in the place now occupied by the corporation'.

[89]   Leiter, n 85, describing the 'core claim' of realism. Cf Anthony Mason, 'Trends in Constitutional Interpretation' (1995) 18 *University of New South Wales Law Journal* 237, 245: '. . . the Constitution is our paramount law, and interpretation requires that we give effect to its language and heed what it says'.

always determined by law, leaving room for choice, the bases for the exercise of which should be acknowledged.[90] On some questions, during this phase, the Court undoubtedly perceived the boundaries within which choice might be made as lying further apart than its predecessors or successors were prepared to do. It is not clear, even so, that the overall outcome of constitutional decisions at this time is a radical departure from a norm.[91]

iii. Realistic Legalism

It is generally assumed that the advantage of legalism in Australia is that it shields courts from the perception that constitutional review entrenches upon spheres of policy and law-making properly left to the elected branches of government.[92] This assumption may have additional force in a constitutional system in which the combination of a culture of parliamentary sovereignty with an entrenched constitution places additional pressures on constitutional review. If the assumption is correct, it follows that the political attacks on the High Court from 1996 were attributable, at least in part, to the change in its interpretive method.

While there is something to be said for this chain of reasoning, the reality is more complex. The culture of parliamentary sovereignty that accompanies responsible government and the constraints of a Constitution that is superior law initially were reconciled with each other on the basis that a federation was the only conceivable form of government that would bring the entire continent together; that an entrenched constitution was necessary for federation; and that constitutional review was necessary to resolve disputes about the federal framework. For almost 80 years thereafter, federal questions dominated Australian constitutional law. Even the conclusion that federal courts cannot exercise non-judicial power was explained in 1956 as a concomitant of a federal form of government.[93] Consistently with this understanding of the purpose and effect of the Constitution, Dixon's commitment to legalism in 1952 was justified as 'the only way to maintain the confidence of all

---

[90] Gray, n 60, 47 ff, acknowledging the influence of the jurisprudential writings of Julius Stone on Australian realism.

[91] M McHugh, 'The Constitutional Jurisprudence of the High Court', n 74.

[92] D Williams, 'The Role of the Attorney-General' (2002) 13 *PLR* 252, 259.

[93] *Boilermakers'* case, n 82, 267–68, 276.

parties in Federal conflicts'.[94] While it seems obvious with hindsight that legalism was likely to be useful for the same reason in relation to other 'great conflicts', at the time almost all of these were federalism-related. Even the highly sensitive issue of the validity of Commonwealth legislation outlawing the Communist Party of Australia in the early years of the cold war presented itself as a question about the federal division of power. The equanimity with which the Court's conclusion of invalidity was met by the government has been attributed to the 'neutral conceptions' of the Court.[95]

Against this background, the interpretive phase that spanned the 1980s and much of the 1990s courted controversy for at least three reasons. Most obviously, by exposing the reasoning of the Court more explicitly it prompted questions about the legitimacy of the judicial role. Equally importantly, however, it revealed ways in which those parts of the Constitution that distribute functions between the institutions of Commonwealth government might also operate as a constraint on power, with no particular federalism rationale, but with rights-protecting effect. The understanding of the first three chapters of the Constitution was transformed during this period as a result. In addition, as Australian constitutional jurisprudence expanded its focus beyond questions of federalism the Court become involved in issues that were more easily understood, on which passions sometimes ran high, and which were more readily perceived as being 'political'.[96] The potential for controversy over constitutional questions was heightened by some of the decisions of the Court in other areas; most obviously those concerning native title.

Criticism of the High Court on the grounds of 'judicial activism' has been stemmed in the last decade. This can be attributed both to the reversion of the Court to a more legalistic style of reasoning and to its renewed emphasis on the federal character of the Constitution as justification for judicial review. Not surprisingly, the variety and flow of constitutional litigation has been stemmed as well. But the Court has been exposed instead to criticism on other grounds: the alleged imprac-

---

[94]   (1952) 85 CLR xiv.

[95]   Williams, n 92, 258.

[96]   Cf Barwick CJ in 1976: 'we have no Bill of Rights and that means that our work is strictly legal work', in Address to the National Press Club, (1976) 50 *Australian Law Journal* 433, 434, quoted in Williams, n 92, 259.

ticality of some of its decisions;[97] the often convoluted nature of its reasons;[98] outcomes that offend human rights standards;[99] and failure to give effect to meaningful constraints on Commonwealth power in general and Commonwealth executive power in particular.[100]

In the light of this experience, it is tempting to suggest that the way forward lies in an amalgam of the approaches of the past 20 years that combines greater transparency in judicial reasoning with somewhat greater caution in the development of the law. This may be a mirage, however. Whatever its original rationale, the Constitution is more than a legal framework for the Australian federation; indeed, it is increasingly less effective in this regard. The Constitution also establishes institutional checks and balances through which the exercise of power is controlled and rights receive a modicum of protection. But it does so obliquely, demanding creativity on the part of the Court and encouraging contestation over constitutional decisions in which the stakes are high.

C. Interpretation and Change

i. An Instrument of Government

Any version of legalism enables some adaptation of the Constitution to contemporary circumstances. A constitution that is written in relatively general terms has a degree of natural flexibility. In addition, it has been accepted from the outset in Australia that the character of the Constitution 'as an instrument of government meant to endure' must be taken into account in the interpretive process.[101] Thanks to the battle over interpretive method during the first 20 years after federation, it is generally assumed that this aphorism requires the Court always to 'lean to the broader interpretation' of a constitutional expression unless

---

[97] *Re Wakim; Ex parte McNally* (1999) 198 CLR 511.

[98] *R v Hughes* (2000) 202 CLR 535.

[99] Eg *Al-Kateb v Godwin* (2004) 219 CLR 562.

[100] *New South Wales v Commonwealth* (*Workchoices* case) (2006) 229 CLR, 1; *Combet v Commonwealth* (2005) 224 CLR 494.

[101] *Australian National Airways Pty Ltd v Commonwealth* (1945) 79 CLR 29, 81; see also *Jumbunna Coalmine, No Liability v Victorian Coal Miners' Association* (1908) 6 CLR 309, 367.

there are clear indications that it should not.[102] This approach has had its principal impact on the ambit of the heads of legislative power allocated to the Commonwealth and accounts for at least part of the expansion of Commonwealth power since the decision in *Engineers*. Its relevance to the interpretation of the few express constitutional guarantees in the Constitution is much less clear and its application has not been consistent.[103] By definition, it has no application at all to principles derived by implication.

Nevertheless, the longevity of a deeply entrenched constitution places an essentially text-based interpretive method under pressure, as the conditions in which the constitution operates change over time. In Australia, this has been further alleviated in at least two ways.

First, principles of statutory interpretation focus not only on the text but also on the context and, sometimes, the purpose of an instrument. In the application of these principles to the very particular case of the Australian Constitution, moreover, context is understood to include what often is described as the 'structure' of the Constitution, which in some instances goes beyond the structure of the instrument itself to the core elements of the principles of government for which it provides. Structure has been critical to the process whereby implications have been drawn from parts of the Constitution establishing the various institutions of government so as to provide a deeper level of protection for the institutions themselves, on which Australian constitutionalism in turn depends.

Secondly, Australian doctrine draws a distinction between the connotation and the denotation of constitutional terms, assisted by the generality with which they often are expressed.[104] Connotation refers to the core meaning and is fixed at the date of the enactment of the Constitution in 1900. Denotation is apt to pick up subsequent developments, as long as they also satisfy the core.[105] The distinction is much criticised, for reasons that can be understood by attempting to use it to resolve the (so far hypothetical) question whether marriage encompasses

---

[102] *R v Commonwealth Court of Conciliation and Arbitration* (1912) 15 CLR 586, 608.

[103] Compare eg *Attorney-General (Vic); ex Rel Black v Commonwealth (DOGS* case) (1981) 146 CLR 599 (s 116: freedom of religion) and *Street v Queensland Bar Association* (1989) 168 CLR 461.

[104] See generally Zines, *The High Court and the Constitution,* n 42, 25–27.

[105] For the philosophical derivation of this distinction and reference to other forms in which it appears see J Goldsworthy 'Originalism in Constitutional Interpretation' (1997) 25 *Federal Law Review* 31.

same sex marriage.[106] It remains an analytical tool on which the Court relies, however and, at least ostensibly, accounts for many, although not all, cases in which Commonwealth legislative powers have been interpreted to embrace post-federation developments.

The distinction between connotation and denotation sometimes also is used to explain how, by 1999, the United Kingdom had become a 'foreign power' for the purposes of s 44 (i) of the Constitution, precluding Australians with British citizenship from election to the Commonwealth Parliament.[107] More plausibly, however, the willingness of the High Court to conceive of the Constitution as an instrument that anticipates an independent Australia provides a discrete explanation for this, together with some other conclusions. Examples include the acceptance of the Australian people as authority for the Constitution; recognition that the Commonwealth executive inherited from the United Kingdom the right to exercise the external sovereignty of Australia; and the distinction now drawn between Australian citizens and other 'subjects of the Queen' in order to identify the community that the Constitution serves.

ii. *Relevance of the Framers*

The origin of Australian legalism in the techniques of statutory interpretation makes the meaning of the Constitution at the time of enactment a key consideration in resolving disputes. It is not surprising in these circumstances that, when originalism emerged as an influential approach to constitutional interpretation during the 1980s in the United States, it attracted some attention in Australia. The temptation to understand Australian interpretive method through the lens of originalism was further encouraged when the High Court decided, in 1988, that historical sources could be taken into account in constitutional interpretation 'for the purpose of identifying the contemporary meaning of the language used'.[108]

---

[106] For an overview of some of the criticisms and a defence, in the context of his theory of 'moderate originalism' see J Goldsworthy, 'Constitutional Interpretation' in HP Lee and P Gerangelos, *Constitutional Advancement in a Frozen Continent* (Annandale, NSW, Federation Press, 2009) 245. On the same sex marriage example see *Re Wakim* (1999) 198 CLR 511, 553; *Grain Pool of Western Australia v Commonwealth* (2000) 202 CLR 479, 529; and for analysis, K Walker, 'The Same Sex Marriage Debate in Australia' (2007) 11 *International Journal of Human Rights* 109.

[107] *Eastman v R* (2000) 203 CLR 1, 45, per McHugh J, explaining the outcome in *Sue v Hill* (1999) 199 CLR 462; cf A Mason, 'Trends in Constitutional Interpretation' (1995) 18 *University of New South Wales Law Journal* 237, 242.

[108] *Cole v Whitfield* (1988) 165 CLR 360, 385.

Originalism comes in a variety of forms. For one of its most famous exponents, Antonin Scalia, it depends not on the intent of the drafters of the Constitution but on more general understanding of constitutional meaning at the time of the founding.[109] The Australian approach to determination of the meaning of constitutional terms in 1900 is comparable insofar as it seeks, not always consistently, to avoid reliance on the subjective intention of the framers of the Constitution.

Even so, Australian legalism is not United States originalism and in 2010 all but one of the Justices of the High Court are legalist, rather than originalist, in their approach.[110] The original meaning of constitutional terms is only one of the considerations taken into account in the interpretive process, albeit an important one. The starting point is the Constitution itself, understood with the aid of the multiple techniques of legalism. Constitutional interpretation in accordance with the tenets of legalism also now requires consideration of more than 100 years of constitutional doctrine. Much of that, moreover, has been settled in the light of constitutional experience elsewhere. Insofar as originalism precludes reference to foreign legal sources that could not have been taken into account when the Constitution was made, it is inconsistent with Australian practice, which has accepted the relevance of the experience of other jurisdictions in resolving Australian constitutional problems since the Constitution came into effect. Even the most thoughtful analyses of the extent to which Australian interpretive method might be able to be understood in terms of originalism have found it necessary to qualify the latter as 'moderate',[111] 'evolutionary'[112] or 'faint-hearted'.[113] In the circumstances, legalism remains a more accurate label, however vulnerable to criticism it may be.

---

[109]   A Scalia and KJ Ring, *Scalia Dissents* (Washington, Regnery Publishing, 2004) 8.

[110]   The occasional exception is Heydon J: see for example *Forge v Australian Securities and Investment Commission* (2006) 228 CLR 45; *Roach v Electoral Commissioner* (2007) 233 CLR 162; *Wong v Commonwealth of Australia* (2009) 236 CLR 573.

[111]   Goldsworthy, n 105.

[112]   J Kirk, 'Constitutional Interpretation and a Theory of Evolutionary Originalism' (1999) 27 *Federal Law Review* 323.

[113]   *Eastman's* case, n 107, 44, per McHugh J, quoting Antonin Scalia, who describes his own originalism in the same terms: 'The Role of a Constitutional Court in a Democratic Society' (1995) 2 *The Judicial Review* 141, 142.

III. SOURCES

A. Precedent

Apart from the Constitution itself, the principal source on which Australian courts draw in resolving constitutional disputes are earlier decisions of courts in the Australian court hierarchy. The High Court is at the apex of that hierarchy. Decisions of the High Court are binding on all other Australian courts and generally are followed by the High Court itself, subject to what is said below.

There are seven Justices of the Court. The quorum for a Full Court is two Justices but a typical minimum is three and in practice at least five Justices are likely to sit on significant cases. All seven Justices generally sit *en banc* for constitutional cases of any degree of importance, whether in the original jurisdiction of the Court or on appeal. It is relatively unusual for the Court to sit with an equal number of Justices, but where this occurs and the Court is evenly divided, the decision of the Court below is affirmed, in the case of an appeal. If this happens when the Court is sitting in its original jurisdiction, the decision of the Chief Justice prevails.[114] While these rules ensure that there is an outcome in such cases, the decisions themselves are not regarded as binding on the High Court.[115]

The Court normally follows its own decisions, in the interests of 'continuity and consistency'.[116] It has always maintained the authority to depart from them for sufficient reason, however, and from time to time has done so.[117] The Court may be more ready to overrule itself in constitutional than other cases, because of the inability of the Parliament to alter a constitutional rule. The considerations that it takes into account in exercising this discretion include the magnitude of the perceived error; the extent to which the challenged precedent has become embedded in

---

[114] Judiciary Act 1903 s 23(2)(a),(b).

[115] *Tasmania v Victoria* (1935) 52 CLR 157, 183. Cf the treatment of *Gould v Brown* (1998) 193 CLR 346 in *Re Wakim* (1999) 198 CLR 511, where the rule was unsuccessfully contested.

[116] *R v Commonwealth Court of Conciliation and Arbitration (Brisbane Tramways* case) (1914) 18 CLR 54, 69.

[117] Examples are given by Aickin J in *Queensland v Commonwealth (Second Territories Representation* case) (1977) 139 CLR 585, 620–631.

the jurisprudence by subsequent decisions of the Court; the practical steps taken in reliance on the challenged precedent; and the degree of inconvenience that overruling would cause. In the past the Court has declined to hear argument about whether an earlier case was wrongly decided. Its right to do so has been contested by individual Justices, however, and it may be that future courts will not take the same view.[118]

B. Extrinsic Materials

The High Court has always taken history into account and, indeed, its interpretive method obliges it to do so. Nevertheless, until relatively recently, the Court precluded itself from examining a range of historical sources for the purpose. It was accepted that in constitutional cases the Court might draw historical inferences from successive drafts of the Constitution before it came into effect. The Court was unable, however, formally to take into account the record of debates of the Constitutional Conventions and other, comparable, extrinsic material.[119] In consequence, after those who had been involved in framing the Constitution left the Court, many of its historical conclusions necessarily were based on assumptions about historical fact, on earlier judicial decisions drawing historical conclusions, or on those historical materials that were acceptable in the Court including, somewhat surprisingly, Quick and Garran.[120] In 1988, however, in the course of a complete revision of the understanding of the guarantee of freedom of interstate trade, commerce and intercourse in section 92, the Court accepted that historical sources were admissible and made extensive use of them.[121] Reference to historical sources, including the Convention Debates, is now a frequent practice.

---

[118] *Evda Nominees v Victoria* (1984) 154 CLR 311; see also *XYZ v Commonwealth* (2006) 227 CLR 532, 561.

[119] The availability of this material made Australia a 'constitutional laboratory': J Waugh, 'Lawyers, Historians and Federation History' in R French, G Lindell and C Saunders *Reflections on the Australian Constitution* (Annandale, NSW, Federation Press, 2003) 25–26.

[120] For the use made of this source, see H Irving, 'The Framers' Vision of the High Court' in P Cane (ed), *Centenary Essays for the High Court of Australia* (Chatswood, NSW, LexisNexis Butterworths, 2004) 17, 34.

[121] *Cole v Whitfield* (1988) 165 CLR 360. For occasional earlier references from the 1970s see C McCamish, 'The Use of Historical Materials in Interpreting the Commonwealth Constitution' (1996) 70 *Australian Law Journal* 638, 654.

The question of the source from which the High Court derives any non-legal information on which its reasoning is based is not confined to history but arises in relation to other forms of information as well: social, economic and commercial data, political facts, community values. In many cases, information is received under a somewhat generous doctrine of 'judicial notice' as a matter of 'general public knowledge'.[122] In general, however, the Court lacks developed procedures whereby such information can formally be presented to it and handled in a way that is consistent with the adversarial process.[123] In part this may be the consequence of assumptions about the extent to which such information is relevant, when decisions are made on legal criteria alone. In this respect it is notable that, even during the period when the Court most explicitly took non-legal considerations into account, there was no corresponding change to its procedures.[124] Consistently with its position as an apex court, procedures in the High Court in any event are designed to avoid the trial of facts as far as possible, even when these are ordinary facts that could arise between the parties in proceedings in the original jurisdiction.[125]

The issue arises in an acute form when a fact is a constitutional fact on which the validity of a challenged law depends. Such a fact is not necessarily an 'ordinary fact' in issue between the parties and thus automatically subject to the rules of evidence.[126] On the other hand, it may be contested by the party claiming invalidity. The difficulty of dealing with material of this kind is compounded in one particular context in which it is likely to arise: a challenge to the validity of security legislation, where the constitutional fact is the existence of a threat to security that provides the necessary link between the legislation and the power on which it relies. The Court must be satisfied of the existence of such a fact and will not rely on assurances by the executive branch. On the other hand, the latter may be unwilling to lead evidence, at least in public.[127] Final resolution of how

[122] *Stenhouse v Coleman* (1944) 69 CLR 457, 469 per Dixon J.

[123] For discussion of some cases in which this difficulty has been manifest see *Thomas v Mowbray* (2007) 233 CLR 307, 483–84.

[124] J Doyle 'Implications of Judicial Law-Making' in C Saunders (ed), *Courts of Final Jurisdiction* (Sydney, NSW, Federation Press, 1996) 84, 97–98.

[125] Sometimes through the use of a 'demurrer', see *Wurridjul v Commonwealth of Australia* (2009) 237 CLR 309.

[126] For the distinction, see *Thomas v Mowbray* (2007) 233 CLR 307, 512.

[127] G Winterton, 'The *Communist Party* case' in HP Lee and G Winterton (eds), *Australian Constitutional Landmarks* (Cambridge, CUP, 2003) 108, 124.

such facts should be determined so far has been avoided either by reliance on an extended doctrine of judicial notice or other 'rational considerations'[128] or by resolving the case on another ground.[129] A more extended analysis of the problem in *Thomas*, in which it was suggested that the rules of evidence do not apply to the determination of constitutional facts but that the information should be made available to all parties in a manner that enables them to present evidence if they wish to do so, is likely to influence future consideration of the issue.[130]

C. Foreign Law

The High Court has always referred relatively freely to the law of other jurisdictions in dealing with questions of both constitutional and non-constitutional law. While statistics are incomplete, it is clear that references to foreign law declined somewhat after the first decade of federation, when they were very high. A study in 2000 suggests that this decline came to an end around 1950 after which the proportion remained more or less steady, at around 25 per cent. These statistics do not indicate how the foreign authority is used and in particular whether it has been accepted or rejected. Anecdotally, treatment is mixed. Anecdotally also, citations of foreign law appear across a wide range of constitutional issues including federalism, separation of judicial power and political rights.

The practice itself is not controversial in Australia. This is unsurprising in relation to the years immediately following federation, given the reliance on foreign models in the drafting of the Constitution. References to British authorities also are unsurprising in the decades prior to independence, when the decisions of the Privy Council were binding and offered a conduit through which constitutional experience elsewhere was brought to bear on comparable Australian constitutional questions.

But neither of these factors explains the prevalence of references to decisions of the Supreme Court of the United States handed down after the Australian Constitution was enacted, which continued throughout

---

[128] *Marcus Clark & Co Ltd v The Commonwealth* (1952) 87 CLR 177, 227.

[129] *Australian Communist Party v Commonwealth* (1951) 83 CLR 1; *Thomas v Mowbray* (2007) 233 CLR 307.

[130] *Thomas v Mowbray* (2007) 233 CLR 307, 512ff.

the twentieth century. Reference to British and Canadian authority also persisted even as a distinctive Australian common law began to emerge and appeals to the Privy Council were severed. In 1986, the relevance of British decisions in Australia was formally considered by the High Court, in terms that are significant for present purposes. British decisions were no longer binding on Australian courts. Nevertheless:

> The history of this country and of the common law makes it inevitable and desirable that the courts of this country will continue to obtain assistance and guidance from the learning and reasoning of United Kingdom courts just as Australian courts benefit from the learning and reasoning of other great common law courts [but] the precedents of other legal systems are not binding and are useful only to the degree of the persuasiveness of their reasoning.[131]

The range of jurisdictions to which the High Court is most likely to refer is relatively narrow: the United Kingdom, the United States, Canada, New Zealand, India, South Africa, Ireland and the European Court of Human Rights. The use that it makes of such authority is broadly comparable to that of other common law courts that follow the same practice, once described by Emeritus Justice Laurie Ackerman of South Africa as: 'seeking information, guidance, stimulation, clarification, or even enlightenment . . . keeping the judicial mind open to new ideas'.[132] Foreign law is always a secondary consideration, especially if there is an Australian authority in point. Obvious legal and structural differences between Australia and other jurisdictions typically are taken into account, although more subtle differences may be missed.

In Australia, as elsewhere, there is some potential for the practice of referring to the law of other jurisdictions to become caught up in the debate on judicial activism. This has been largely avoided so far; not least because references to foreign law have always been considered compatible with Australian legalism.[133] The practice is presently under pressure from various quarters, however, which in time may affect the extent and manner of its use. These include the perception of the growing distinctiveness of the Australian legal and constitutional system and the palpable, if so far limited, influence in Australia of the United States debate

---

[131]   *Cook v Cook* (1986) 162 CLR 376, 390.

[132]   LH Ackermann, 'Constitutional Comparativism in South Africa: A Response to Sir Basil Markesinis and Jorg Fedtke' (2005) 80 *Tulane Law Review* 169, 183.

[133]   Dixon, 'Concerning Judicial Method' n 54, 470–71; see also the use made of foreign authorities by Dixon J in *Melbourne Corporation v Commonwealth* (1947) 74 CLR 31, 81–83.

on originalism, with its implications for the use of foreign law. The present picture is further confused by some acerbic exchanges within the High Court about the relevance of international law to constitutional interpretation, to which the Court takes a quite different approach.

D. International Law

Australia adheres to a distinctively dualist theory of the relationship between domestic and international law. International law is not part of the domestic legal system; treaties must be given effect by statute in order to affect rights and interests under Australian law; and there is uncertainty about whether customary international law also requires legislative implementation.[134] While this approach has historical roots, it draws its contemporary rationale from the separation of powers, under a Constitution that leaves the authority to make and ratify treaties with the executive alone and constrains the scope of judicial power.

Even without incorporation, international law may indirectly affect Australian general law in ways that are explained in chapter eight, in the context of the protection of rights. As a general rule, however, it is not used as an aid in constitutional interpretation. This was established by earlier decisions of the High Court, when it was still accurate to describe international law as 'a law for the intercourse of States with one another and not a law for individuals'.[135] The view that international human rights law should now be taken into account in cases where the meaning or application of the Constitution is unclear was pressed strongly by Michael Kirby, as Justice of the High Court, until his retirement in 2009.[136] In the absence of constitutional rights, however, such arguments typically are directed to restriction of the scope or application of Commonwealth heads of legislative power.[137] Thus in *Kartinyeri*, Kirby J held that the answer to the question of whether the power to make laws with respect to the 'people of any race for whom it is deemed necessary to make

---

[134]   *Nulyarimma v Thompson* (1999) 165 ALR 621.

[135]   *Polites v Commonwealth* (1945) 70 CLR 60, 75.

[136]   *Newcrest Mining (WA) Ltd v Commonwealth* (1997) 190 CLR 513. The issue had been raised just before his appointment to the Court in 1996 in the particularly stark context of the *Stolen Generations* case: *Kruger v Commonwealth* (1997) 190 CLR 1.

[137]   Although cf *Al-Kateb v Godwin*, where the meaning of the separation of judicial power also was in issue: (2004) 219 CLR 562.

special laws' could be used to discriminate against an Indigenous group should be answered in the negative, in the face of both customary international law and treaty.[138]

In this as in other cases, the remaining Justices remained unpersuaded of the applicability of international law. The resulting, sometimes hostile, exchanges reveal the following reasons. There is no proper analogy between the use of international law for the purposes of constitutional interpretation and statutory construction because the former operates as a constraint on power that the Parliament cannot overcome; most current rules of international law postdate the making of the Constitution; to take them into account in interpreting the Constitution would be to amend the Constitution without using the formal alteration procedure; in any event, international law is now too voluminous to be practically useful for this purpose; Australia is not necessarily represented on the committees by which some of the international instruments are interpreted and applied.[139]

Some of these points might also be made about the use of foreign law and occasionally the two are run together. Generally, however, they are distinguished; a phenomenon that might be explained in a variety of ways. Judicial reference to foreign decisions presents no challenge to the separation of executive and legislative power. Unlike international treaties, foreign law has no claim to be binding and represents only a source of ideas. References to foreign law lie within the established repertoire of legalism; international law is not only a relative newcomer but was linked by Kirby J to a different approach to constitutional interpretation that recognised the Constitution as a 'living force'.[140] International law represents a new source of restrictions on Commonwealth heads of power, unsupported by the text or structure of the Constitution. It thus presents a new challenge to the 'plenary' character of Commonwealth power that was settled in *Engineers*.

There is some interpenetration of international and domestic law in Australia, even in the constitutional context. Most notably, international law was a medium for the dramatic expansion of Commonwealth power vis-à-vis the States, when the external affairs power in section 51(xxix)

---

[138] *Kartinyeri v Commonwealth* (1998) 195 CLR 337.

[139] *Al-Kateb v Godwin* (2004) 219 CLR 591ff, per McHugh J. The latter point is made by Heydon J in *Roach v Electoral Commissioner* (2007) 233 CLR 162, 225.

[140] M Kirby, 'Constitutional Interpretation and Original Intent: A Form of Ancestor Worship' (2000) 24 *Melbourne University Law Review* 1.

of the Constitution was interpreted to authorise Commonwealth legislation to implement any international agreements to which Australia
is a party.[141] The extent to which the legislation gives effect to such an
agreement in turn became a measure of validity.[142] Very occasionally,
international law is raised in relation to other constitutional questions
as well. In *XYZ* the extent to which international law recognises the
extraterritorial jurisdiction of states was considered in rejecting a challenge to the validity of Commonwealth legislation criminalising sexual
acts with persons under 16, outside Australia, on the part of Australian
citizens or residents.[143] In *Bradley* Gleeson CJ referred to international
law sources, amongst others, to demonstrate the 'fundamental importance' of judicial independence.[144] These are minor instances, however.
For the foreseeable future, more extensive use of international law in
constitutional interpretation is likely to be inhibited by a combination of
the content of the Constitution and the prevailing interpretive approach.

SELECTED READING

Australian Law Reform Commission, *Beyond the Door-keeper: Standing to Sue
for Public Remedies* (Report No 78, 1996)
Australian Law Reform Commission, *The Judicial Power of the Commonwealth*
(Report No.92, 2001)
Blackshield T, Coper, M and Williams, G, *The Oxford Companion to the High
Court of Australia* (Oxford, OUP, 2001)
Cowen, Z and Zines, L, *Federal Jurisdiction in Australia,* 3rd edn (Sydney,
NSW, Federation Press, OUP, 2002)
Galligan, B, *Politics of the High Court: A Study of the Judicial Branch of
Government in Australia* (St Lucia, University of Queensland Press, 1987)
Gray, R, *The Constitutional Jurisprudence and Judicial Method of the High Court
of Australia* (Adelaide, SA, Presidian Legal Publications, 2008)

---

[141] *Commonwealth v Tasmania* (*Tasmanian Dam* case) (1983) 158 CLR 1. The Court
will not consider whether the treaty itself is valid in international law: *Horta v
Commonwealth* (1994) 181 CLR 183.
[142] Ibid, 259; see generally Zines, *The High Court and the Constitution* n 42, 392.
[143] *XYZ v Commonwealth* (2006) 227 CLR 532, 536–37.
[144] *North Australian Legal Aid v Bradley* (2004) 218 CLR 146, 152. The sources were
the *Universal Declaration of the Independence of Justice* and the *Beijing Statement of Principles
of the Independence of the Judiciary in the Lawasia Region.*

Gummow, W, *Change and Continuity* (Oxford, OUP, 1999)

Opeskin, B and Wheeler, F (eds), *The Australian Federal Judicial System* (Melbourne, Vic, MUP, 2000)

Patapan, H, *Judging Democracy: The New Politics of the High Court of Australia* (Cambridge, CUP, 2000)

Saunders, C (ed), *Courts of Final Jurisdiction* (Sydney, NSW, Federation Press, 1996)

Zines, L, *The High Court and the Constitution* (Sydney, NSW, Federation Press, 2008)

4

Representative Democracy

———⟫•⟪———

Principle – Institutions – Legislative Function – Political Rights

I. PRINCIPLE

A. Significance

REPRESENTATIVE DEMOCRACY IS one of the pillars of the Australian constitutional system.[1] It is secured through the Parliaments, which in Australia are the only elected institutions above the local level of government. It is twinned with the principle of responsible government, under which the executive government holds office because it has the support of a majority in the House of Parliament deemed to be the more representative, described in Australia as the 'lower' House. Representative democracy nevertheless is a critical principle in its own right. It is the source of legitimacy for both parliament and government. It provides the justification for the supremacy of the legislature in the exercise of its law-making function and the basis for the assumption that this power will not be abused.[2] Together with responsible government and the rule of law, it provides a foundation for an approach to the protection of rights that so far has relied almost entirely on the allocation of power between institutions of government, rather than on rights instruments that limit what the institutions collectively may do.

[1] Paul Finn describes it as 'our primary form of governance: 'A Sovereign People, a Public Trust' in PD Finn (ed), *Essays on Law and Government, Vol 1* (Sydney, NSW, Law Book Company Limited, 1995) 1, 24.

[2] AV Dicey *Introduction to the Study of the Law of the Constitution*, 8th edn (1915) 30; *Amalgamated Society of Engineers v Adelaide Steamship Co (Engineers* case) (1920) 28 CLR 129.

The democratic character of the Commonwealth Constitution was a cause of pride when it came into effect in 1901. In large part this was attributable to the requirement for both Houses to be 'directly chosen by the people' on the basis of the same franchise, which the Commonwealth, and not the States, would prescribe.[3] Much important detail, however, which elsewhere is found in written constitutions, was left to future legislation. It was also evident on the face of the Constitution that something less than universal adult suffrage was contemplated; in particular, that the vote would not necessarily be extended to either women or Aboriginal Australians.[4] These provisions have long since been overtaken by legislation although, in the case of the latter, not until 1962. Nevertheless, they are inconvenient contextual evidence of the more limited representative democracy for which the Constitution originally provided.

The extent to which it is rational to rely on the representatives of a current majority to protect rules of representative democracy that may jeopardise their own incumbency is a familiar conundrum, even in systems that otherwise are inclined to place confidence in elected institutions. Over the past 30 years or so, the question of the extent of constitutional protection for democratic rules has come before the High Court in three contexts in particular: the fairness of constituency boundaries; freedom of political communication about political and governmental affairs; and voting rights. The outcome in each case will be examined in the course of this chapter.

These cases are important not only for their outcome, but also for the pressure that they placed on the interpretive method of the High Court. They have required the Court to consider whether the concept of democracy in 1901 could evolve over time so as to affect the meaning or application of the Constitution; whether indications of a more restricted conception of representation in 1901 inhibits a contemporary understanding of the general constitutional requirement for the Houses of Parliament to be 'directly chosen by the people'; and whether and how core features of representative democracy that are not spelt out in the Constitution are nevertheless protected by it. For a time, these tensions caused a reaction against the terminology of democracy

---

[3] Sections 7 and 24; the same franchise is mandated by s 8.
[4] For women, the signs are in ss 41 and 128; for Aboriginal Australians in s 25 and the now repealed s 127.

altogether, in favour of 'representative government'.[5] Given the significance of democratic principle in Australian constitutionalism, both historically and now, this seems inappropriately cautious. Concern that the constitutional prescription cannot be equated with democracy is also unnecessary, if minimalist democratic theory is used as a measure.[6] In any event, this seems to have been a passing phase; the terminology of 'representative democracy' is back in occasional use.[7]

B. Characteristics

The following three parts of this chapter examine, respectively, the institution of Parliament in Australia, its functions, and the few political rights that have a basis in the Constitution. The chapter focuses largely on the Parliament of the Commonwealth, with only occasional reference to the Parliaments of the States, which are broadly similar in design and operation, albeit on a smaller scale. The remainder of this part identifies three characteristics of Australian representative democracy that are shared by all Australian Parliaments and that assist to inform the discussion that follows.

i. The Concept of Representation

As in other parliamentary systems, Australian parliaments are deemed to represent their respective polities as a whole. As in other parliamentary systems also, however, there is the usual ambiguity about the nature of the constitutional relationship between representatives and those that are represented. The traditional view is that Members of Parliament are not delegates of the voters, at least in the sense of being subject to instruction by them, and thus may make decisions 'which are contrary to

---

[5] *Theophanous v Herald & Weekly Times* (1994) 182 CLR 104, 200; *Lange v Australian Broadcasting Corporation (Lange)* (1997) 189 CLR 520; T Blackshield, 'The Implied Freedom of Communication' in G Lindell (ed), *Future Directions in Australian Constitutional Law* (Annandale, Federation Press, 1994) 232.

[6] For example, J Dunn, *Setting the People Free* (London, Atlantic Books, 2005) 176.

[7] For example in *Roach v Electoral Commissioner* (2007) 233 CLR 162 at 173, 211; cf 186. Cf also N Aroney, 'Justice McHugh, Representative Government and the Elimination of Balancing' (2006) 28 *Sydney Law Review* 505.

popular prejudice'.[8] In practice, however, regular elections and a sense of self-preservation ensure that Members individually and collectively keep a close eye on public opinion.

The traditional position in any event has long since been overlaid by the operation of political parties. In Australia, these are a formidable force, although recognised in the Constitution only in passing (s15). While a Greens Party is progressively gathering strength, there are only two major political groupings, the Australian Labour Party (ALP) and the Liberal Party of Australia (LP), which often is in coalition with the much smaller National Party. These groups broadly represent the left and the right of politics respectively. They are national parties, in the sense that government alternates between them in the Commonwealth and in all States. Party discipline is tight and it is extremely rare for a member of a parliamentary party to flout it in a parliamentary vote. Parties issue policies, between which voters can choose if they so wish. Party discipline ensures that government measures will pass any House in which the governing party has a majority. There are occasional controversies over the extent to which governments have implemented the platforms on which they were elected and over the impact of upper Houses on their ability to do so.[9] In response to the latter the Constitution of the State of Victoria recognises a non-justiciable 'principle of Government mandate', which requires the Legislative Council to respect both the government's 'specific mandate' and its 'general mandate' to govern for Victoria.[10]

Representation also is essentially territorial. Members of lower Houses typically are elected from single member divisions. Upper House electorates generally are larger multi-member electorates and the Senators for each State are elected from the State as a whole.[11] Historically, there has been a struggle in Australia over the extent to which geographical size is relevant in drawing division boundaries. That struggle has now effectively been resolved in favour of a standard that aims at rough equality of the numbers of enrolled voters in each division, subject to a 10 per cent margin of tolerance above or below an average, which can be

---

[8]   Constitutional Commission *Final Report 1988,* para 13.81.
[9]   See generally J Nethercote 'Mandate: Australia's Current Debate in Context' Commonwealth Parliamentary Library, *Research Paper 19, 1998–99.*
[10]   Constitution Act 1975 (Vic) s 16A.
[11]   s 7 enables the Commonwealth Parliament to divide the States into divisions for Senate elections, but the power has not been used.

used to accommodate factors that encourage a 'community of interests' within divisions.[12] In Australia as elsewhere, the mobility of people and the diversity of their interests combine to undermine the cohesion of territorially based political communities and thus the extent to which voters identify closely with their local Members of Parliament.

In recent decades, the extent to which the Parliaments mirror the communities they represent has attracted greater attention, with particular reference to the proportional representation of women, more recent immigrant communities, often identified by reference to non-English speaking background (NESB) and Indigenous Australians. Some improvement in the proportion of seats held by women has been effected through political practice including, in the case of the ALP, the imposition of minimum targets. In June 2010, 30.6 per cent of the Members of all Australian Parliaments were women, although the proportions varied considerably between parties, jurisdictions, and upper and lower Houses of Parliament.[13] Representation of NESB communities also is gradually increasing, although they are almost everywhere underrepresented in comparison with their presence in the population. Here, too, there is considerable variation between spheres of government, jurisdictions and parties. Factors inhibiting representation include the difficulty of securing preselection by the major parties and the Commonwealth constitutional prohibition on the candidacy of dual citizens (s44(i)).[14]

Indigenous representation in Parliament remains very low. There have been only three Aboriginal Members of the Commonwealth Parliament since 1901, two of whom were in the Senate and the most recent of whom was elected to the House of Representatives in 2010. In 2009 there were only eight Aboriginal Members of State and Territory legislatures, four of whom were in the Northern Territory, two in Western Australia and one each in New South Wales and Tasmania. Opinion is divided over whether seats should be reserved for Indigenous Australians

---

[12] Variations between State electoral divisions in Western Australia are larger: A Vromen, K Gelber, A Gauja, and F Katauskas, *Powerscape* (Crows Nest, NSW, Allen and Unwin, 2008) 110–13.

[13] Politics and Public Administration Group, 'Composition of Australian Parliaments by Party and Gender, as at 23 June 2010', Commonwealth Parliamentary Library, 2010.

[14] K Anthony, 'The Political Representation of Ethnic and Racial Minorities', New South Wales Parliamentary Library Research Service, Briefing Paper 3/06, March 2006.

or whether efforts should be redoubled to increase their representation through the traditional political process.[15]

ii. Centrality of Elections

A second characteristic of representative democracy in Australia is the centrality of elections. These are held frequently; in the case of the Commonwealth, at least every three years. Parliamentary terms have now been extended to four years in most States, but these are not synchronised with each other. The result is that each voter participates in an election every 18 months or so, in what has been described as 'unprecedented level of voting among the advanced democracies'.[16]

To the same end, the design of the electoral system is inclusive, broadening the democratic base from which lower Houses derive their support. Voting is effectively compulsory and the requirement is enforced.[17] Widespread use of a full preferential voting or alternative vote (AV) electoral system ensures that each Member can claim the support of a majority of voters in his or her constituency and that the governing party generally can claim the support of a majority of voters overall, although not necessarily on the basis of first preference votes. Coupled with a proportional single transferable vote (STV) system that is used in the Senate and, with variations, in most State upper Houses, these arrangements also offer voters a greater range of initial choice than the dominance of two major parties normally would suggest. Necessarily, to make such a system work, the administration is efficient and voting procedures relatively convenient. Elections are held on Saturdays; polling places are numerous; and procedures are available for pre-poll, postal and absentee voting.

As a corollary, however, once a Parliament is elected, representative democracy is subordinated to the demands of responsible government, at least as far as the institution of Parliament is concerned. A new Prime Minister or Premier is commissioned by the representative of the

[15] B Lloyd, 'Dedicated Indigenous Representation in the Australian Parliament' Commonwealth Parliamentary Library Research Paper No.23, 2008–09.

[16] DM Farrell and I McAllister, *The Australian Electoral System: Origins, Variations and Consequences* (Sydney, NSW, UNSW Press, 2006) 14.

[17] Commonwealth Electoral Act 1918 s 245; the current fine is $50. As the act of voting itself is private, in practice the enforceable obligation is met once a voter is recorded as having attended the polling place: s 232; but cf *Judd v McKeon* (1926) 38 CLR 380.

Crown, who typically calls on the leader of the party with a majority in the lower House, generally on the advice of the leader of the former government. The electoral system makes it more likely than not that the governing party will have a clear majority in the lower House of the Parliament without reliance on complex coalition arrangements; an inconclusive election result in 2010 was the first for 70 years. Party discipline is such that the executive government can count on members of its party to support all its measures throughout its term of office, at least in the lower House. Parliamentary proceedings can be lively, as a result of the confrontation between government and opposition, but the object of these manoeuvrings is victory at the next election, rather than public deliberation on current policy proposals.

In consequence, leaving aside for a moment the complication of upper Houses in which the government lacks a majority, Australian Parliaments typically are acquiescent rather than deliberative, in a way that favours unity and efficiency over diversity and institutional balance, even when the operation of parliamentary committees are taken into account. These are characteristics of many parliamentary systems. They are exacerbated in Australia, however, by the relatively small size of most Parliaments[18] and relatively short parliamentary sessions of around 80 days per year at best.[19] Both are products of population size and geographical distance, but both also maximise executive control.

iii. Modified Westminster

The Commonwealth and all State Parliaments originally were modelled broadly on the Parliament at Westminster and they continue to share its functions and many of its procedures. Most Australian parliaments, for example, adopted the privileges of the House of Commons at the date of their establishment, including the protection for freedom of speech in Parliament in article 9 of the Bill of Rights 1688. In the case of the Commonwealth these have since been modified by legislation, to clarify the purpose of parliamentary privileges and immunities, the

---

[18] The numbers range from around 226 in the Commonwealth Parliament to 17 in the Northern Territory legislature.

[19] J Uhr, *Deliberative Democracy in Australia* (Cambridge, CUP, 1998) 239. Uhr reports an average of 61 sitting days per year for the House of Representatives in 1993–95, with an average of 2.3 bills passed each day in 1995. In 2009, around 71 sitting days were scheduled for the House.

circumstances in which they apply and the penalties that may be imposed, with particular reference to freedom of speech in Parliament.[20]

In other respects, however, the structure and operation of Australian Parliaments differ from Westminster. One of the most significant differences is the way in which bicameralism has evolved. Bicameralism is, of course, a feature of the Westminster Parliament too. The original colonial legislative councils were modelled loosely on the House of Lords, in the sense that they were designed to protect property interests and to moderate impulsive tendencies on the part of their lower Houses. Over the course of the twentieth century, however, the upper Houses were democratised to a greater or lesser degree in all States except Queensland where, in 1922, the Council was abolished instead. The more democratic a House, the greater is its claim to substantive power and the greater the potential for conflict with the lower House, from which the government derives its authority to govern. In the case of the Commonwealth Parliament, the Senate draws greater authority still from its role as the House in which the States are equally represented for the purposes of the Australian federation.

Conflict between the Houses of bicameral legislatures has been a recurrent theme of Australian constitutional history. In the latter part of the twentieth century, efforts to craft a distinctive role for upper Houses as Houses of 'review' led to further changes in their composition, functions and powers. One was the introduction of proportional voting systems in the Senate and four of the five State Legislative Councils, which facilitates the election of independents and members of minor parties and ensures that the pattern of membership in the two Houses is different. Another limited the effective power of Legislative Councils in some States to veto bills appropriating money for the ordinary annual services of government, which threaten the capacity of a government with the confidence of the lower House to continue in office and thus strike at the core principle of responsible government. In all jurisdictions, however, the power to veto other legislation remains, often subject to complex deadlock-breaking procedures, which for the Commonwealth are discussed in the next part.[21]

---

[20] Parliamentary Privileges Act 1987 (Cth). See generally EM Campbell, *Parliamentary Privilege* (Annandale, NSW, Federation Press, 2003).

[21] In relation to the States see G Carney, *The Constitutional Systems of the Australian States and Territories* (Cambridge, CUP, 2006) 89–93.

Constitutional evolution thus has produced a system in which Australian upper Houses have authority to 'review' proposed legislation and government action, backed by powerful sanctions. How they exercise this authority depends on their composition from time to time. On any view, however, this is a departure from a model under which a government with a clear majority in the lower House of Parliament governs without hindrance during its term of office. Australian opinion is divided over whether an upper House should be regretted as a blot on the constitutional landscape or welcomed for its contribution to the deliberative potential of a Parliament. Consistently with the latter view, it has sometimes been suggested that the State of Queensland should re-establish its upper House, to enhance the quality of its representative democracy.[22]

A second difference between Australian Parliaments and the Westminster prototype lies in the combination of representative government with Australian federalism. Some consequences have been noted already: the limitation of parliamentary sovereignty under a federal Constitution and the creation of the Senate as a powerful second Chamber to represent the States. Another, which will be examined more closely in chapter seven, is the impact on all Parliaments, and in particular on State Parliaments, of the myriad intergovernmental arrangements that typify the practical operations of government in a modern federation.

II. INSTITUTIONS

A. Structure and Composition

i. House of Representatives

Membership of the House of Representatives is determined on a population basis. Under section 24 the members are 'directly chosen by the people of the Commonwealth'. The Constitution does not specify how they are to be chosen, but the centrality of population as a criterion is evident. The number of Members from each State must be proportionate to the population of the State, subject to a guarantee of at least

---

[22] For example, N Aroney and S Prasser, 'An Upper House for Queensland: An Idea Whose Time Has Come', Democratic Audit of Australia, Discussion Paper 1/07.

five members from each of the Original States (s.24). It follows that each electorate must be enclosed within the boundaries of a State. The Constitution also specifies that in the absence of electoral divisions, each State comprises a single electorate (s.29).

The total number of Members is tied to the membership of the Senate by a requirement for the size of the House to be 'as nearly as practicable' twice the number of Senators (s.24). The original purpose of the 'nexus' was to protect the significance of the Senate. Initially, it caused the size of the Senate to grow from six to twelve Senators for each State, to enable an increase in the number of Members of the House in response to population movement.[23] Further increase in the number of Senators is hard to justify, however, so that the nexus effectively now limits the size of the House. In 2010, the House had 150 Members, including two from each of the mainland territories, who are not included in the nexus calculations.[24]

House of Representatives elections are governed entirely by Commonwealth, rather than State legislation. The AV electoral system that has been in use since 1918 tends to produce clear majorities in the House.[25] The hung Parliament following the 2010 election is, for the moment, the exception that proves the rule. Neither of the two major political groupings secured a majority, leaving independents and representatives of minor parties with the balance of power. It is too early to know whether this presages a continuing change in Australian voting patterns and whether, if so, it will change the dynamics of the operation of the Parliament as the independent Members hope.

ii. Senate

By contrast, the Senate is designed to represent the States. In a counterpart to section 24, section 7 requires Senators to be 'directly chosen by the people of the State'. The six Original States are entitled to equal representation, irrespective of population size. Tasmania, with a population of 485,000 people thus has the same Senate entitlement as New South Wales, where the population is 6.8 million people. New States do not have an automatic entitlement to equal representation and if and

---

[23] A proposal to break the nexus failed at referendum: Constitution Alteration (Parliament) 1967.

[24] *Attorney-General (NSW); ex rel McKellar v Commonwealth* (1977) 139 CLR 527.

[25] The system is described in detail in Farrell and McAllister, n 16, 3–4.

when the Northern Territory, with its population of 206,000, again seeks statehood, the tension between federal and democratic equality is likely to be resolved in favour of the latter.[26]

The federal rationale for the Senate now lies in its composition, rather than its operation, which is dominated by party allegiance.[27] The equal representation of the Original States in the Senate is not only symbolic but it also ensures a significantly larger numerical representation of the smaller States in the Commonwealth Parliament than would otherwise be the case. The federal design of the Senate is evident in other ways as well. State Governors issue writs for Senate elections (s 12); the time and place of Senate elections are determined by State Parliaments, although the Commonwealth has power over the 'method of choosing Senators' (s 9); casual Senate vacancies are filled by State Parliaments or Governors (s15); and the President of the Senate has a deliberative but not a casting vote, so as not to disadvantage the State from which he or she comes (s 23). The motion passes in the negative if the votes are equal.

On the other hand, the decline in the significance of the federal rationale for the Senate is demonstrated by the way in which each of these provisions now operates in practice. The timing of Senate elections and the issue of writs is carried out under broadly complementary Commonwealth and State legislation, in accordance with an election timetable determined by the Commonwealth.[28] Casual Senate vacancies are filled by the nominee of the party of the retiring Senator, following a constitutional amendment in 1977, itself prompted by the failure of certain States to comply with a convention to this effect that had been evolving since 1949.[29] The conception of the Senate as primarily a States' House was further eroded in 1975 when the High Court upheld the validity of Commonwealth legislation providing for the election of Senators from the two mainland territories, in effect favouring the Commonwealth power in section 122 to provide for the 'representation'

---

[26] For an overview of the arguments either way see House of Representatives, Standing Committee on Legal and Constitutional Affairs 'Federal Implications of Statehood for the Northern Territory', June 2007, ch.6.

[27] On the various functions of the Senate see H Evans (ed), *Odgers Australian Senate Practice,* 12th edn (Canberra, NSW, Parliament of Australia Senate, 2008) esp. ch.1.

[28] For an instance where a State threatened not to co-operate see G Sawer, *Federation Under Strain,* (Carlton, Vic:, MUP, 1977) ch.3.

[29] Constitution Alteration (Senate Casual Vacancies) 1977. The story is told in Sawer, ibid.

of a territory in 'either House of the Parliament' over the apparently equally prescriptive requirements in section 7 for the Senate to be composed of Senators for the States.[30]

Each State constitutes a single electorate for the purpose of Senate elections. The broadly proportional STV electoral system that has been used for Senate elections since 1949 makes the Senate a more accurate reflection of the electoral preferences of voters than the House of Representatives. The Senate is more likely than the House to have members who are independent or who belong to minor parties. It is unusual for either of the major political groupings to have a majority in the Senate.[31] This pattern of party representation has encouraged the evolution of a relatively strong Senate committee system and has enabled the Senate to develop a significant review role.

B. Fair and Regular Elections

i. *Regularity*

Consistently with the Australian focus on electoral democracy, elections for the House of Representatives must be held every three years and may be held more often if the Governor-General dissolves the House earlier (ss.5, 28). In exercising this power, the Governor-General invariably acts on the advice of a Prime Minister as long, at least, as the Prime Minister has a majority in the House.

By contrast, Senators have fixed six year terms, which run from 1 July and which are staggered, so that one half of the Senators for each State normally face election every three years. The expense and political disruption of separate House and half-Senate elections generally can be avoided by taking advantage of the leeway under section 13 for elections to be held within one year before Senate places fall vacant, although at cost of a significant time-lag before newly elected Senators take their seats. Where this is not possible, because the timing of the two Houses is seriously out of sync, the elections can be brought back into alignment

---

[30]   *Western Australia v Commonwealth (First Territories Representation* case) (1975) 134 CLR 201; *Queensland v Commonwealth (Second Territories Representation* case) (1977) 139 CLR 585.
[31]   Unusually, an incumbent government had a Senate majority from 2005–2008, for the first time since 1980.

by dissolving the House of Representatives even earlier than usual, at obvious cost to the stability of government. The disadvantages of both these options have encouraged four attempts to amend the Constitution to mandate 'simultaneous' elections, by tying the term of Senators to one or two terms of the House of Representatives. All four proposals attracted opposition on grounds that included their effect on the independence of the Senate and all four failed, although two attracted national majorities.[32]

The frequency of elections in Australia sometimes attracts criticism because of its impact on the willingness of governments to take long term decisions. It has been suggested that the term of the House of Representatives should be extended to four years, following the lead of most of the States and, more ambitiously still, that Commonwealth and State elections should be synchronised.[33] Neither seems likely to happen. Four year terms for the House would necessitate some change to Senate terms if the elections are to continue to be aligned. Eight year Senate terms are unacceptably long, while four year terms are likely to be seen as an attack on the Senate; and one such proposal has already been rejected on this ground.[34] Politically, also, it would be difficult for the Commonwealth to extend the term of the House without also fixing it, so as to remove or limit the discretion of the executive to call an early election. This has already been done in New South Wales, South Australia and Victoria. In any event, it can be argued that the frequency of elections in Australia is a quid pro quo for the extent to which power is concentrated between elections and has evolved as an integral element of the constitutional system.

ii. Electoral Boundaries

In a constituency based electoral system, electoral boundaries can affect the fairness of elections. The 'relative parity' of people or voters in each electorate necessarily is the dominant consideration although

---

[32] The referendum dates were 1974, 1977, 1984 and 1988: Australian Electoral Commission, *Referendum Dates and Results 1906–Present,* http://www.aec.gov.au/index.htm (viewed 30 July 2010).

[33] House of Representatives, Standing Committee on Legal and Constitutional Affairs, *Inquiry into Constitutional Reform* 2008, ch.3.

[34] Constitution Alteration (Parliamentary Terms) 1988.

other factors may also have a bearing on 'effective' representation.[35] In Australia, the only explicit constraint on the constitutional power of the Commonwealth to determine electoral divisions is that a division 'shall not be formed out of parts of different States' (s.29). In practice, however, a degree of protection for the fairness of electoral boundaries has developed from the interaction of several of the other constitutional provisions relating to the composition of the House of Representatives.

As so often, doctrinal development initially was prompted by extraordinary political circumstances. In 1975, there were very substantial differences between the numbers of people in House of Representatives electoral divisions; in some cases by a factor of two to one.[36] The existing divisions had been drawn under old electoral legislation that allowed a 20 per cent variation above and below a quota. An embattled Labour government, disadvantaged by these divisions and with an election pending, was unable to persuade the Senate to approve new electoral boundaries. A challenge to the constitutional validity of the boundaries was only weakly defended by the government, which also provided an Attorney-General's fiat to one of the plaintiffs.

The plaintiffs had two principal arguments. The first was that the requirement in section 24 for Members of the House to be 'directly chosen by the people' required effective equality of the numbers of people, or at least voters, within electorates. While the argument was rejected, a majority of Justices accepted that section 24 required more than direct rather than indirect election. Importantly one majority Justice, Stephen J, observed that the opening words of the section suggested 'three great principles', one of which was representative democracy.[37] The constitutional requirements might be satisfied by a wide variety of electoral arrangements. Nevertheless, there were 'finite limits'; and two Justices, McTiernan and Jacobs JJ, thought that these might vary over time. The limits were not exceeded on this occasion, but their very existence was significant. In the event of breach, each State would become a single electorate, with unpredictable political results.

As the final part of this chapter shows, while the first argument of the plaintiffs failed, the reasoning of the court had significant doctrinal

---

[35] *Reference re Electoral Boundaries Commission Act* (1991) 81 DLR (4th) 16, 36, quoted with approval in *McGinty v Western Australia* (1996) 186 CLR 140, 267, Gummow J.

[36] *Attorney-General (Cth); Ex rel. McKinlay v Commonwealth* (*McKinlay's* case) (1975) 135 CLR 1.

[37] Ibid, 56.

consequences in the longer term. The second argument succeeded and, although it did not affect the forthcoming election, it had beneficial, longer term effects as well. Section 24 of the Constitution requires the number of members in the several States to be 'in proportion to the respective numbers of their people' and provides that proportionality is to be 'determined, whenever necessary'. The challenged legislation provided for the number of Members of the several States to be redetermined whenever a census was taken, every ten or, at best, five years. Worse still, it was clear that a new determination based on recent population figures would not come into effect until any necessary redistribution of electoral divisions occurred and that this might never happen. The plaintiff argued and the Court accepted that the Constitution required a new determination of the number of Members to which each State was entitled to be made and given effect every three years, in time for each regular election.[38] Parts of the challenged legislation therefore were invalid, although the pending election was not affected 'in view of the overriding constitutional duty to hold elections'. Gibbs J expressed 'no doubt' that the Parliament would 'act to give effect to the requirements ofs 24, now that they have been pointed out'.

His confidence was not misplaced. In the wake of *McKinlay,* the relevant legislation was completely reconceived. The Commonwealth Electoral Act 1918 now prescribes a procedure to ensure that a redetermination is made every three years and that a redistribution occurs every seven years or whenever the number of members for State changes or divisions are 'malapportioned'.[39] The ground rules for distribution impose a margin of allowance of no more than 10 per cent above or below a quota. After an elaborate consultation process the new divisions come into effect by determination of an independent Electoral Commission.

The arrangements for the determination of Commonwealth electoral boundaries thus depend largely on ordinary legislation administered by an independent and effective institution. They work well; they are responsive to Australian conditions; and the standards they secure are broadly accepted as fair. Although the arrangements outlined above apply only to Commonwealth electoral boundaries, they subsequently became the model for other Australian jurisdictions. To this extent, the manner in which Australian electoral boundaries are drawn is consistent

---

[38] The leading judgment on this point is that of Gibbs J, n 36 at 51–53.
[39] Part III, Divs. 3 and 4.

with the Australian tendency to rely on the political process to protect values that elsewhere might be framed as constitutional rights. On the other hand, the impetus for the changes to the electoral laws that laid the framework for the current arrangements derived from constitutional provisions that were interpreted to provide some protection, however minimal, for electoral democracy. Absent the constitutional requirements, it is unlikely that agreement on either the criteria or the independent process for drawing electoral boundaries would have been reached so quickly; or, perhaps, reached at all.

The existence of such requirements also provides a degree of ongoing protection. However generous the constitutional limits, they operate as a reminder of the need for electoral procedures to be justifiable by reference to some standards of representative democracy that lie beyond the power of an incumbent majority. These received further endorsement in 1996, when at least three Justices in a court of six confirmed that the Constitution provides protection against malapportionment and that the perception of malapportionment for constitutional purposes may vary over time.[40] In passing, the reasons of Gummow J also reinforced the role of the Electoral Commission, as a 'specialist body' charged with the determination of electoral divisions in accordance with legislative criteria that on the face of it are constitutionally compliant.[41]

C. Power and Disagreement

i. *Power*

The two Houses of the Commonwealth Parliament have almost equal power to initiate, amend and reject proposed legislation (s.53). The powers of the Senate are limited in relation to certain categories of financial legislation, however. Bills appropriating funds or imposing taxation must originate in the House of Representatives and only the House can amend legislation appropriating revenue for the 'ordinary annual services of the

---

[40] *McGinty v Western Australia* (1996) 186 CLR 140, Toohey, Gaudron and Gummow JJ. The issue in the case was the validity of Western Australian boundaries, to which Commonwealth constitutional standards were only indirectly relevant, enabling Brennan CJ to assume limits on Commonwealth power without finally deciding the point.

[41] Ibid, 288.

Government' or in a way that increases a 'proposed charge . . . on the people'.[42]

The greater authority of the House of Representatives over financial legislation is attributable both to its character as the more representative chamber and to its role as the seat of executive government in a system of responsible government. The limitations on the power of the Senate ensure that the government has the initiative in financial matters and controls budget design.[43] The ability of the Senate to veto any legislation, however, means that a government with the confidence of the House of Representatives may not be able to secure the passage of financial legislation through the Parliament, threatening its capacity to remain in office. To the extent that the powers of the Senate are attributable to its role as a States' House, this somewhat curious feature of Australian constitutional arrangements can be understood as a product of tension between responsible government and federalism, which has had considerable consequences, as described below.

ii. Disagreement and Deadlock

The differences in the composition of the two Houses make disagreement on some matters inevitable over time. Their almost co-extensive power means that disagreement may lead to deadlock in such cases. The Australian decision to provide a mechanism to attempt to resolve deadlocks again reflects the influence of the principles of responsible government, although the mechanism itself is designed to strike a balance that respects the authority of both Houses.

The deadlock procedure prescribed by section 57 applies only to deadlocks over ordinary legislation that begin in the House of Representatives.[44] The procedure is lengthy and cumbersome, with political ramifications that extend well beyond the disputed legislation. In brief, it requires the fact of a deadlock to be first established by a prolonged period of demonstrated disagreement during which a bill is twice passed by the House and twice effectively rejected by the Senate with a

---

[42] Sections 54 and 55 prevent the tacking of other measures to such laws. In the case of bills that it cannot amend, the Senate can suggest amendments to the House and also assumes the power to 'press' such requests.

[43] See also the requirement in s 56 for the Governor-General to 'recommend' appropriation legislation to the House.

[44] See also s 128, adapting it for deadlocks over constitution alteration bills.

three month interval between the first rejection by the Senate and the decision of the House to persevere with the measure by passing it again.[45] Once these conditions are satisfied, the Governor-General may dissolve both Houses, including the whole Senate, and thus precipitate an election.[46] After the election, which necessarily takes some months, the legislation may again be introduced into the House, although whether this happens depends on the electoral outcome. If the House again passes the bill and it is again rejected by the Senate, the Governor-General may convene a joint sitting of both Houses.[47] The disputed legislation must be passed by an absolute majority in this rare unicameral formation of the legislature in order to be signed into law.

The deadlock procedure has been used infrequently; there have been only six double dissolutions since federation and only one joint sitting. Nevertheless, there is now a small body of case law and practice that clarifies the meaning and operation of the section.[48] More importantly for present purposes, it is also possible to make some evaluation of the role that the procedure plays in relations between the two Houses.

As a generalisation, the utility of the procedure for the purpose of resolving disagreement over particular measures has proved to be limited. Most obviously, it is too slow to resolve deadlocks over key appropriation bills that make funds available for the 'ordinary annual services of the Government'. As a result, ironically, there is no constitutional process for dealing with the one category of legislation that is critical to the survival of a government under a system of responsible government. On the one occasion when a hostile Senate blocked the budget, in 1975, the Governor-General resolved the deadlock by dismissing the Prime Minister and dissolving both Houses on the basis of other legislation that, fortuitously, had fulfilled the section 57 requirements.[49]

---

[45] The section refers to rejection by the Senate, failure to pass the bill, or passage with amendments to which the House will not agree. See generally *Victoria v Commonwealth* (1975) 134 CLR 81.

[46] Dissolution may not occur within six months of the end of the term of the House of Representatives; otherwise, there is no restriction on timing: *Western Australia v Commonwealth (First Territories Representation* case) (1975) 134 CLR 201.

[47] The joint sitting may deliberate on multiple bills that have fulfilled the section 57 requirements: *Cormack v Cope* (1974) 131 CLR 432. For a critique of use of the procedure to 'stockpile' double dissolution bills see Evans, n 27, ch.23 .

[48] For an overview of all six double dissolutions and associated case law see Evans, n 27, ch.23.

[49] Sawer, *Federation Under Strain,* n 28, ch.7.

The repercussions of this draconian solution, which will be examined more closely in the next chapter, continue to be felt, not least because they complicate the design of the powers of the Head of State in an Australian republic.

In any event, the deadlock procedure is rarely invoked for the purposes of settling disagreement over a particular proposal, although the implicit threat of a double dissolution no doubt is a factor in many of the negotiations between parties in the Senate. The stakes in an election are too high to be wagered on a single policy proposal, or even a group of proposals, however significant. The merits of a particular proposal have little chance of emerging as a significant issue in a general election campaign. In consequence, a government that wishes to safeguard the passage of its legislation is more likely to use persuasion and compromise than to rely on the deadlock procedure for the purpose. Instead, section 57 is used for wider tactical political purposes. When a government would like an early election, which it calculates (rightly or wrongly) that it can win, a double dissolution offers both an excuse for the election and an opportunity to dissolve the whole Senate to try to improve the position of the governing party. To that end, it is relatively common for a Commonwealth government to ensure that there are one or more bills that have satisfied the double dissolution requirements that can be used as a 'trigger' should a suitable occasion arise.

There have been many proposals to reform the manner in which deadlocks are handled under the Commonwealth Constitution. Most of them involve limitation of the power of the Senate in some way. In the wake of the events of 1975, for example, a latter day Constitutional Convention considered mechanisms to deal with deadlocks over key appropriation bills, one of which would have limited the power of the Senate to a suspensory veto of one month.[50] Neither this, nor any other mechanism attracted cross party support, however, and no action was taken. More recently, in 2003, a government irritated by obstruction of its proposals in the Senate initiated public consultations on a proposal to remove the requirement for a double dissolution from the section 57 procedure, to enable a joint sitting to be held on disputed bills, in which the preferences of the House of Representatives would be likely to prevail. This attempt also was abandoned, despite some cross-party

---

[50] Australian Constitutional Convention, *Proceedings, 1978*, Resolution 5. For a list of such proposals see House of Representatives Standing Committee on Legal and Constitutional Affairs, *Constitutional Change,* Miscellaneous Paper 8442, March, 1997.

interest in it, in the face of evidence of lack of 'any substantial measure' of public support for it.[51]

As the latter episode demonstrates, there is deep ambivalence in Australia about the role of the Senate. On the one hand, it clearly runs counter to majoritarian democracy and interferes with the traditional assumptions of responsible government. On the other, it dilutes the concentration of authority in an executive government that can rely on the support of the House of Representatives and scrutinises both proposed legislation and government action in a way that is beyond the capabilities of the House. These contradictions are embedded in the Australian constitutional system and could not now be removed without triggering multiple consequential effects.

III. LEGISLATIVE FUNCTION

A. Legislative Process

The Commonwealth Parliament typically enacts around 180 statutes each year. The detailed and prescriptive drafting style that typifies much common law legislation is prevalent in Australia and many statutes are lengthy and complex. On one calculation of the volume of legislation passed by all Australian jurisdictions in the 12 month period beginning 1 July 2007, the Commonwealth Parliament enacted 198 statutes covering 8,198 pages in all.[52]

Proposals for government legislation with 'significant policy implications' must be approved by Cabinet; other proposals may be approved by the Prime Minister or in some cases by the Minister alone.[53] Government legislation is drafted by the statutory Office of Parliamentary Counsel (OPC), which is formally attached to the Attorney-General's Department. The OPC drafts legislation in response to agency instructions and is responsible for ensuring that there is executive policy authority for it. Constitutional and other legal difficulties with the proposed legislation may be raised at this stage but will not necessarily prevent a proposal

---

[51] Prime Minister Howard, Ministerial Statement, 'Resolving Deadlocks: The Public Response', House of Representatives, *Hansard,* 1 June 2004, 29656.

[52] Productivity Commission, *Performance Benchmarking of Australian Business Regulation: Quantity and Quality* December 2008.

[53] Department of the Prime Minister and Cabinet *Legislation Handbook* 2000, ch.4.1.

proceeding.[54] Legislation is supposed to be considered by the relevant committee of parliamentary members of the governing party before it is introduced into the Parliament.[55]

A bill generally is introduced into the House of which the responsible Minister is a member, subject to the limitations on Senate authority in section 53. Each bill is accompanied by an explanatory memorandum, which may later be taken into account in the interpretation of the legislation, together with other extrinsic materials, including the Minister's 'second reading' speech.[56] A bill passes through three 'readings' in each House, as in most parliamentary systems in this tradition, before presentation to the Governor-General for the royal assent.[57] All bills are examined for compliance with certain standards by the Senate Standing Committee for the Scrutiny of Bills. A bill also may be referred to a standing or select committee in either House for consideration in substance. Committee consideration is more likely in the Senate where, nevertheless, only around 35 per cent of bills are so referred.[58] Committees may, but need not, invite submissions from the public. There is no other systemic procedure for public consultation on proposed legislation.

Government proposals typically dominate the legislative work of both Houses. By 2010 only 20 non-government bills had been enacted since federation, although some other private members bills may have been taken up in government legislation.[59] Most questions in the House are determined on party lines, although occasionally the parties allow their members a free vote. *House of Representatives Practice* lists 22 free votes, although the list is not necessarily complete. Two of the most recent concerned the establishment of a republic in 1999 and research involving human embryos in 2002. For obvious reasons, non-government legislation is more likely to pass the Senate. Twelve of the 20 private members bills that ultimately became law began in the Senate and another 60 or so

---

[54] Office of Parliamentary Counsel, *Working with OPC: A Guide for Clients,* 3rd edn (2008) para 28: 'OPC would not, in the end, refuse to draft . . . constitutionally suspect provisions'.

[55] *Legislation Handbook,* n 53, ch.11.

[56] Acts Interpretation Act 1901 (Cth) s 15AB. The Explanatory Memorandum is not prepared by OPC.

[57] For the procedure in the House in detail, including possible consideration by the 'Main Committee', see IC Harris (ed), *House of Representatives Practice,* 5th edn (Canberra, NSW, Department of the House of Representatives, 2005) ch.10; for detail of the Senate procedure see Evans, n 27, ch.12

[58] Evans, n 27, 244.

[59] Harris, n 57, ch.16.

were accepted by the Senate but failed in or before introduction to the House.[60]

B. Legislative Power

The Constitution confers the 'legislative power of the Commonwealth' on the Parliament. The base conception of legislative power for this purpose is derived from the common law, under which legislative authority is required to create legal rights and duties, to impose taxation, and to alter existing law. Nevertheless, 'legislative power' is a constitutional term and its scope may be affected by the constitutional context. Thus in *West's* case a unanimous Court suggested that the provision of benefits for Members of Parliament might require an exercise of legislative power as an inference from the text or structure of the Constitution although in the end it was not necessary finally to decide the point.[61]

The legislative power of the Commonwealth necessarily is subject to the Constitution. Most obviously, it can be exercised only in areas in which authority has been allocated to the Commonwealth for the purposes of the federal division of power. Most of these are listed in section 51 and will be examined more closely in chapter seven, in the context of Australian federalism. In addition, an exercise of power under section 51 is subject to other parts of the Constitution, including the separation of powers and implications drawn from the system of representative democracy for which the Constitution provides, both of which are dealt with below.

These constraints aside, the Commonwealth Parliament is supreme in the exercise of its legislative powers, in a typically Diceyan sense. As the conception of legislative power presently is understood, there is no enforceable requirement for legislation to be general,[62] certain, equitable, prospective or territorially bounded. It may yet be, however, that further standards for the exercise of legislative power will be drawn from the text and structure of the Constitution in response to particular issues that come before the Court, framed by reference to federalism, separation of powers or the rule of law.

---

[60] Evans, n 27, Appendix 5.

[61] *Brown v West* (1990) 169 CLR 195.

[62] A bill of attainder, adjudging the guilt of particular persons, would be contrary to the separation of judicial power: *Polyukhovich v Commonwealth* (1991) 172 CLR 501.

C. Separation of Legislative Power

i. Doctrine

It is settled as a matter of principle that there is a three way separation of powers under the Commonwealth Constitution. The separation of judicial power is considered in detail in chapter six. In brief, however, the Parliament cannot itself exercise judicial power and there are limits on its capacity to regulate the manner in which judicial power is exercised. Conversely, with minor exceptions, the judiciary cannot act in a way that involves it in the exercise of legislative or executive power.[63] The impact of the doctrine of separation of powers on the relationship between legislative and executive power is considerably less severe. In part this is attributable to the institutional fusion of the branches and in part to the common law conception of legislative power in a system of responsible government. It is typically taken for granted, for example, that Commonwealth legislation can control the exercise of the general executive power to which section 61 of the Constitution refers.[64]

The main context in which this question has been explored is the delegation of legislative power. The foundation case illustrates the influence of the underlying conception of legislative power and the structure of responsible government on the constitutional separation of powers.[65] In *Dignan*, the issue before the Court was the validity of delegation to the executive of what Dixon J characterised as a 'complete . . . power, over a large and by no means unimportant subject, in the exercise of which . . . [the executive] is free to determine from time to time the ends to be achieved and the policy to be pursued as well as the means to be adopted'. Significantly, under the terms of the delegation, the power could be 'exercised in disregard of other existing statutes, the provisions of which concerning the same subject matter may be overridden'.[66] Nevertheless, the validity of the delegation was upheld.

---

[63] *Strickland v Rocla Concrete Pipes Ltd* (1971) 124 CLR 468; *Minister for Aboriginal Affairs v Peko-Wallsend* (1986) 162 CLR 24.

[64] Eg *Barton v Commonwealth* (1971) 131 CLR 477; and see generally L Zines, *The High Court and the Constitution*, 5th edn (Annandale, NSW, Federation Press, 2008) 359–69. It is unlikely that legislative power can control the exercise of specific powers conferred on the executive in eg sections 5, 57, 72.

[65] *Victorian Stevedoring & General Contracting Co Pty Ltd v Dignan* (1931) 46 CLR 73.

[66] Ibid, 100.

No member of the Court held that the doctrine of separation of powers imposed limits on delegation of legislative power to the executive. Justices Dixon and Evatt, however, suggested that limitations could be derived from the concept of law-making itself. The empowering statute must not be so broad or uncertain that it is not a law with respect to a head of power or, in Evatt's Terms, that amounts to an 'abdication' of power. While these limits are weak and impose little effective constraint, in one case an extensive delegation was described as being 'very close to the boundary'.[67]

In his reasons, Dixon J confronted the apparent 'inconsistency' in the Court's approach to the separation of legislative and executive power. While he justified his decision in part by reference to previous cases in which the power to delegate had been accepted without question, his analysis rested primarily on the character of legislative power. Unlike in the United States, the legislative power of an Australian Parliament is not conceived as a delegation from the people but as power of a 'plenary and absolute nature'. More importantly still, once delegated to the executive a power, however extensive, lacks 'the independent and unqualified authority which is an attribute of true legislative power' in the sense that, for example, the delegated authority is controlled by the empowering statute and will lapse if the statute is repealed.[68]

ii. Practice

Parliamentary control of delegated legislation through repeal of the empowering statute, as envisaged by the court in *Dignan*, is too blunt an instrument to be effective for the purpose. It is now supplemented, however, by other relatively sophisticated parliamentary procedures. These originated in the 1920s, at a time of rising concern about the volume of delegated legislation in Australia, as elsewhere. The phenomenon is now even more pervasive: *Australian Senate Practice* notes that 2,982 such instruments were made in 2007–2008 at the Commonwealth level alone and that they are denoted by more than 100 terms in enabling

---

[67]   *Giris Pty Ltd v Federal Commissioner of Taxation* (1969) 119 CLR 365, 385. See also the observation of five Justices in *Plaintiff S157/2002 v Commonwealth* that an Act that conferred 'a totally open-ended discretion' on the Minister to make 'any decision respecting visas' might lack the 'hallmark of the exercise of legislative power': (2003) 211 CLR 476, 512.

[68]   *Dignan*, n 65, at 101–02.

legislation.[69] Since their initial introduction, the procedures have been progressively refined by the Commonwealth Parliament and adopted and adapted by the Parliaments of the States.

In their present form, Commonwealth parliamentary procedures for the control of delegated legislation have three principal elements. First, legislation requires all subordinate instruments of a legislative character to be registered on the Legislative Instruments Register, as a prerequisite to enforcement.[70] Secondly, all registered instruments must be tabled in both Houses of Parliament and are subject to disallowance by either House, within prescribed time limits. Disallowance in the House of Representatives is rare, but the real possibility of disallowance in the Senate gives that House a formative influence on policy-makers in developing subordinate legislative instruments. Thirdly, the Senate Standing Committee on Regulations and Ordinances is charged with the responsibility of scrutinising all instruments by reference to stipulated standards, with a view to recommending disallowance to the Senate if necessary.[71] In practice, notice of a motion of disallowance by the Committee generally sparks negotiations with the Minister, leading to some remedial action, so that the notice of motion is withdrawn; a risky procedure if the Minister fails to comply.[72] Once disallowed, an instrument may not be remade within six months.

D. Financial Control

The requirement for legislatures to approve the appropriation of public funds is attributable to their representative character. In a parliamentary system, it is critical to the capacity of the legislature to hold the executive

---

[69] Evans, n 27, 326–27.

[70] Now the Legislative Instruments Act 2003 (Cth), Part 4, Divs 2–4. For exceptions, see ss 6, 7 and 9. The Act also seeks to control the drafting quality of such instruments (s 16); to encourage consultation before they are made (ss 17–19); and to ensure that they are reconsidered through a sunsetting device every ten years (Part 6).

[71] Under Senate Standing Order 23 the Committee may examine compliance of the instrument with the enabling statute; whether it trespasses 'unduly' on personal rights and liberties; whether it does 'unduly' make rights and liberties dependent on unreviewable discretions; and whether it is more appropriate for enactment by Parliament.

[72] Thus in 2003–2004 the Committee examined 1,561 instruments; raised concerns about 121 of them; and gave notice of motion to disallow 18. No disallowance ultimately occurred: Senate Standing Committee on Regulations and Ordinances, 112th Report, 2005, ch.2.

government to account. The potential for appropriation to be refused underpins the central design feature of responsible government, that the government must have the confidence of the lower House and that if it loses the confidence of the House it must resign.

The constitutional framework for the Commonwealth appropriation process centres on sections 81 and 83. Section 83 requires 'appropriation made by law' for the dispersal of public funds. Under section 81, moneys raised by the government must be credited to a central fund, 'to be appropriated for the purposes of the Commonwealth'. The requirement in section 56 for the 'purpose' of an appropriation to be recommended to the Parliament by the Governor-General means that only the government can initiate an appropriation. The division of authority between the House and the Senate under sections 53 and 54 makes it necessary to distinguish between bills that appropriate moneys for the 'ordinary annual services of the Government', which may not be amended by the Senate, and other appropriation bills. The Houses have agreed on a list of matters that must be included in appropriation bills that the Senate can amend, including grants to the States and 'new policies not authorised by special legislation'.[73] The compact is not legally enforceable and misallocations occur.[74]

A panoply of parliamentary practice, which would be broadly familiar elsewhere, has grown up around these provisions. Appropriations may be authorised by special legislation or as part of the annual budget process. Appropriations may provide continuing authority for expenditure, as standing appropriations, or require annual approval. The proportion of the former has grown, to an estimated 80 per cent in 2002–3, with obvious implications for parliamentary control.[75] Appropriations for the Parliament itself are now included in separate, budget legislation. Elaborate procedures cover debate on the budget in the House and the budget estimates are scrutinised by Senate Standing Committees, providing what the clerk of the Senate has described as an opportunity for 'twice-yearly general inquisitions into government operations'.[76]

---

[73] For the present terms of the 'compact of 1965' see Evans, n 27, 285–86.

[74] Examples include tsunami relief and the controversial Work Choices advertising campaign, of which more below: A Murray, *Review of Operation Sunlight: Overhauling Budgetary Transparency*, a report to the Minister for Finance, June 2008.

[75] Evans, n 27. 292.

[76] Ibid, 311. The procedures in the House of Representatives are outlined in Harris, n 57, 416 ff.

Compliance is monitored by a Joint Committee on Public Accounts and Audit, which reviews all financial statement audits by an independent audit office, which also conducts performance audits. Each Australian jurisdiction has similar arrangements. The sensitivity of the role of Auditor-General makes the office vulnerable to political inroads into its independence, which caused a constitutional amendment in one State, Victoria, to protect the integrity of the audit function.[77]

The appropriation provisions have long been at the centre of dispute over the extent to which the Commonwealth can spend on programs that fall outside its allocated legislative powers. This issue raises questions about both the scope of executive power and federalism and will be examined from these perspectives in chapters five and seven. More recently, however, the significance of the requirement for moneys to be appropriated by reference to 'purposes' has been raised also in the context of relations between the government and the Parliament.

There is a tension between the interests of a Parliament in appropriating money to a purpose and the need for government to have some flexibility in the management of its expenditure and in responding to unanticipated needs. This tension has been played out for some time in the use made of a statutory procedure whereby the Finance Minister may approve additional funding that was not included in the original budget and that has the effect of amending the appropriation legislation.[78] It was exacerbated when, towards the end of the 1990s, the Commonwealth moved to accrual accounting, with appropriations by reference to 'outcomes' rather than to programs.

The problem came to a head in 2005 in a challenge to the validity of the expenditure of around $50 million on government advertising for highly controversial forthcoming industrial relations legislation.[79] The majority of the Court interpreted the appropriation legislation as authorising appropriation at the very general level of 'departmental expenditure' rather than by reference to particular 'outcomes' themselves also described in general terms.[80] While it remains unclear whether

---

[77] Constitution Act 1975 (Vic) ss 94A–94C.

[78] For an analysis of one such controversy, see G Lindell, 'Parliamentary Appropriations and the Funding of the Federal Governments' Pre-election Advertising in 1998' (1999) 2(2) *Constitutional Law & Policy Review* 21.

[79] *Combet v Commonwealth* (2005) 224 CLR 494.

[80] The 'outcome' potentially in issue here was defined as 'Higher Productivity, higher pay workplaces'.

the majority decision obviates the need for prescription of a purpose altogether, the dismissal of the challenge suggests that the responsibility for monitoring the constitutionality of appropriation legislation has now largely been abandoned by the Court.[81] If this proves to be the case, it adds to the already considerable political and legal incentives for governments to use spending, rather than legislative instruments to implement their programs where possible.

IV. POLITICAL RIGHTS

The Commonwealth Constitution makes very little provision for the core political rights: to vote, to stand for election, to engage in political debate and protest. The explanation lies largely in political culture at the time the Constitution was made, although with hindsight it also is relevant that the scope of the political community was not settled until well after federation, when the status of Australian citizen was legally created. Rights directly linked with representation were left largely to decision by the Commonwealth Parliament, after a transitional period in which they were determined by State law. Questions of freedom of speech, assembly and association were presumed to be governed by the common law.

On the other hand, at a more abstract level, the Constitution clearly provides for an elected legislature; less clearly but no less definitely mandates responsible government; and prescribes approval by referendum as the mechanism for constitutional change. Representative and responsible government, moreover, are relied on to safeguard other constitutional values. The question of the extent to which the constitutional framework provides protection for the key democratic principles on which the Constitutions rests began to be explored in the 1970s, in cases concerning fair electoral boundaries, examined earlier in this chapter. It was raised again in the 1990s, first by reference to freedom of political communication[82] and subsequently in relation to the right to vote. The chapter concludes by examining these.

---

[81] G Lindell, 'The *Combet Case* and the Appropriation of Taxpayers' Funds for Political Advertising—An Erosion of Fundamental Principles?' (2007) 66 *Australian Journal of Public Administration* 307.

[82] The rationale for freedom of political communication also supports protection for freedom of political association on which there is still, however, very slight case law: *Mulholland v Australian Electoral Commission* (2004) 220 CLR 181.

A. Political Communication

i. Evolution

The 'public interest in freedom of information and discussion' is a recognised value in Australian law.[83] A sign that it might also be constitutionally protected emerged in 1988, when the Court invalidated legislation that gave the Australian Bicentennial Authority the right to control the use of certain common expressions that also were relevant to the bicentennial celebrations.[84] The ground for the decision was that the extent of intrusion into freedom of expression meant that the law could not be supported as an exercise of the power incidental to the executive power, pursuant to which the Authority was established. This is a federalism argument, albeit bolstered by proportionality analysis.[85] And federalism played a role again four years later, in the next freedom of speech case, when the Court held that the incidental power did not support Commonwealth legislation that created an offence to 'use words calculated' to bring the Industrial Relations Commission into 'disrepute'.

But both this and its companion case, *Australian Capital Television,* also recognised a constitutional guarantee of 'freedom of communication, at least in relation to public affairs and political discussion'.[86] Political communication was an 'indispensable' concomitant of representative government in a polity in which the people are sovereign and was necessarily implied from those parts of the Constitution that made provision for representative government, including sections 7 and 24.

Australian Capital Television itself involved a challenge to the validity of Commonwealth legislation prohibiting paid political broadcasts in the approach to Commonwealth and State elections; in this case, as in *Nationwide News,* the constitutional guarantee therefore operated as a constraint on legislative power. Two years later, however, when the freedom was invoked in actions for defamation of Members of Parliament,

---

[83] Eg *Attorney-General (UK) v Heinemann Publishers Australia Pty Ltd (Spycatcher* case) (1988) 165 CLR 30, 45; see also the liberalisation of freedom in information legislation in 2010 in order to 'promote Australia's representative democracy', now in Freedom of Information Act 1982 (Cth) s 3.

[84] *Davis v Commonwealth* (1988) 166 CLR 79; a prescribed expression included, for example, use of the word 'Sydney' in conjunction with '1988'.

[85] On which see A Stone, 'Australia's Constitutional Rights and the Problem of Interpretive Disagreement' (2005) 27 *Sydney Law Review* 29.

[86] *Australian Capital Television Pty Ltd v Commonwealth* (1992) 177 CLR 106, 138.

a narrow majority of the Court held that the freedom also 'controls' the common law.[87] This departure from the traditional conception of the Constitution as either conferring or limiting governmental power was treated as confirmation that the implied freedom had broken free from its contextual roots and exacerbated controversy over the legitimacy of the doctrine.[88]

Another three years later, in another defamation case, the rifts in the Court were healed, or at least concealed, in a unanimous decision in what now is the foundation case.[89] *Lange* confirmed that the Constitution protects 'freedom of communication . . . concerning political or governmental matters'. The freedom is derived from those parts of the Constitution that deal with representative government, responsible government and the referendum requirement for constitutional change. It applies to communications between people and between people and officials and it applies between elections, as well as at election time. The freedom is not absolute; a law that burdens political communication will be valid if it is 'reasonably appropriate and adapted to serve a legitimate end the fulfilment of which is compatible with the maintenance of the constitutionally prescribed' system of government. The freedom is a limit on 'legislative or executive power' that creates an 'area of immunity from legal control' rather than a right 'in the strict sense'.[90] On the other hand, as the common law 'cannot run counter to constitutional imperatives' the common law can be developed by the Court to comply with a constitutional standard. In *Lange*, the common law of qualified privilege was so developed, to protect communications to the public that are reasonable and not actuated by malice, in the sense in which both terms were defined by the Court.

---

[87]   *Theophanous v Herald & Weekly Times Ltd* (1994) 182 CLR 104; *Stephens v Western Australian Newspapers* (1994) 182 CLR 211. Other cases decided in the interim include *Cunliffe v Commonwealth* (1994) 182 CLR 272; *Langer v Commonwealth* (1996) 186 CLR 302; *Muldowney v South Australia* (1996) 186 CLR 352.

[88]   See for example McHugh J in *McGinty* at 234: '[The doctrine] appears to be a free-standing principle, just as if the Constitution contained a [provision] which read: "Subject to this Constitution, representative democracy is the law of Australia, notwithstanding any law to the contrary"'.

[89]   *Lange v Australian Broadcasting Corporation* (1997) 189 CLR 520, from which the following quotations are taken.

[90]   Ibid, 560. For a critique, see A Stone, 'Rights, Personal Rights and Freedoms: The Nature of the Freedom of Political Communication' (2001) 25 *Melbourne University Law Review* 374.

ii. *Application and Scope*

Ostensibly at least, the constitutional freedom of political communication remains in place, broadly in the terms that were settled in *Lange*.[91] It has been invoked in a range of cases dealing with the validity of, for example, the regulation of entry into duck-hunting areas, which inhibited protests against hunting;[92] the arrest of a person for an offence of using 'insulting words' in a public place by accusing a police officer of corruption;[93] a prohibition on advertising legal services relating to personal injury claims;[94] restriction of the right to be registered as a political party so as to be mentioned by name on the ballot paper.[95] In each of these cases most members of the Court engaged with the arguments based on an implied freedom.[96] But only in *Coleman* did it make a difference to the outcome, causing three Justices to read the legislation down and a fourth to decide that it was invalid. In terms of both quantity and quality, the implied freedom of political communication has had a relatively limited impact on constitutional adjudication since *Lange* was decided.

In some respects, moreover, the contours of the doctrine remain surprisingly uncertain. In part this reflects the difficulty of the absence of a text from which doctrinal markers can be derived.[97] In part it appears also to be due to ambivalence about the freedom within the post-*Lange* Court, affecting enthusiasm for its conceptual coherence.

One question that requires resolution is the scope of the communications protected by the freedom. It is clear from *Lange* itself that the protection extends beyond communications about the conduct of

---

[91] Subject to a reformulation in 2004 to protect laws that are 'reasonably appropriate and adapted to serve a legitimate end in a manner which is compatible with the maintenance of the constitutionally prescribed' system of government: *Coleman v Power* (2004) 220 CLR 1, 51, 78, 90.

[92] *Levy v Victoria* (1997) 189 CLR 579.

[93] *Coleman v Power* (2004) 220 CLR 1.

[94] *APLA Limited v Legal Services Commissioner (NSW)* (2005) 224 CLR 322.

[95] *Mulholland v Australian Electoral Commission* (2004) 220 CLR 181.

[96] Others in which the doctrine also attracted some consideration include *ABC v Lenah Game Meats* (2001) 208 CLR 199; *Roberts v Bass* (2002) 212 CLR 1.

[97] Adrienne Stone points also to the significance of interpretive materials that typically accompany a text, including historical context: 'Australia's Constitutional Rights and the Problem of Interpretive Disagreement' (2005) 27 *Sydney Law Review* 29.

Ministers and the public service to 'the affairs of statutory authorities and public utilities which are obliged to report to the legislature or to a Minister who is responsible to the legislature'.[98] It is not clear, however, whether it extends further still, to other public bodies, including tribunals and courts.[99] This outstanding question in turn masks a deeper uncertainty about how tightly the scope of protected communication is tied to the need to ensure that voters can make an informed choice at an election, or whether it also provides a more general safeguard for interaction between people and officials and the active engagement of people in the public sphere.[100]

A second unresolved issue concerns the impact of the freedom on the States. It draws its rationale from the constitutional framework for the Commonwealth system of representative and responsible government. These parts of the Constitution do not prescribe conditions for State systems of government, which are structured by the Constitutions of the States. Even so, the Commonwealth Constitution must preclude State legislative or executive action that would interfere with political communication in the Commonwealth sphere. The outstanding question, however, is whether it is feasible to divide political communication along jurisdictional lines, within a federation in which the government and politics of all levels of government are highly interdependent. A majority thought not, in *Australian Capital Television,* and many of the subsequent cases have challenged restrictions on communication emanating from State Parliaments or from the common law. On the other hand, there is an observation in *Lange* that suggests that not all 'discussion of government or politics' at the State level 'bears on matters' at the Commonwealth level.[101] If this view is maintained, it will make it necessary to try to identify a link with the Commonwealth for any

---

[98] See n 89, 561.

[99] In Australia the former lie within the executive branch and fall literally within the *Lange* formula: see also *Nationwide News v Wills* (1992) 177 CLR 1. Courts were specifically excluded by McHugh J in *APLA,* n 94, 361. Cf Kirby J in *APLA,* n 94, 440 and see also the criticism in Zines, n 64, 543.

[100] Consider the division of view in *Cunliffe v Commonwealth* over whether restrictions on assistance by immigration agents before tribunals fell within the scope of the protection: (1994) 182 CLR 272, 298, 329.

[101] See n 89, 571. The modification of the common law in *Lange* affected communications that fall outside the scope of the freedom including 'discussion of matters concerning the United Nations or other countries': 571

communication for which protection is sought, however convoluted the link may be.[102]

A third issue concerns the manner in which the validity of a burden on protected communication is determined. Ostensibly, this was settled in *Lange*, with the adoption of the 'appropriate and adapted' test. In fact, however, the test has been under attack on a number of fronts. One is the use of the terminology of 'appropriate and adapted', instead of the somewhat more comprehensible concept of 'proportionality', although the Court has insisted that they are much the same.[103] Another, advanced by Adrienne Stone in the wake of the decision in *Lange,* is that the test leaves considerable discretion to the Court to balance the burden on the freedom against the objective of the challenged law, which in the long run is unsatisfactory.[104] This criticism prompted a not entirely convincing attempt in *Coleman* to explain the test further as one that does not involve balancing once the relatively narrow scope of the freedom is infringed.

In any event, as Stone also has observed, the Court sometimes has categorised laws in different ways in determining whether the freedom is infringed.[105] This tendency was evident again in *Coleman*, despite the reaffirmation, with modifications, of the appropriate and adapted test.[106] Neither the definition of these categories nor their doctrinal status is yet clear. It may be that the narrow scope of the implied freedom will enable Australian courts to avoid some of the jurisprudential complexity that

---

[102] As in *Coleman v Power,* n 93, 45, 78. Determination of this question also affects the issue of whether Commonwealth restrictions on communication in the State sphere are precluded by the implied freedom of political communication or by implications drawn from federalism alone: see generally *Australian Capital Television,* n 86, where the Court was divided on the rationale for the invalidity of Commonwealth legislation restricting paid political advertising in the approach to State elections.

[103] See for example, Kirby J in *Coleman*, n 93 at 90ff, and the references to *Lange* there cited.

[104] A Stone, 'The Limits of Constitutional Text and Structure: Standards of Review and the Freedom of Political Communication' (1999) 23 *Melbourne University Law Review* 668.

[105] Stone, 'The Limits of Constitutional Text and Structure', ibid, 678–80, with reference to *ACTV* and *Levy* in particular; see also *Kruger v Commonwealth* (1997) 190 CLR 1, 128.

[106] Gleeson CJ, n 93, at 30–31, adopting the distinction of Gaudron J in *Levy* between laws with a direct and indirect effect on political communication, although without endorsing her test for the former category; McHugh J, at 52, distinguishing laws that 'promote or protect' communication and others.

attends more general guarantees of freedom of speech elsewhere. Even so, the doctrine inevitably will become more nuanced as the case law develops and the freedom is invoked in different contexts.

B. Voting

i. *Legal and Constitutional Framework*

The Constitution makes relatively little specific provision for the franchise. The voting requirements for the House and the Senate must be the same; each voter has only one vote for each House; elections must be direct, rather than indirect. At first glance section 41, which provides that 'no adult person' with a right to vote in State elections shall 'be prevented by any law of the Commonwealth' from voting in Commonwealth elections offers a guarantee on which voters in States with more progressive voting rules might be able to rely. The High Court has held, however, that the section was transitional, protecting the position of those who acquired the right to vote for the Commonwealth Parliament under State legislation before the first Commonwealth franchise was established, with a particular eye to the voting rights of women.[107] In so doing, the majority gave priority to the need for a uniform Commonwealth franchise over whatever advantage might have accrued to individual voters had the section been given a continuing operation.[108]

These provisions aside, on the face of the Constitution, the determination of the franchise was left to the Commonwealth Parliament and has been governed by Commonwealth legislation since 1902. In policy terms, the legislation is notable for enfranchising white women early but denying the vote to Aboriginal Australians until 1962. Citizenship finally became the core qualification for voters in 1981, although other British subjects who were on the electoral role before 26 January 1984 retained the franchise and do so still.[109] The voting age was lowered to 18 in 1973. Dual citizenship is permitted and Australians with dual

---

[107] *R v Pearson; Ex parte Sipka* (1983) 152 CLR 254.

[108] For a detailed critique on historical and contextual grounds see A Twomey, 'The Federal Constitutional Right to Vote in Australia' (2000) 28 *Federal Law Review* 125.

[109] See now Commonwealth Electoral Act 1918 s 93(1)(b)(ii). They must have remained on the roll since: *Paulding and the Australian Electoral Commission* [2000] AATA 202. In 2006, at least 164,000 voters qualified on this basis.

citizenship who are based in Australia are both entitled and expected to vote, although the Constitution precludes them from standing for election (s.44(1)).

The relatively inclusive franchise is consistent with the reliance of the Australian constitutional system on the legitimacy that is derived from elections. Nevertheless, in Australia as elsewhere, there are pressures to extend the franchise further, to non-citizen residents and to Australian expatriates and to lower the voting age to 16. Ironically, extensions are complicated by the requirements for compulsory registration and voting: in each case it is necessary to consider whether a right to vote should be accompanied by a corresponding duty.[110]

In the absence of constitutional protection, moreover, important details of the franchise can be changed by an incumbent government that has the support of both Houses, in ways that may give it an electoral advantage. Amendments to the electoral legislation in 2006 that shortened enrolment deadlines and disqualified convicted prisoners from voting were controversial for this reason.[111] In a further demonstration of the dynamics of the interaction between politics and the Constitution in Australia, however, the ensuing litigation confirmed long-standing speculation that the constitutional requirement for an elected Parliament has some implications for the right to vote.

ii. Constitution and the Franchise

It has seemed likely that the Constitution provides some protection for the franchise since 1975, when the potential of chapter 1 began to be explored in *McKinlay's* case, as an admittedly meagre framework for representative democracy. More than twenty years later, in *McGinty*, a majority of the Court appeared to accept that the requirement for the Houses to be 'chosen . . . by the people' could now be met only through universal adult franchise, irrespective of the position in 1901.[112] This ambulatory standard derived further support from the decision in *Cheatle* that the core requirement for trial by jury within the meaning of section 80 of the Constitution was that it be 'truly representative' and that 'in contemporary Australia,

---

[110] Most proposals to lower the voting age, for example, suggest that voting should be optional for those under 18.

[111] Electoral and Referendum Amendment (Electoral Integrity and Other Measures) Act 2006.

[112] *McGinty v Western Australia* (1996) 186 CLR 140.

the exclusion of females and unpropertied persons would be inconsistent' with the constitutional rule.[113]

In none of the earlier cases, however, was the franchise directly in issue. But in *Roach* the plaintiff challenged the validity of legislation that disqualified any person serving a sentence in full-time detention from voting in Commonwealth elections.[114] The previous legislation had disqualified persons serving terms of three years or more. The plaintiff herself was serving a six year term. A majority of the Court held that the legislation was invalid. In doing so it confirmed that universal adult suffrage was a constitutional requirement, derived from the description of the Houses as 'chosen by the people' in sections 7 and 24. The Parliament retains power to prescribe disqualifications but these must be rational and not arbitrary or, in terms of a familiar test adapted for the purpose by the joint judgement, 'reasonably appropriate and adapted to serve an end which is consistent . . . with the maintenance of the constitutionally prescribed system of representative government'.[115] In this case, disqualification purely by reference to incarceration after sentence offered no rationale that could 'reconcile the disenfranchisement with the constitutional imperative of choice by the people'.[116] Invalidation of the 2006 amendment, however, revived the legislation in its earlier form, the validity of which was upheld, partly because it relied on a 'criterion of culpability'[117] and partly because disqualification of prisoners serving three year terms had been a familiar practice in 1901.

Roach is important for its substantive outcome. And in 2010 it became clear that this line of authority is likely to develop further, when a majority of the Court invalidated Commonwealth legislation requiring the electoral rolls to be closed to new voters on the day election writs are issued.[118] Nevertheless *Roach* itself is also, in many ways, a typically restrained example of contemporary Australian constitutional reasoning in cases concerning political rights. The joint judgement denied that an individual right is at stake, as opposed to a limit on power.[119] Gleeson CJ

---

[113]   *Cheatle v R* (1993) 177 CLR 541.

[114]   *Roach v Electoral Commissioner* (2007) 233 CLR 162.

[115]   Ibid, 174, 199.

[116]   Ibid, 182, Gleeson CJ. Variations in sentencing practice around the country meant that incarceration alone was an inadequate measure of culpability.

[117]   Gummow, Kirby and Crennan JJ, at 204.

[118]   *Rowe v Electoral Commissioner*; the decision of the Court was announced on 6 August, leaving the reasons to be published at a later date.

[119]   Gummow, Kirby and Crennan JJ at 199–200; cf Gleeson CJ at 174.

went to some lengths to justify a change in the constitutional standard since the Constitution came into effect, by characterising adult suffrage as a 'fact' in the sense of a 'historical development of constitutional significance' akin to the process by which Britain became a foreign power.[120] Both sets of reasons relied in part on historical practice in upholding the validity of the earlier version of the law. And the doctrine that emerged, in response to an egregious law, left the Parliament with considerable discretion to prescribe criteria for disqualification, as long as they can reasonably be justified in some way.

SELECTED READING

Campbell, EM, *Parliamentary Privilege* (Annandale, NSW, Federation Press, 2003)

Democratic Audit of Australia, *Discussion Papers,* http://democraticaudit.org.au/

Department of the Prime Minister and Cabinet, *Legislation Handbook* 2000

Evans, H (ed), *Odgers Australian Senate Practice,* 12th edn (Canberra, NSW, Parliament of Australia Senate, 2008)

Farrell, DM and McAllister, I, *The Australian Electoral System: Origins, Variations and Consequences* (Sydney, NSW, UNSW Press, 2006)

Finn, PD (ed), *Essays on Law and Government, Vol 1* (Sydney, NSW, Law Book Company Limited, 1995)

Gelber, K and Stone, A, *Hate Speech and Freedom of Speech in Australia* (Annandale, NSW, Federation Press, 2007)

Harris, IC, *House of Representatives Practice,* 5th edn (Canberra, NSW, Department of House of Representatives, 2005)

Lindell, G and Bennett, RL (eds), *Parliament: The Vision in Hindsight* (Annandale, NSW, Federation Press, 2001)

Orr, G (ed), *Realising Democracy: A Century of Australian Electoral Law* (Annandale, NSW, Federation Press, 2003)

Sawer, G, *Federation Under Strain* (Carlton, Vic, MUP, 1977)

Uhr, J, *Deliberative Democracy in Australia* (Cambridge, CUP, 1998)

---

[120] For a critique, see Zines, n 64, 561–63.

5

Responsible Government

————◆◆◆————

Principle – Crown – Government – Power

I. PRINCIPLE

A. Significance

RESPONSIBLE GOVERNMENT PLAYS a central role in Australian constitutionalism. Most obviously, it provides the framework of principle through which representative democracy is translated into effective government in the Commonwealth and all States. In addition, however, this is the feature of the Australian constitutional system that is said to justify extensive reliance on political, rather than legal constitutionalism.[1]

This chapter therefore has two purposes. The first is to explain the structure and operation of the executive branch. In this context, the chapter also draws attention to moves to establish an Australian republic, with particular reference to the challenge of designing a model for a republic that meets public expectations and that adequately fills the niche left in the constitutional system by the removal of the Monarch and the Governor-General. The second is to show how the Australian system of responsible government works from the standpoint of claims that it offers safeguards for the integrity of government and respect for constitutional principles, including the protection of human rights. In a

---

[1] On the general concept, see R Bellamy, *Political Constitutionalism: A Republican Defence of the Constitutionality of Democracy* (Cambridge, CUP, 2007); for a critique see D Dyzenhaus, 'How Hobbes met the "Hobbes Challenge"' (2009) 72 *Modern Law Review* 488.

classic statement to this effect, former Prime Minister Robert Menzies once explained to an American audience that: 'responsible government in a democracy is regarded by us as the ultimate guarantee of justice and individual rights', constituting a 'basic difference' between government in Australia and the United States.[2] In a less usual application, responsible government has been claimed as 'a mechanism of constitutional constraint capable of operating in relation to issues of federalism'.[3]

The defining feature of responsible government is the dependence of a government, based in the Parliament in accordance with the Westminster parliamentary tradition, on the continuing support of a democratically elected lower House. Ministers are responsible to the Parliament, individually and collectively, for the conduct of the business of government, defined broadly to include both policy-making and implementation under the auspices of apolitical, continuing departments of state and other agencies. Ministers are held regularly to account by the House of which they are a member during their term of office. A government that loses the confidence of the lower House cannot continue, but must either seek re-election or surrender office to another group of ministers whom the House is prepared to support.[4]

There is also a second dimension of responsible government, which governs the relationship between Ministers and the Crown. This aspect of the doctrine is a necessary corollary of an arrangement that vests formal executive power in the Queen or her vice-regal representatives. In the United Kingdom, the retention of executive power by the monarch is the end product of a process of constitutional evolution that democratised the system of government, leaving the outward forms intact. The acceptability and workability of this dichotomy between executive form and function requires the Monarch to act on the advice of ministers in all but a small and dwindling range of matters in which she retains a discretionary or 'reserve' power[5] and requires ministers in turn to take responsibility for the actions of the Monarch. Adoption of the same

[2] R Menzies, *Central Power in the Australian Commonwealth* (London: Cassell, 1967) 49–55.

[3] S Gageler, 'Foundations of Australian Federalism and the Role of Judicial Review' (1987) 17 *Federal Law Review* 162, 164.

[4] The complication of a government that retains the confidence of the House but that cannot secure 'supply' from the Senate, is examined below.

[5] Geoffrey Sawer notes that the term derives from the 'residue' of personal power still retained by the monarch: *Federation Under Strain* (Melbourne, Vic, Melbourne University Press, 1977) 153.

format in colonial Australia had the practical advantage for the Imperial authorities of enabling part of the executive power pertaining to the colonies to be exercised on British, rather than Australian ministerial advice.[6] As British control slackened, the requirement for the Australian representatives of the Queen to act on the advice of local ministers produced what Henry Parkes described as a system under which 'the actual government of the State is conducted by officers who enjoy the confidence of the people'.[7] In Australia, as in the United Kingdom, holders of vice-regal office have some reserve powers, although these are not necessarily co-extensive with those exercisable by the Queen in relation to the United Kingdom. There is an open and topical question whether the reserve powers and, more generally, the retention of formal executive power by vice-regal representatives, have a contemporary rationale.

It is a commonplace that the business of government became increasingly complex over the course of the twentieth century, heightening pressure on the political process and prompting new approaches to public sector management. The ramifications with constitutional significance in Australia have included greater disinclination by Ministers to take individual responsibility for error in the absence of personal culpability; a linked tendency for public servants to be exposed to public scrutiny and criticism; some politicisation of the upper echelons of the public service with implications for the impartiality and expertise of the service as a whole; the corporatisation or privatisation of a growing number of governmental functions in forms that diminish ministerial control; a higher incidence of intergovernmental co-operation, blurring lines of both political and legal accountability; increasing reliance on regulation through incentives provided by contract or government funding; and a leaching of power to higher levels of policy-making, to deal with trans-border phenomena.

The principles and practices of responsible government have adjusted in a variety of ways in response to these changed conditions. Much of the innovation has taken place within the sprawling executive branch: in more elaborate procedures for the 'internal control' of both ministry and bureaucracy and in the establishment of independent institutions

---

[6] For reaction against this arrangement in the struggle for a more complete measure of responsible government see *Toy v Musgrove* (1888) 14 VLR 349.

[7] H Parkes, 'Notes on Australian Federation', 1896, 17–18, quoted in J Quick and RR Garran, *Annotated Constitution of the Australian Commonwealth* (Sydney, NSW, Angus and Robertson, 1901) 704.

to monitor the integrity of public bodies or to provide more effective redress for individual grievances. Without detracting from the significance of many of these developments individually, collectively they do not have the coherence of the relatively simple accountability chain provided by responsible government in its traditional form, and it would be unrealistic now to expect that this is possible.

The remainder of the first part of this chapter outlines the constitutional framework for responsible government in Australia, only a portion of which is set out in the constitutional text, leaving the rest to be drawn from the structure of the Constitution or supplied by constitutional convention. The next two parts deal respectively with the two limbs of responsible government: the office of Governor-General and its relationship with the ministry and the relationship between the government and the Parliament, in the light of the structure and operation of the executive branch as a whole. The final part examines the power of the executive, with particular reference to the concept of inherent executive power and the relationship between legislation and executive power.

As in earlier chapters, for reasons of space, this chapter focuses largely on the Commonwealth sphere of government. In this instance, however, it is a pity. Each State has its own executive branch, its own Parliament and its own vice-regal representative,[8] functioning within the parameters of a system of responsible government. While the State systems are broadly similar to those of the Commonwealth there are significant differences as well. Some are a product of different evolutionary paths, but others are the consequence of more recent experimentation in constitutional design that may be gradually and perhaps unintentionally modifying the template for responsible government in Australia.[9] The introduction of fixed term parliaments by three of the States, necessitating some codification of constitutional convention, is an example.

---

[8] Cf the ACT, in which there is no such office: Australian Capital Territory (Self-Government) Act 1988 (Cth); GJ Lindell, 'The Arrangements for Self-Government for the Australian Capital Territory: A Partial Road to Republicanism in the Seat of Government?' (1992) 3 *Public Law Review* 5.
[9] There is good coverage of the field in G Carney, *The Constitutional Systems of the Australian States and Territories* (Cambridge, CUP, 2006) ch.8.

B. Constitutional Framework

i. Constitutional Text

The Constitution provides a skeletal framework for responsible govern-ment. Both limbs of the doctrine are mandated, although the signs can easily be missed. The dependence of the government on the Parliament derives from section 64, which precludes 'Ministers of State' from hold-ing office for more than three months without having a seat in one or other of the Houses of Parliament. This section also equates ministers with the 'officers' who 'administer' the departments of State. In another supporting indication, section 44(i) excepts 'Ministers of State' from the disqualification of Members of Parliament who hold an 'office of profit under the Crown'. Sections 65–67 make interim provision for the num-ber and salaries of ministers and for the appointment of civil servants 'until the Parliament otherwise provides'.[10]

The Constitution makes somewhat more fulsome, but equally obscure, provision for the other limb of responsible government, dealing with the relationship between the Governor-General and ministers. Its focus is on the Governor-General as the formal repository of executive power, rather than on the working rule of responsible government that requires the Monarch and her representatives to act on ministerial advice. The Constitution makes no reference to the two most significant institutions in the executive branch: the cabinet and the office of Prime Minister. Instead, it provides for a 'Federal Executive Council' to 'advise the Governor-General in the government of the Commonwealth' (s 62).

The Executive Council is another survivor from colonial times.[11] It began as an institution in which a powerful Governor received advice from local officials, whom he appointed to the council, and has been adapted over time to become the body in which advice on a range of matters already determined by cabinet or a minister is formally conveyed to and accepted by the Governor or Governor-General.[12] In practice, a meeting of the Federal Executive Council usually involves attendance

---

[10] See now Ministers of State Act 1952 (Cth); Remuneration Tribunal Act 1973 (Cth); Public Service Act (Cth) 1999.

[11] P Boyce, *The Queen's Other Realms: The Crown and its Legacy in Australia, Canada and New Zealand,* (Sydney, NSW, Federation Press, 2008) 52.

[12] Department of the Prime Minister and Cabinet *Executive Council Handbook,* 2009.

by only two members.[13] In most, although not all, cases it is chaired by the Governor-General.[14] Section 64 requires ministers to be members of the council, thus squaring the circle. Membership of the council is not co-extensive with that of the cabinet or even with those who hold the status of full minister, however. Parliamentary secretaries also are appointed to the council and bear much of the brunt of attendance at council meetings.[15] Because appointments are during the 'pleasure' of the Governor-General and thus in most cases for life, ministers of former governments also are Executive Council members, albeit not 'under summons' for the purpose of attending meetings or giving advice.

The constitutional provision for an Executive Council makes it clear that the Governor-General is expected to act on advice in some circumstances, but it does not necessarily determine when. Some sections of the Constitution confer power on the 'Governor-General in Council': the appointment of judges under section 72 is an example. Other sections confer power on the Governor-General with no reference to the council. These include the general executive power in section 61 and a range of specific powers, of which dissolution of the House of Representatives (s 28) or both Houses (s 57), prorogation of the Parliament (s 5), recommendation of the purpose of an appropriation to the Parliament (s 56), and submission of a constitution alteration bill to referendum (s 128) are examples. Section 68 also vests the 'command in chief' of the armed forces in the Governor-General, with no reference to ministerial advice.[16]

In fact, however, the distinction drawn by the Constitution between powers conferred on the Governor-General in Council and those conferred on the Governor-General alone is not an accurate guide to the circumstances in which the Governor-General must act on advice and those in which he or she has discretion.[17] It does not even serve to

[13] For significant variations in the Executive Councils of the States see Carney, n 9, 294 ff.

[14] Boyce notes that this practice began in 1914 and is now (almost) invariably followed: n 11 above, 52.

[15] Parliamentary secretaries now are ministers, but do not exercise all ministerial responsibilities: IC Harris, *House of Representatives Practice*, 5th edn (Canberra, NSW, Department of the House of Representatives, 2005) 69 ff.

[16] s 68. For confirmation that this is merely 'titular command' see former Governor-General Ninian Stephen, 'The Governor-General as Commander-in-Chief', an address to the Joint Services Staff College, Canberra, NSW, 21 June 1983.

[17] The decision to allocate powers to one or other category in 1901 was deter-

identify actions taken directly under the Constitution that in practice are finalised through the Executive Council, although it identifies those that must be dealt with in this way.[18] It thus does not determine the scope of the discretionary or reserve powers of the Governor-General under the Constitution, which is left to constitutional convention.

ii. Constitutional Convention

The working rules of responsible government are not unique in their reliance on constitutional convention. The phenomenon is most evident in this context, however. This is the part of the Constitution that draws most directly on British constitutional arrangements, infused by the assumptions of an uncodified constitution and reliant on the flexibility that conventions provide. Conventions underpin the operation of both limbs of responsible government: the relationship between Ministers and Parliament and the Governor-General and Ministers. In addition, as chapter one shows, they govern relations between the Governor-General and the Queen.

In Australia, as elsewhere in the common law world, a convention is understood as a practice associated with the Constitution, which may be critical to its operation and is regarded as binding by those to whom it applies.[19] A convention is generally, but not necessarily, unwritten. It is not a rule of law although it may qualify a rule of law by, for example, structuring the way in which a legal power should be used. In theory, a convention can be distinguished from a behavioural practice of lesser status by employing the three factors identified by Jennings: the extent to which a practice has been followed; whether the relevant actors consider themselves bound by it; and, most importantly, the rationale for it.[20] In practice, however, except in the strongest case in which the system is unworkable unless a practice is followed, difficulties may arise in

mined by British practice; powers vested in the Governor-General alone were prerogative powers in the UK, uncontrolled by statute: J Quick and RR Garran, *Annotated Constitution of the Australian Commonwealth* (Sydney, NSW, Angus and Robertson, 1901) 707.

[18] See for example, *Executive Council Handbook,* n 12, 4 noting that some matters arising under s 61, including entry into treaties, may be dealt with through the Executive Council.

[19] *Re Resolution to amend the Constitution* [1981] 1 S.C.R. 753, 853–58.

[20] I Jennings, *The Law and the Constitution,* 5th edn (London, University of London Press Ltd, 1959) 134–36.

determining not only whether a practice is a convention but also its precise scope.

These difficulties have been borne out by experience in Australia, where politics are aggressive and pragmatic and public figures are more accustomed to the demands of positive law. Writing in the aftermath of the constitutional crisis of 1975, during which a series of apparently established practices had been either broken or redefined, Geoffrey Sawer argued that, in Australia, the 'fuzzy . . . concepts' associated with convention 'should be used with caution'.[21]

There has been some experimentation with the codification of conventions in Australia, in a variety of forms. Section 16A of the Acts Interpretation Act 1901 (Cth) requires the Governor-General to act 'with' the advice of the Executive Council in the exercise of statutory powers[22] although this section does not affect the exercise of constitutional power. Some conventions have been reduced to written form within the executive branch; obligations created by the collective responsibility of ministers and the constraints on new policy and appointments during the 'caretaker' period after the Parliament is dissolved for an election are examples.[23] Relevantly, the periodic revision of these documents points to an assumption that the practices are fluid, at least to a degree. By contrast, in 1977, failure to comply with an alleged convention to fill casual Senate vacancies with someone from the same political party as the retiring Senator, during the heady events of 1975, led to a rare constitutional amendment to codify the practice in what now is section 15.

The dismissal of the Governor-General in 1975 also prompted an attempt to codify the conventions associated with the Constitution by way of a declaration in non-justiciable form by a body representative of all Australian Parliaments, the Australian Constitutional Convention (ACC).[24]

---

[21] G Sawer, *Federation Under Strain* (Melbourne, Victoria, Melbourne University Press, 1977), 121

[22] Despite the cautious wording, it seems obvious that the Governor-General is required to act on the advice; although cf *FAI Insurances v Winneke* (1982) 151 CLR 342, 365.

[23] Department of the Prime Minister and Cabinet, *Cabinet Handbook*, 6th edn (2009) 3–7; also Attachment 2, dealing with caretaker conventions.

[24] For the history of the ACC see C Saunders, 'The Parliament as Partner: A Century of Constitutional Review' in G Lindell and R Bennett (eds), *Parliament, The Vision in Hindsight* (Sydney, NSW, Federation Press, 2001) 454. For critique of the codification exercise see CHG Sampford, '"Recognise and Declare": An Australian

After considerable negotiation, in both committee and plenary, successive sessions of the ACC in 1983 and 1985 recognised a range of 'principles and practices [to be] observed as Conventions in Australia'.[25] Although the ACC was unable to agree on the critical question of when, if ever, a Governor-General may constitutionally dismiss a Prime Minister who retains the confidence of the House, this remains a useful and authoritative statement, not least because it grounds all the conventions on which the ACC agreed in the core expectations of responsible government.

However bare the bones of the provision for responsible government in chapter two, their inclusion in the Constitution at all raises a question of the extent to which they are enforceable through the courts. The possibility that such an action might be dismissed on the grounds that the involvement of the Governor-General makes it non-justiciable has receded in the face of cases that make it clear that a decision cannot be shielded from review for that reason alone, although other bases for non-justiciability may be arguable.[26] This possibility aside, where form and practice coincide there seems no reason why a section could not be enforced on its terms, in the unlikely event that an appropriate case arose. Given the terms of section 72, for example, a federal judge could not lawfully be appointed by the Governor-General without the advice of the Executive Council,[27] or by the Prime Minister without the consent of the Governor-General.

The difficulty arises in relation to those sections where the text of the Constitution does not advert to the convention by which it is qualified, including the conferral of general executive power on the Queen and the Governor-General in section 61. A requirement to act on advice is effectively unenforceable through judicial review under such provisions, unless a court is prepared to take constitutional convention into account. The orthodox view has been that, while a court may recognise a convention for the purposes of the resolution of other legal questions it will not

---

Experiment in Codifying Constitutional Conventions' (1987) 7 *Oxford Journal of Legal Studies* 369.

[25] Most of the practices declared in 1985 are reproduced in Carney, n 9, Appendix 1.

[26] G Lindell, 'Responsible Government and the Australian Constitution: Conventions Transformed into Law?' Centre for International and Public Law, Law and Policy Paper 24, (Annandale, NSW, Federation Press, 2004).

[27] Even in this case, however, the composition of the Executive Council depends on convention, which limits the discretion of the Governor-General under s 62 to 'choose and summon' members of the Executive Council.

enforce it directly.[28] Nevertheless, this issue received considerable attention after 1975, when the Governor-General dismissed a Prime Minister who retained the confidence of the House of Representatives but who could not secure passage of budget legislation by the Senate, presumably by withdrawing his 'pleasure' under section 64.[29] While opinion was, and remains, divided, some scholars argued strongly at that time that the centrality of responsible government in the Constitution meant that at least some conventions would be given effect by the courts if a suitable action were brought.[30]

This view has been strengthened more recently by the decision in *Lange,* in which a unanimous High Court accepted that an implied protection for political communication can be derived from the constitutional requirements for responsible, as well as representative government.[31] *Lange* raises the possibility that the core requirements of responsible government can be derived from the structure of the Constitution even if they are not clearly stated in the text. To take an obvious example: it can readily be argued that it is necessary for the executive power in section 61 to be exercised on ministerial advice, given the logic of the responsibility of government to Parliament that can be derived from section 64. To go much further down this path, however, would involve the Court in settling disputes about contested constitutional practices that it would be likely to seek to avoid, possibly on the grounds of non-justiciability or separation of judicial power or a combination of the two.

---

[28]   See for example, *FAI Insurances Ltd v Winneke* (1982) 151 CLR 342; and generally, G Lindell, 'Responsible Government', n 26; PD Finn, *Essays on Law and Government, Vol 1,* (Sydney, NSW, Law Book Co Ltd, 1995) 75, 80–89, including the cases there cited.

[29]   See chapter 4; also G Winterton, '1975: The Dismissal of the Whitlam Government' in HP Lee and G Winterton (eds), *Australian Constitutional Landmarks* (Cambridge, CUP, 2003) 229.

[30]   G Winterton, *Parliament, The Executive and the Governor-General* (Melbourne, Vic, Melbourne University Press, 1983) ch.1, also 125–27; cf G Lindell, 'Book Review Article' (1983) 6 *University of New South Wales Law Review* 261.

[31]   *Lange v Australian Broadcasting Corporation* (1997) 189 CLR 520, 557–59, 561.

II. CROWN

A. Office of Governor-General

i. Nature of the Office

On the face of the Constitution, the Governor-General is the represent-ative of the Queen in the Commonwealth sphere. He or she is appointed by the Queen under section 2. Since 1930, the appointment has been made on the advice of the Australian Prime Minister. Section 2 describes the Governor-General as holding office during the Queen's 'pleasure', although in practice the initial appointment is generally for five years. Like the Queen herself, the Governor-General carries out a mixture of constitutional, ceremonial and community-oriented functions.[32]

By the process of evolution described in chapter one, the Governor-General has become the de facto head of state.[33] The formal legal posi-tion remains significant, however, not least as the explanation for the unusual situation whereby the person who performs the role of head of state is effectively appointed and removable by the Prime Minister, through advice to the Queen.[34] Almost as unusual and attributable to the same cause, is the absence of any grounds or stipulated process for the removal of a Governor-General before the end of his or her term. The Constitution also provides for an Administrator (s 4),[35] appointed on the advice of the Prime Minister, to act when the Governor-General is physically unable to do so or, since amendments to the Letters Patent in 2003, has 'absented himself . . . temporarily from office for any reason'.[36]

---

[32] G Winterton, 'The Evolving Role of the Governor-General' in M Groves (ed), *Law and Government in Australia* (Annandale, NSW, Federation Press, 2005) 44, 50.

[33] G Winterton, 'Who is Australia's Head of State?' (2004) 7 *Constitutional Law and Policy Review* 45.

[34] On the problem of recall see Winterton, 'The Evolving Role', n 32, 47 noting, without accepting, arguments that the Queen has a reserve power to refuse to accept advice to remove a Governor-General in exceptional cases.

[35] See also s 126, providing for deputies for short term purposes. In practice, State Governors fill these roles.

[36] Letters Patent Relating to the Office of the Governor-General of the Commonwealth of Australia, *Gazette,* S 179, 9 September 2008, cl.III. The changes were prompted by the early resignation of Governor-General Hollingworth: see G Winterton, 'The Hollingworth Experiment' (2003) 14 *Public Law Review* 139.

Partly for these reasons it is not possible to fully equate the function of the Governor-General with that of the Queen in the United Kingdom. There are logical reasons why a representative of the monarch who holds office for a limited term may be less inhibited in dealing with the government of the day than the Monarch herself, who risks the institution of the monarchy by defying a government with the confidence of the Parliament. The received wisdom in Australia that the Governor-General is kept in check by the possibility that the Prime Minister might cause the Queen to remove her might (or might not) be correct, but creates an entirely different dynamic.[37] Ironically, the existence of a written Constitution in Australia weakens the argument for the Governor-General to have discretionary powers in some areas where they may theoretically still be useful in the United Kingdom, as an ultimate safeguard against an abuse of power. Refusal of assent to legislation that seeks to extend the life of a Parliament is one obvious example.

The Governor-General is now always an Australian. Typically, the holder of the office has been a lawyer, a former politician, or a retired military officer. The Governor-General is expected to be independent of politics, not only for the effective performance of her constitutional functions, which are considered below, but in order to provide a symbol of unity or, in the words of one former Governor-General, to 'represent . . . the Australian nation to the people of Australia'.[38] In the face of the bitterness that followed the dismissal of the Prime Minister in 1975, successive Governors-General gave priority to this aspect of the office, in a generally successful effort to restore respect for it. The profile of the office appears to have lessened in recent years reflecting, perhaps, ambiguity about its status and significance.[39]

B. Governor-General and Ministers

i. Advice

Almost all the decisions of the Governor-General under constitutional or statutory power are taken on government advice. Advice is normally

---

[37] Winterton, 'The Evolving Role', n 32, 47–48, noting that this is 'no carefully constructed constitutional architecture, but rather an accident of history'.
[38] Ninian Stephen, quoted in Winterton, 'The Evolving Role', n 32, 55.
[39] Ibid, 57.

conveyed through the Executive Council, constituted as previously described. On some matters, of which dissolution of the House of Representatives is an example, the Governor-General is advised by the Prime Minister directly. The Governor-General gives assent to legislation on the basis of assurances from a clerk of the Parliament that the bill has passed both Houses and a certificate from the Attorney-General that amendments are not required and that there is no need to reserve the bill for the Queen's assent.[40]

There is a question about what this process adds to the quality and integrity of government. One answer is that the checking and co-ordination required to prepare material for the Council is a form of quality control, although this could be accomplished by other means. Another is that the Council is the forum through which the Governor-General exercises her right to 'be consulted, to encourage and to warn' before ministerial advice is accepted.[41] There is anecdotal evidence in Australia that some vice-regal representatives have paid considerable attention to this aspect of the role, raising questions with the Council secretariat, if not in a meeting of the Council itself.[42] On the other hand, both the interests and capacities of successive Governors-General vary and in the end a Governor-General is likely to have no option but to accept the advice of a government with the confidence of the House.

The question of the appropriate limits of the Governor-General's role arises in acute form if she is advised to take action that may be unlawful or have unlawful consequences. Examples that have arisen in practice include advice to approve authority for an unlawful borrowing[43] and to dissolve both Houses of the Parliament in circumstances where there is doubt whether a deadlocked bill has fulfilled the requirements of section

---

[40] Department of Prime Minister and Cabinet, *Legislation Handbook* 76–77. On the complications that arise if the government does not want the Governor-General to assent see (in the context of New South Wales) A Twomey, *The Constitution of New South Wales* (Annandale, NSW, Federation Press, 2004) 224 ff.

[41] Structure of Government Sub-Committee, *Report to the Standing Committee*, August 1984, in *Proceedings*, Brisbane 1985, Vol II Australian Constitutional Convention, 25, quoting Walter Bagehot, *The English Constitution* (London, Collins/Fontana, 1963) 11.

[42] See the references cited in eg Winterton, 'The Evolving Role', n 32 51–52; on the latter point see M Hazell, 'The Role of the Governor-General' (2008) *Public Administration Today* 63.

[43] For detail of the Khemlani loan affair see Winterton '1975: The Dismissal of the Whitlam Government', n 29, 233–34.

57.[44] Even in cases of this kind, it is widely accepted that the Governor-General should act on the advice, on the assumption that the illegality can eventually be resolved in the courts and that the Governor-General in any event is not equipped to make decisions of this kind. On the other hand, it is also accepted that the Governor-General is entitled to ask for advice about the legality of a proposal that gives rise to concern; preferably from the Solicitor-General, as the more independent and professional of the two Law Officers of the Crown.[45] Matters become more complicated in the relatively unlikely event that a question of unlawfulness cannot be resolved through the courts or if the Solicitor-General's opinion is not persuasive. Opinion is divided over whether the Governor-General may constitutionally reject advice in such cases. In practice, at least in the recorded cases, the advice has been accepted. In practice also, once again, the Governor-General has little effective choice.

One partial solution is to focus more attention on the propriety of the advice that the Governor-General is given, using transparency both as a deterrent and as a means to strengthen political accountability. Transparency is not a general panacea, because much of the communication between the ministers and the Governor-General is confidential. Nevertheless, it has been used to effect in one key area, where it has reduced and perhaps eliminated the need for a reserve power.

As explained in chapter four, the Governor-General may dissolve both Houses of the Parliament if a bill has been rejected twice by the Senate, in accordance with the procedures laid down in section 57 of the Constitution. This is a disruptive action in two respects: it cuts short the three year cycle for general elections and, very exceptionally, it interrupts the rotation of Senate membership, by dissolving the Senate as a whole. Perhaps for this reason, there was a tendency even in the early years of federation for the advice of the Prime Minister to be made publicly available, to enable voters to draw their own conclusions. This practice has been consistently followed in more recent double dissolutions[46] and has been extended to early dissolutions of the House as well.

---

[44] This situation arose in relation to the 1974 double dissolution: see A Mason, 'The Double Dissolution Cases' in Lee and Winterton, n 29, 213, 218–24.

[45] There are varying views on whether the Governor-General may also seek independent legal advice: see Winterton, 'The Evolving Role', n 32, 53.

[46] H Evans, *Odgers Australian Senate Practice*, 12th edn (Canberra, NSW, Parliament of Australian Senate, 2008) ch.21; the double dissolution of 1951 was an exception. In relation to the House, see Harris, n 15, ch.1, Table 1.1. See also the statement of constitutional practices approved by the ACC: Carney, n 9.

Its value was enhanced by the request of the Governor-General in 1983 to receive advice not only on the legality of what he was being asked to do but also on the importance of the bills in issue and on the 'workability' of the Parliament.[47] The corollary of transparency is that the advice is invariably accepted. As Lindell has observed, it would be consistent with the logic of these developments for any related advice of the Law Officers of the Crown to be published at the same time.[48]

ii. Reserve Powers

Reserve or discretionary powers may be exercised by the Governor-General without or against the advice of the incumbent government. Responsibility for their exercise thus lies with the Governor-General, who is deprived of both the protection and the legitimacy that comes from reliance on the advice of democratically elected representatives. Necessarily, therefore, the powers are limited and exercised in rare and extreme circumstances.

There is consensus on the existence of a small central core of reserve powers, all of which can be explained as necessary to protect the 'basic principle' of responsible government that the Ministry must have the confidence of the lower House of Parliament.[49] Reserve powers in this category can be used to commission a new Prime Minister, following an election, if an outgoing Prime Minister is not available or willing to give the requisite advice; to dismiss a Prime Minister who has lost the confidence of the House but refuses to resign;[50] and, perhaps, to refuse an early dissolution to a Prime Minister who has lost the confidence of the House, if another Member is able to command a majority.[51] Given a Constitution that makes no other provision to deal with these matters, the reserve powers thus recognise a role for the Governor-General as constitutional guardian, albeit one that is limited to the effectuation of responsible government.[52]

[47] G Lindell, 'Governor-General' in T McCormack and C Saunders (eds), *Sir Ninian Stephen: A Tribute*, (Melbourne, Vic, The Miegunyah Press, 2007) 26, 46.

[48] See Lindell, 'Governor-General', ibid. 46–51, noting a range of views on whether there nevertheless is a reserve power to refuse a double dissolution.

[49] Declaration of Constitutional Practices, n 46, para A.

[50] On the complications of determining loss of confidence see Carney, n 9, 285–86.

[51] Declaration of Constitutional Practices, n 46, E and F.

[52] Cf Winterton, *Parliament, The Executive and the Governor-General*, n 30, describing the rationale as action 'absolutely necessary to ensure the effective operation of

In addition, however, Australian experience points to the possibility of a reserve power in at least two other sets of circumstances, on which there is much less agreement and that cannot be justified on the same basis. The first is to dismiss a government that retains the confidence of the lower House but is acting, or perceived to be acting, illegally.[53] On most accounts, the illegality must be 'serious' and 'persistent' and a reserve power should not be exercised if the question of legality can be resolved by a court.[54] The second is to dismiss a government that has obtained supply from the House but is unable to obtain it from the Senate and is unwilling to resign or to advise an election. This is the precedent of 1975, in which Governor-General Kerr dismissed Prime Minister Whitlam and commissioned leader of the opposition, Fraser, on condition that he could secure supply and would advise a double dissolution. The double dissolution that ensued was technically based on Fraser's advice, although hardly in a way that accords with the principles of responsible government. The Governor-General had been obliged to 'shop around' for an adviser that would give him this advice and Fraser did not have the confidence of the House: a fact starkly emphasised when the House voted no confidence in the new government before it was dissolved.

The circumstances that led to the dismissal of the government in 1975 were made possible by the combination of responsible government with the powerful Senate that federalism was thought to require. The Constitution makes no effective provision to resolve such a deadlock, in part because the framers did not anticipate that a Senate performing a distinctively federal role would have cause to reject bills appropriating moneys for the 'ordinary annual services' of the government. The development of the Senate primarily as a house of review rather than a federal chamber means that such a deadlock may occur when a non-government majority in the Senate considers it politically feasible to reject budget legislation in order to try to force the government to an election. Such a deadlock might be resolved by the Houses between themselves, as the political consequences of the failure to enact a budget begin to bite. In the circumstances of 1975, the wisdom of hindsight

parliamentary democracy': 152. Cf also Hazell, n 42, referring to the 'Governor-General's clear role to protect the Constitution'.

[53] For an account of the dismissal of Premier Lang by Governor Game on these grounds in 1932 see Twomey, n 40 642 ff.

[54] Carney, n 9, 286–89, citing authors to broadly similar effect.

suggests that the Governor-General acted too early, for this reason. A variant of this view would deny the power to dismiss a Prime Minister unless and until the absence of an appropriation for the ordinary annual services of government caused the government to act unlawfully, thus linking the two sets of circumstances in which the Governor-General may dismiss a Prime Minister who retains the confidence of the House.[55]

A reserve power to dismiss a government on the grounds of illegality nevertheless raises complex considerations. If there is such a power, its justification presumably lies in the rule of law and it implies a considerably expanded role for the Governor-General as a guardian of the Constitution. Unlike the reserve powers that are attributable to responsible government, however, this power is not necessary to deal with questions of legality, which generally can be left to the courts. Nor is the office of Governor-General appropriately designed to enable the holder to fulfil this role, by reference either to the qualifications for office or the security of tenure of the incumbent. Retention of the theoretical possibility of a reserve power in such a case is arguably misleading, creating an illusion of a check and balance in the Constitution that does not exist in reality.[56]

iii. The Republican Dilemma

The problem of the design of an Australian republic, in the sense of breaking Australian links with the monarchy and adopting alternative arrangements for a head of state, can be understood only against the background of the current system.

When a republic was first mooted in the 1990s, considerable faith was placed in 'minimalism', although for a variety of different reasons. In its most extreme form, minimalism would break the link with the Crown and replace the Governor-General with a President but would otherwise make relatively little change to existing arrangements. Minimalism fits with what is assumed to be an Australian preference for evolutionary change. It was considered by many to be the best strategy for success at referendum. It was attractive to political leaders, as a way of retaining effective control over the appointment and removal of the person performing the functions of head of state.

---

[55] Sawer, n 5, 161–62.
[56] Thus Hazell, n 42 describes the reserve powers as providing 'perhaps the most significant checks and balances in our system of governance'.

In essence, therefore, the proposal that was put to referendum in 1999 was an incremental development of the status quo.[57] It would have severed the links with the Crown in the Commonwealth sphere, leaving each State to take action on its own behalf. It would have provided for a President, to be appointed by a two thirds majority of a joint sitting of the Commonwealth Parliament, on a motion by the Prime Minister, seconded by the leader of the opposition. These requirements would have gone a long way to ensuring consensus on the appointment. Nevertheless, the choice of nominee would have rested with the Prime Minister, subject to an obligation to consider a short-list of proposals from a statutory Presidential Nominations Committee, more than one half of the members of which would have been appointed by the Prime Minister or the governing party.[58] The President would have been appointed for a five year renewable term and would have been removable by the Prime Minister with 'instant' effect, subject to an obligation to seek the approval of the House of Representatives within 30 days; refusal of approval by the House, however, would not have reinstated the President. The President would have been required to act on ministerial advice, codifying convention at least to this extent. The Constitution also would have recognised, however, that the 'President may exercise a power that was a reserve power of the Governor-General in accordance with the constitutional conventions relating to the exercise of that power'. Transitional provisions were designed to enable the 'evolution' of these conventions to continue and to prevent them from being justiciable, to any greater degree than they were justiciable before. The referendum was rejected in all States and approved by only 45.13 per cent of voters overall.

It is widely believed that the referendum failed in part because many voters prefer a directly elected President.[59] On the assumption that, on any view, a less easily manipulated process for both appointment and removal is likely to be required, the problem of designing an acceptable

[57] Constitution Alteration (Establishment of a Republic) 1999.

[58] A draft of the Presidential Nominations Committee bill was published at the same time. Of the 32 members of the Committee, 16 would have been community representatives appointed by the Prime Minister; the eight members from the Commonwealth Parliament would have been determined in accordance with the proportional representation of the parties in the Parliament.

[59] Warhurst reports an AES survey in 2007 in which 80% of respondents favoured direct election, with 50% strongly in favour: J Warhurst, 'The Trajectory of the Australian Republic Debate', Senate Occasional Lecture March 2009.

model is as follows. The more democratic the method or mechanism for appointing a President, the greater the legitimacy of the President, in his or her own right. If responsible government is to be preserved, it is undesirable in these circumstances to leave the President with broad legal powers, especially if the sanction of instant dismissal is removed. This problem could be overcome by specifying the manner in which presidential powers are to be exercised. Codification of the existing practices is difficult if not impossible, however, partly because of uncertainty about their scope and partly because of the disagreement that persists over whether the Senate should retain power to reject key appropriation bills and how such a deadlock should be resolved.

To meet these difficulties, it would seem preferable to consider what powers a President should have, in both form and substance, rather than to try to reach agreement on the past. This would be a good idea in any event, in view of the inadequacies of this part of the Constitution.[60] But it is a more creative exercise, which requires patience and committed leadership and which is susceptible to misrepresentation in a referendum campaign. The alternative is to resort to a minimalist model that retains the status quo as far as possible, but that already, in one form, has been resoundingly defeated. Since the rejection of the referendum, most of the focus, such as it is, has been on the process by which these decisions should be made, rather than on the substance of the model.[61]

III. GOVERNMENT

A. Composition

The executive branch is constructed around a 'Cabinet system',[62] with a Prime Minister at its head, which drives the development of policy and the management of government and which supplies the critical link in the explanation for the legitimacy of an exercise of executive power. The Cabinet itself comprises senior Ministers with portfolio responsibilities

---

[60] C Saunders, 'Beyond Minimalism' in S Murray (ed), *Constitutional Perspectives on an Australian Republic* (Annandale, NSW, Federation Press, 2010) 54.

[61] Senate Finance and Public Administration Committee, *Report of an Inquiry into a Plebiscite for an Australian Republic Bill 2008*, (2009) which proposes a national plebiscite to ask voters whether they support Australia becoming a republic as a prelude to further debate on design.

[62] See generally *Cabinet Handbook* n 23 above.

and others as determined by the Prime Minister. It meets weekly and is the forum in which decisions are taken on matters sufficiently significant to be deemed appropriate for determination at this level, including new policy proposals; expenditure; proposals for legislation; and treaty negotiations. The precise scope of Cabinet business, the nature and use of Cabinet committees and extent of Prime Ministerial authority vis-à-vis Cabinet vary between governments and over time.[63] The system presently also allows for two other categories of Ministers: those in the 'outer' Ministry without Cabinet responsibilities and parliamentary secretaries, who have limited ministerial functions.[64] In early 2010 the government comprised 40 ministers, 16 of whom were cabinet ministers (some with multiple responsibilities) and 11 of whom were parliamentary secretaries. All Ministers are elected Members of Parliament and remain Members of the House to which they were elected during their term in office.

Ministers are supported by what in Australia is termed a public service, organised in departments by executive arrangement, each of which is headed by a Secretary, who holds statutory office.[65] In addition to these, there are a large number of other agencies, statutory authorities and incorporated bodies, performing regulatory, scrutiny, adjudicatory, managerial or advisory functions and subject in varying degrees to ministerial direction and financial control. An Administrative Arrangements Order, issued by the Governor-General, specifies the matters to be dealt with by each of what presently are 19 departments and the legislation to be administered by each portfolio Minister. A distinctive feature of the Commonwealth approach to separation of powers is that administrative tribunals are not categorised as courts and are located entirely within the executive branch.

The claim that responsible government is a safeguard for the quality of government centres on this aspect of the system, rather than on the role of the Governor-General, speculation about the protective effect of the reserve powers notwithstanding. While no doubt it is important not

---

[63] On the relationship between Prime Minister and Cabinet see P Weller, *Cabinet Government in Australia 1901–2006*, (Sydney, NSW, UNSW Press, 2007) 277.

[64] For confirmation of the validity of the appointment of parliamentary secretaries to assist ministers in the management of departments see *Re Patterson* (2001) 207 CLR 391. On the rationale for this 'paradoxical' category of Minister see Evans, *Odgers Australian Senate Practice*, n 46. ch.19.

[65] Public Service Act 1999 (Cth) s 56.

to oversimplify the complex dynamics of the system, at the very least it assumes that the relationship of Ministers to Parliament, which is its defining feature, operates either as a quality control for legislation and executive action or as a mechanism through which fault can publicly be exposed for consideration by the voters at the next election. As the remainder of this part shows, however, the claim is overdrawn. Responsible government plays a role in ensuring quality and accountability but its effectiveness is necessarily patchy, on both counts. It is further undermined by a tendency of governments increasingly to rely on the exercise of executive power, in ways that are described in the next part.

B. Ministers and Parliament

i. *Collective Responsibility*

Ministers have both collective and individual responsibility to the Parliament. The critical features of the former are that ministers are appointed on the basis that they have the confidence of the House and that if this is lost, they vacate office altogether. Collective responsibility in turn both requires and fosters solidarity between ministers and thus strengthens the internal cohesion of the government. Cabinet Ministers are bound by Cabinet decisions, whatever stance they took in Cabinet and are obliged to support Cabinet decisions publicly and in the party room. Cabinet solidarity is reinforced by the confidentiality of cabinet deliberations; to that end, cabinet documents are shielded from both freedom of information legislation and discovery procedures in the course of litigation.[66] The obligations to maintain solidarity and respect confidentiality are extended to other ministers by co-opting them to cabinet when matters relevant to their responsibilities are under consideration. According to the *Handbook,* only one very senior official and two 'note-takers' attend cabinet meetings and the latter may be asked to leave if ministers wish to discuss issues privately.

Given political party discipline, a government is highly unlikely to be defeated in the House of Representatives and defeat in the Senate,

---

[66] Freedom of Information Act 1982 (Cth) s 34. Cabinet documents are not exempt from discovery as a class, but a court is unlikely to order their production in the absence of 'exceptional circumstances': *Commonwealth v Northern Land Council* (1993) 176 CLR 604, 605.

which is more usual, will not cause the government to fall.[67] It is more plausible that a government is placed under pressure from its own back-benchers in the privacy of the party room, if its actions are electorally unpopular and the opinion polls unfavourable. As such meetings are not public, the extent to which this occurs in practice is difficult to gauge, but the potential for it do so is clear. In this regard it also is relevant that in Australia the Prime Minister can be changed during a parliamentary term by a vote of the parliamentary party, leading to the formation of a new ministry, from the same party, but under a new leader. In a spectacular example, in June 2010 a Prime Minister elected with a sixteen seat major-ity in late 2008 was effectively forced to resign when it became clear that his deputy would win a leadership vote in caucus the next morning, in the face of adverse opinion polls.[68]

In normal times, however, the operation of cabinet solidarity in the party room strengthens the position of the Prime Minister and the cabi-net. The unlikelihood that change to government policy will result from party deliberations is suggested by provision in the *Legislation Handbook* for ministers to be reminded, in the week before a bill is due to be intro-duced into the Parliament, to send it to the relevant parliamentary party committee.[69] No procedure is suggested, should the party committee propose change. Other tools for backbench control over which the Prime Minister has some influence include the carrot of promotion to the ministry, the stick of loss of preselection and the blunt instrument of early dissolution of the House.

The opposition also has a role to play, as counterpoint to the cohesion of the governing party in the House of Representatives. Responsible government enables an opposition to publicly present itself as an alter-native government. Where the opposition is strong and co-ordinated, which is by no means generally the case, it may be able to use the presence

[67] For the (long) list of such occasions, see Evans, n 46, ch.19. The proposition in the text is subject to the exceptional case of defeat of a supply vote in the Senate, as in 1975.

[68] On the relative vulnerability of a Prime Minister where election remains in the hands of the parliamentary party, see Weller, n 63. 277. See also the replacement of Bob Hawke by Paul Keating as Prime Minister in 1991, allegedly in fulfilment of a prior agreement between the two, which would not be possible under more inclusive arrangements for selecting the Prime Minister.

[69] Department of the Prime Minister and Cabinet, *Legislation Handbook 2000*, ch.11.

of the ministers in the Parliament to flush out information, highlight flaws in the government's performance and prompt a sense of insecurity amongst the backbench. Particularly significant for this purpose is what John Uhr has described as the 'raw power' of question time,[70] which in the Commonwealth Parliament occurs each sitting day, involves all the ministers in each House and is televised live.

On the other hand, the government exercises substantial control over the procedures as well as the deliberations of the House of Representatives. Government business takes precedence over other business, including censure motions, on all except one day per week. The government can use its numbers in the House to close debate and, for that matter, to bring question time to an end. Questions alternate between opposition and government members, offering any harassed minister the promise of regular reprieve; and there is limited opportunity for supplementary questions.[71] The Speaker is a member of the governing party and may attend party meetings. While the Speaker nevertheless is expected to be 'impartial in the Chair', party affiliation makes a difference at the margin.[72] Again, the government has less control in the Senate when, as is usually the case, it lacks a majority there.

ii. Individual Responsibility

Ministers are also individually responsible to Parliament. Exactly what this requires when things go wrong is likely to be the subject of dispute, but it is unquestionably a key feature of the system. The Constitution describes ministers as 'officers to administer . . . departments of State' (s 64). Each Minister is assigned at least one area of government for which he or she is responsible. While the most important questions that arise are considered in cabinet and thus fall directly within the ambit of collective responsibility, the vast majority are not. Ministers are individually responsible to Parliament for these.

In relation to the areas assigned to them, ministers introduce bills, make parliamentary statements, answer questions, and appear before

---

[70] J Uhr, 'Ministerial Responsibility in Australia: 2005', quoted in P Rasiah, 'Does Question Time fulfil its role of ensuring accountability?', Democratic Audit of Australia, Discussion Paper 12/06, 2006, 6.

[71] For an analysis of the deficiencies of question time in the context of a case study on questions over the Iraq war, see Rasiah, ibid.

[72] Harris, n 15, 164.

parliamentary committees.[73] These procedures often are less comfort-
able for ministers in the Senate than in the House, where the government can use its numbers to control the outcome of a vote. Thus the
Senate is the site of an ongoing struggle between what a former Senate
clerk has described as 'the executive's claim for confidentiality and the
Parliament's right to know' in relation to claims of public interest immunity for government information.[74] Problems may be exposed through
these procedures in either House, weakening a minister and, if the matter is serious enough, affecting the government as a whole.

The ultimate sanction is loss of ministerial office. Resignation would
necessarily follow from passage of a censure motion in the House,
although in the Senate it has no constitutional consequences. Censure by
the House is effectively impossible as long as the government continues to
support the minister, however. If it ceases to do so, the Prime Minister is
likely to persuade or force the minister to resign rather than leaving it to the
House. In this situation, there is room for considerable debate about when
a minister should surrender office, voluntarily or involuntarily, in accordance with the principle of ministerial responsibility. The principal point
of difficulty is the extent to which a minister should be held to account
for serious errors in program administration. On the face of it, this would
be unreasonable, given the complexity of modern government. On the
other hand, the logic of assigning ministers departments to 'administer'
and requiring them also to be Members of Parliament suggests that they
are expected to take some form of responsibility for errors of this kind.

One relatively recent official statement of the position in Australia is
that where a minister 'neither knew, nor should have known about matters of departmental administration which come under scrutiny it is not
unreasonable to expect that the secretary or some other senior officer
will take the responsibility'.[75] The devil is in the application of this test:
it is not always easy to determine what a minister, as opposed to his
or her advisers or officers, has personally done and in the case of any

---

[73] A House may order one of its own members to appear before a committee. On
the procedures for inviting ministers from the other House to do so, or for seeking
leave from the other House, see Evans, n 46, chs. 2, 17.

[74] Evans, n 46, ch.19. For the outcome of a similar struggle between the upper
and lower Houses in New South Wales see *Egan v Willis* (1998) 195 CLR 424; also
Twomey, n 40, 27 ff.

[75] Prime Minister Howard, 'A guide to key elements of ministerial responsibility',
December 1998, ch.6; this part of the guide was not affected by the 'Standards of
Ministerial Ethics' issued by Prime Minister Rudd in 2008.

significant error it is generally possible to argue that a minister 'should' have done more. In relation to a controversy over whether the privatised Australian Wheat Board had made payments to the Iraqi government in breach of UN sanctions, for example, it could not be established that ministers had personal knowledge of what had occurred and it could not be agreed that they could or should have prevented it happening.[76]

In the absence of indisputable fault, of which misleading Parliament is an example, forced resignation of a minister depends on the political judgement of the Prime Minister, who in turn can rely on the solidarity of the government as a whole. The potential for sustained parliamentary criticism of a minister's failure to comply with public expectations of ministerial behaviour is a component of the political calculation. The gap thus exposed in the matters for which it is possible to hold individual ministers to account has been partly filled in other ways that are outlined in the next two sections.

C. Departments and Other Agencies

Traditionally, the public service was permanent, impartial and face-less, acting as advisers to ministers who in turn were responsible to Parliament. Typically, it derived its structure from an exercise of executive power, thus avoiding the conflict that may arise between political and legal authority if civil servants are empowered in statutory form.

To the extent that this 'ideal type'[77] ever existed in Australia, it has long since changed in important respects. Impartiality is listed as the first of the Australian Public Service (APS) values[78] and becomes even more important during the caretaker period leading to an election and in the event of transition to a new administration. But the most senior positions are no longer permanent and departmental secretaries may be changed by an incoming administration. Politicisation is encouraged not only by such changes at the top but by the greater exposure of public servants and, through them, their ministers, to parliamentary and public

---

[76] *Report of the Inquiry into Certain Australian Companies in Relation to the UN Oil-For-Food Program* (Cole Inquiry), November 2006.

[77] H Patapan and J Wanna, 'The Westminster Legacy: Conclusion' in H Patapan, J Wanna, P Moray Weller (eds), *Westminster Legacies: Democracy and Responsible Government in Asia and the Pacific* (Sydney, NSW, UNSW Press, 2005) 242, 245.

[78] Public Service Act 1999 (Cth) s 10.

scrutiny. Departmental heads have a range of both general and particular statutory responsibilities. Many government entities are established
by statute, sometimes to give them distance from the political process,
raising questions about how they are best accommodated within the
accountability chain.[79]

There are several respects in which departments and officers now have
a direct link with the Parliament, although both have been tailored with
ministerial responsibility in mind. First, every department and agency
is required to prepare an annual report for tabling in the Parliament,
through the minister.[80] The guidelines for annual reports are approved
by the statutory Joint Parliamentary Committee for Public Accounts and
require, for example, 'sufficient information . . . for the Parliament to
make a fully informed judgement on departmental performance'.[81] All
reports automatically stand referred to the relevant Standing Committees
in each of the Houses, although the attention they receive is somewhat
patchy.[82] Secondly, public service officers regularly appear as witnesses
before parliamentary committees. There are tensions over the evidence
that public servants may properly be asked to give. Government and
Parliament agree that while officials can be asked to explain government
policy they may not be asked their opinion about it, but they disagree
over the scope of public interest immunity that can be claimed.[83] Any
claim for immunity must be made by a minister 'who can accept political
responsibility' if a dispute arises.[84]

Uncertainty about the implications of responsible government for
the relationship between ministers and agencies where one or the other
has statutory power occasionally surfaces in legal doctrine. Where power
is conferred on an officer or agency, questions sometimes arise about
whether and to what extent the holder of the power can 'take into account
and act upon the views of the Government or a minister'.[85] Conversely,

[79] For the problem of directing questions to ministers concerning statutory
authorities see Evans, n 46, 502.

[80] Public Service Act 1999 (Cth) ss 63(2), 70(2).

[81] Department of the Prime Minister and Cabinet, *Requirements for Annual Reports*
(2008) 3.

[82] Evans, n 46, ch.16, dating more systematic scrutiny in the Senate to 1989. For
the House, see Harris, n 15, ch.18.

[83] Evans, n 46, 477; Department of the Prime Minister and Cabinet, *Government
Guidelines for Official Witnesses Before Parliamentary Committees and Related Matters,*1989.

[84] Evans, n 46. 431.

[85] *Bread Manufacturers of NSW v Evans* (1981) 180 CLR 404, 429–30 and the cases
there cited.

where a power is conferred on a minister, there may be implied authority to delegate all or part of it to a departmental officer, in recognition of 'the special position of constitutional responsibility that Ministers occupy'. But this is the case only where the nature of the function makes it 'unlikely' that Parliament intended it to be exercised personally by the minister.[86] In neither case is there an answer with 'universal application'.[87]

D. Integrity Institutions

Over the past 30 years or so, innovation in public institutional design has gathered pace, supplementing the traditional institutions of government with others, in order to deal more effectively with individual grievances, investigate claims of maladministration, enhance transparency, combat corruption, protect electoral democracy and regulate key services in the public interest. These sometimes are described as components of an 'integrity system' or, more ambitiously still, an 'integrity branch'.[88] The concept of integrity has been defined for this purpose as including, but going beyond, legality to require 'fidelity to . . . public purposes [and] . . . the application of public values'.[89]

Interest in integrity systems is a world-wide phenomenon. Three dimensions of the Australian arrangements deserve particular mention because of their implications for the operation of the executive branch.

The first is the system for review of administrative action, particularly as it operates at the Commonwealth level. From the mid 1970s a comprehensive reform package introduced an integrated review system comprising judicial review, tribunal review, an ombudsman and, ultimately, freedom of information, under the supervision of an advisory Administrative Review Council.[90] Of particular interest for present purposes is the generalist Administrative Appeals Tribunal (AAT), designed to accept jurisdiction from any area of Commonwealth

---

[86] *Minister for Aboriginal Affairs v Peko-Wallsend* (1986) 162 CLR 24. The question does not arise if, as is common, an express power to delegate is used.

[87] *Bread Manufacturers,* n 85, 429.

[88] On the integrity system generally, see BW Head, AJ Brown and C Connors, *Improving Integrity* (Oxford, Ashgate Publishing, 2008); on the concept of an 'integrity branch' see JJ Spigelman, 'The Integrity Branch of Government' (2004) 78 *Australian Law Journal* 724.

[89] Ibid, Spigelman, 725.

[90] Administrative Appeals Tribunal Act 1975 (Cth), Part V.

decision-making and thus equipped to offer a constant and high standard of 'merits' review. In exercising merits review the AAT and the small
range of specialist tribunals associated with it may substitute their own
view of what is 'correct or preferable' in the particular case and are not
bound by government policy, although in practice they is likely to follow
it.[91] Merits review has become a significant mechanism for responding
to individual grievances, thereby enhancing the accountability of public
decision-making.[92] It is sharply differentiated from judicial review, with
implications for the scope of the latter that are examined in chapter six.[93]

Freedom of information (FOI) deserves mention in its own right.
The Commonwealth introduced its Freedom of Information Act in
1992 and there is now broadly comparable legislation in all Australian
jurisdictions. The legislation requires agencies to make certain categories
of information publicly available; creates a right of access to personal
information; and also creates a right of access to public information,
subject to a range of exemptions, which include cabinet documents.
It has transformed the availability of information about the executive
branch. Nevertheless, there has been continuing controversy over the
scope of the exemptions and the techniques through which they are
given effect, including the use of conclusive certificates by ministers.
Transparency International has attributed some of the more restrictive
features of the Australian arrangements to the introduction of FOI legislation modelled on that of the United States into a parliamentary system in which the public service has a greater culture of secrecy. Major
changes to the Commonwealth Act in 2010, however, have tilted the
balance much further towards the release of information and may also
encourage cultural change. The objects of the legislation have been
linked to representative democracy; many previously exempt categories
of documents have been reclassified as 'conditionally' exempt, requiring
release unless access would be contrary to the public interest, which also
is narrowly defined; and conclusive certificates have been abolished.[94]

---

[91] See generally D Pearce, *Administrative Appeals Tribunal,* 2nd edn (Chatswood,
NSW, LexisNexis Butterworths, 2007).

[92] For the linkage with an integrity system, see R Creyke, 'Administrative Justice—
Towards Integrity in Government' (2007) 31 *Melbourne University Law Review* 705.

[93] P Cane, *Administrative Tribunals and Adjudication* (Oxford, Hart Publishing, 2009).

[94] Freedom of Information (Removal of Conclusive Certificates and Other
Measures) Act 2009; Freedom of Information Amendment (Reform) Act 2010.

The third of the new institutional initiatives is the range of anti-corruption bodies established at the State level. The establishment of bodies of this kind initially was a response to concern about corruption in several States in the 1980s, which in Queensland and Western Australia was exposed by major public inquiries.[95] New South Wales, Queensland and Western Australia now have independent bodies charged with dealing generally with questions of corruption, and consideration has been given to establishing similar bodies in other States as well.[96]

In 2004, Australia was ranked third on a public integrity index maintained by Global Integrity.[97] From the standpoint of institutional design, however, these are still early days. The concept of a distinctive grouping of integrity institutions is not yet sufficiently coherent to enable the intellectual construct of a 'system' to be used to develop and protect it. According to the three way categorisation of public functions that is dominant in Australia, all of the new institutions are located within the executive branch in the sense that they are not part of either the legislature or the judiciary. Interesting and generally effective steps have been taken to secure the independence of particular institutions, of which the Independent Commission Against Corruption (ICAC) of New South Wales provides an illustration: the commissioners must be former judges, with the independence that that implies; the Commission reports to the presiding officers of the two Houses of the Parliament; and a dedicated joint parliamentary committee has the responsibility of examining the Commission's reports and vetoing proposals for appointment by the Governor.[98] Even in this case, however, the committee has a majority of members from the governing party; the government initiates appointments; and the Commission depends on the executive branch for its budget allocation. The difficulty of creating an effective separation of powers within the executive branch is an old problem for constitutional law that has not yet been resolved, despite signs of minor progress.

---

[95] Fitzgerald Commission of Inquiry, 1987–1989 (in relation to Queensland), Kennedy Royal Commission into the Commercial Activities of Government and Other Matters, Western Australia, 1992.

[96] Z Gill, 'Corruption and Integrity Systems Throughout Australia', South Australian Parliamentary Research Library, October 2007.

[97] Australia, 'Integrity Scorecard', http://www.globalintegrity.org/reports/2004/2004/scores564a.html?cc=au&act=scores (viewed 30 July 2010).

[98] Independent Commission Against Corruption Act 1988 (NSW), Sch. 1; Part 8; ss 5, 5A; Part 7.

IV. POWER

A. Inherent Executive Power

i. The Nature of the Problem

The scope of executive power is a complicated question in any common law system, both because of its dependence on historical evolution and because of the variety of demands and opportunities for executive action. In Australia, these complications are overlaid by the effects of transition from colony to independence, shifting views within the Court about the relationship between the Constitution and the common law and the division of executive power between the Commonwealth and the States for federal purposes. The scope of executive power is explained against this background in the next section. The section that follows deals with a further complication: the impact of legislation on general executive power.

The starting point is section 61 of the Constitution, the relevant part of which provides that federal executive power 'extends to the execution and maintenance of this Constitution, and of the laws of the Commonwealth'. Insofar as the section recognises that executive power derives from statute, no difficulty arises. In practice every statute confers power on some person or agency within the executive branch and the reality need simply be noted. The debate turns on the rest of the clause. 'Execution' involves carrying out executive powers and duties under the Constitution: summoning the Parliament to meet after an election, for example, in accordance with section 5. 'Maintenance' has overtones of protection, at least against 'conduct antagonistic to the maintenance of Federal institutions and authority' but the activities that may be embraced by the concept of maintaining a Constitution potentially are very wide.[99] In any event, the choice of the verb 'extends' suggests that the components of executive power that are specified may not be exhaustive. Once this is accepted, it becomes necessary to decide what falls within the 'inherent' executive power conferred by section 61.

---

[99] The quotation is from *Australian Communist Party v Commonwealth* (1951) 83 CLR 1, 192; for a significantly wider construction of the phrase see *Victoria v Commonwealth and Hayden* (*AAP* case) (1975) 134 CLR 405–06.

George Winterton has helpfully analysed this problem as having two dimensions.[100] The first is the depth of executive power vis-à-vis Parliament: in other words, what can the executive do without parliamentary authority? The second concerns the width of the executive power of the Commonwealth vis-à-vis the executive power of the States or, in other words, the subjects with which federal executive power may deal. The first thus engages the principles of representative and responsible government and the second the principles of federalism. Most of what is a relatively small number of cases deal with one dimension or the other, often without clearly distinguishing between them, contributing to the complexity of the resulting doctrine.[101]

ii. Depth

The question of what can be done by the executive without parliamentary authority is an old and important problem in common law constitutionalism. In the United Kingdom itself there are competing analyses, which spill over into Australian jurisprudence. There is broad agreement that the inherent powers can be divided into two categories: prerogative powers, including, for example, the power to enter into treaties and other 'common law powers not unique to the Crown',[102] which arguably include powers to contract and spend, subject to justifiable scepticism about whether the exercise of such powers by government can ever be equated to their exercise by private individuals. There is, however, deep disagreement about whether the prerogative should be understood, following Dicey, as the 'residue of . . . authority . . . left in the hands of the Crown' or (also) as 'a discretionary power to be exercised for the public good', following Locke.[103] The answer on this point assists to determine the depth of executive power as a whole.

---

[100]   Winterton, *Parliament, the Executive and the Governor-General,* n 30, 29–30, 40–44.

[101]   C Saunders, 'The sources and scope of Commonwealth power to spend' (2009) 20 *Public Law Review* 256.

[102]   Winterton, *Parliament, the Executive and the Governor-General,* n 30, 121–22. In *Davis v Commonwealth* (1988) 166 CLR 79, 108 Brennan J distinguished between 'prerogative' power and 'mere capacities'.

[103]   AV Dicey, *Introduction to the Study of the Law of the Constitution,* 10th edn (1959) 424; *Laker Airways Ltd v Department of Trade* [1977] QB 643, 705, Denning MR, citing Locke. For detailed analysis of the differing views, see S Payne, 'The Royal Prerogative' in MauriceM Sunkin and S Payne (eds), *The Nature of the Crown: A Legal and Political Analysis* (Oxford, OUP, 1999) 77.

Whether or not the dichotomy between prerogative power and 'capacities' is accepted, it is settled that executive powers spanning both categories are conferred by section 61: thus the Commonwealth can enter into treaties, incorporate companies and make contracts, subject to the considerations of breadth, which are dealt with below. It is still far from clear, however, how the outer limits of executive power are determined, from the perspective of depth. The ambiguity of the common law in relation to the scope of the prerogative is exacerbated in Australia by uncertainty about the ambit of the concept of 'maintenance'. Moreover there are signs that the sands are shifting further, as the idea gradually takes hold that the common law on the prerogative is not the yardstick by which to determine the scope of the executive power 'in a written Constitution for an independent nation'.[104] There is some resonance between this development and the insistence in *Marquet*, noted in chapter two, that 'constitutional norms . . . are now to be traced to Australian sources'.

An approach to the construction of section 61 that begins with the text and places it in constitutional context is obviously sensible and appropriate. Equally, however, determination of its limits must surely take the common law as a base. Far from avoiding the 'intellectual agonies attending British constitutionalism'[105] current Australian doctrine is the source of considerable uncertainty about what the executive branch can do without parliamentary authority. The point is illustrated by the reasoning in the *Tampa* litigation in which the majority and minority justices were divided over both the tests by which executive power is determined and the relevance of the common law, in dealing with a challenge to the validity of the interception and boarding of a Norwegian ship carrying asylum seekers in Australian territorial waters and the expulsion of the asylum seekers from Australia. Black CJ in the minority identified the prerogative as the residue of authority left to the executive; found that it was 'doubtful' that the necessary prerogative existed at common law; and noted that it would be a 'very strange circumstance' if such a power were to emerge 'in a strong modern form' under section 61.[106] French J, with whom Beaumont J agreed, placed greater emphasis on the primacy of section 61 and appeared to adopt a more open-ended view of its

---

[104]   *Pape v Federal Commissioner of Taxation* (2009) 238 CLR 1, 60, French CJ.
[105]   W Gummow, 'The Constitution: Ultimate Foundation of Australian Law?' (2005) 79 *Australian Law Journal,* 167, 171.
[106]   *Ruddock v Vadarlis,* (2001) 110 FCR 491, 500–01.

scope, drawing on 'the idea of Australia as a nation'.[107] A similar notion is used to determine the breadth of executive power. While it plays a useful role in that context it is not yet clear how it helps to determine the boundaries of executive with legislative power.

iii. Breadth

However deep the executive power of the Commonwealth, it is tailored further by reference to its breadth. While this is, essentially, an aspect of the division of powers between the Commonwealth and the States it is convenient to deal with it here. Its impact on the scope of Commonwealth power to spend without authorising legislation is taken up again in chapter seven.

Logically enough, the principal yardstick is the Commonwealth's legislative powers, which are listed in greater detail in sections 51 and 52. Thus an executive power to declare war is the counterpart of the legislative power with respect to defence, whereas the right to exploit mineral resources typically lies with the States as the corollary of their power over land.[108]

Nevertheless, two questions arise. One, tracking the old division between forms of executive power, is whether considerations of breadth apply to executive 'capacities', or only to powers in the nature of the prerogative. The question is important because it determines the limits of the power of the Commonwealth to contract and to spend. While the answer is not settled, the stronger view is that considerations of breadth are relevant in assessing all claims of executive power so that, for example, a valid Commonwealth contract requires a link with a subject of legislative power.

The second question is whether and if so how far the breadth of executive power extends beyond the ambit of Commonwealth legislative powers. It is settled that it does so to some degree. While there have been various formulations, there is now broad acceptance that the executive power also extends to 'responsibilities . . . ascertainable from . . . the character and status of the Commonwealth as a national government', that are 'peculiarly adapted' to national government and that 'cannot otherwise be

---

[107] L Zines, *The High Court and the Constitution* 5th edition, (Annandale, NSW: Federation Press, 2008), 539.

[108] L Zines, *The High Court and the Constitution,* 5th edn (Annandale, NSW, Federation Press, 2008) 348.

carried on for the benefit of the nation'.[109] The 'nationhood' dimension of the power enables the Commonwealth to enter into agreements with the States, subject to the rest of the Constitution.[110] It also supported incorporation of a company to commemorate the bicentenary of European settlement in Australia.[111] In both examples, the activity is inherently national in character and in neither is it in competition with the States.

The potential for sometimes dramatically different views about exactly what this approach implies for the breadth of executive power was demonstrated graphically in 2009. In *Pape* a narrow majority of the Court upheld the validity of an economic stimulus measure that relied on the executive power to pay a 'bonus' of up to $900 to eligible taxpayers. For French J, who occupied the middle ground in the Court, critical features in favour of validity were that the stimulus was to be delivered 'on a scale and within a time-frame peculiarly within the capacity of the national government'.[112] The reasons of the other three majority justices on this point are more difficult to interpret but it is clear that they go at least this far.[113] By contrast, the remaining three members of the Court rejected the executive power as a basis for the tax bonus scheme, suggesting a significantly more restrictive view of the nationhood aspect of Commonwealth executive power.

To the extent that the scope of federal executive power exceeds federal legislative power, problems of principle arise for both responsible government and federalism. Responsible government assumes that Parliament can legislate to override executive power, which on the face of it would be precluded if executive power were broader. This problem is partly resolved by the legislative power in section 51(xxxix), which enables the Parliament to legislate for 'matters incidental to the execution of any power vested by this Constitution in . . . the Government'. The more effective section 51(xxxix) is for this purpose, however, the greater the potential for the extended executive power, reinforced by the incidental legislative power, to undermine the federal division of legislative power. This was also an issue in *Pape*, where the challenged

---

[109] *Victoria v Commonwealth and Hayden* (*AAP* case) (1975) 134 CLR 396–97, Mason J, accepted with varying degrees of enthusiasm by a majority of the Court in *Pape v Federal Commissioner of Taxation* (2009) 238 CLR 1.

[110] *ICM Agriculture Pty Ltd v Commonwealth* (2009) 240 CLR 140.

[111] *Davis v Commonwealth* (1988) 166 CLR 79.

[112] *Pape v Federal Commissioner of Taxation* (2009) 238 CLR 1, 23.

[113] C Saunders, 'The sources and scope of Commonwealth power to spend' (2009) 20 *Public Law Review* 256, 261.

legislation was arguably based on section 51(xxxix) in support of the executive power. Significantly, those justices who took a more restrictive view of the scope of executive power were able to take a correspondingly more robust approach to the scope of legislative power to control its exercise.[114]

B. Executive Power and Legislation

This final section makes three concluding observations about the relationship between executive power and legislation. In Australia, as in other common law systems, this relationship is in a state of flux. As the earlier section shows, under the Commonwealth Constitution it is also affected by the unsettled jurisprudence on the federal division of executive power and its relationship with the incidental legislative power. Insofar as Commonwealth executive power is broader than its substantive legislative power, it offers additional incentive to the Commonwealth government to rely on the former to achieve its policy goals.

The first and most obvious point is that, in principle, legislative power can be used to control activities supported by the general executive power. An example is the executive power to request a foreign state to surrender a fugitive offender to Australia, which the High Court accepted in *Barton* might be overridden by legislation, although as a matter of interpretation this had not occurred.[115]

Secondly, this point of principle in turn raises a question how to determine whether, as a matter of interpretation, legislation overrides executive power. The point is generally taken only in cases dealing with the impact of legislation on executive power in the nature of the prerogative and is thus affected by uncertainty about the actions that fall within this category.[116] In this context, the interpretive hurdle is surprisingly high, given the constitutional relationship between the executive and the Parliament. In *Barton*, Mason J referred to the need for a 'clearly expressed intention' to override the prerogative in accepting

---

[114] *Pape v Federal Commissioner of Taxation* (2009) 238 CLR 1, 120–21, Hayne and Kiefel JJ; cf the limitations on the incidental power recognised by Gummow, Crennan and Bell JJ at 87.

[115] *Barton v Commonwealth* (1974) 131 CLR 477.

[116] G Winterton, 'The Limits and Use of Executive Power by Government' (2003) 31 *Federal Law Review* 421.

that the executive retained power to request a foreign state to detain a fugitive offender with which Australia had no extradition treaty.[117] The *Tampa* litigation introduced an additional nuance. In holding that provisions of the Migration Act 1958 dealing with the detention of unlawful non-citizens and related matters left the claimed executive power intact, French J, with whom Beaumont J agreed, noted that the 'greater the significance of a particular executive power to national sovereignty, the less likely it is that, absent clear words or inescapable implication, the parliament would have intended to extinguish the power'.[118]

Finally, there is a distinct but related interpretive question concerning the circumstances in which legislation that 'regulates the conduct or rights of individuals' should be construed to apply to members of the executive government.[119] The emphasis of the applicable test for this purpose changed in 1990, from a requirement for express words or 'necessary implication' to a focus on the intention of the Parliament, as derived from the text and context of the statute.[120] As Winterton has observed, the contemporary conditions that drove this development are relevant to the impact of legislation on executive power in the nature of the prerogative as well and call for re-evaluation of the present doctrine.[121]

SELECTED READING

Cane, P, *Administrative Tribunals and Adjudication* (Oxford, Hart Publishing, 2009)

Commonwealth of Australia, Department of the Prime Minister and Cabinet, *Executive Council Handbook*, 2005

Commonwealth of Australia, Department of the Prime Minister and Cabinet, *Cabinet Handbook*, 2009

Lindell, G, 'Responsible Government' in Paul Finn, *Essays on Law and Government, Vol.1* (Sydney, NSW, Law Book Co. Ltd, 1995) 75

---

[117] *Barton,* n 115, 501.

[118] *Ruddock v Vadarlis* (2001) 110 FCR 491, 540.

[119] *Commonwealth v Western Australia (Native Title Act* case) (1999) 196 CLR 392, 410.

[120] *Bropho v Western Australia* (1990) 171 CLR 1.

[121] Winterton, 'The Limits and use of Executive Power', n 116 . There is an indication of movement in this direction in the *Native Title Act* case, 410–11, to which Winterton also draws attention.

——, 'Responsible Government and the Australian Constitution: Conventions Transformed into Law', CIPL Law and Policy Paper 24, (Annandale, NSW, Federation Press, 2004)

Murray, S (ed), *Constitutional Perspectives on an Australian Republic* (Annandale, NSW, Federation Press, 2010)

Sawer, G, *Federation Under Strain* (Melbourne, Vic, Melbourne University Press, 1977)

Weller, P, *Cabinet Government in Australia 1901–2006: Practice, Principles, Performance* (Sydney, NSW, UNSW Press, 2007)

Winterton, G, *Parliament, The Executive and the Governor General* (Melbourne, Vic, Melbourne University Press, 1983)

——, '1975: The Dismissal of the Whitlam Government' in HP Lee and George Winterton (eds), *Australian Constitutional Landmarks* (Cambridge, CUP, 2003) 229

6

Separation of Judicial Power

———➤●◄———

Principles – Commonwealth – States – Rule of Law

I. PRINCIPLES

A. Separation of Powers

S EPARATION OF POWERS has been described as a 'dominant principle' of the Commonwealth Constitution.[1] While its consequences for the relationship between the legislature and the executive have been severely restricted by the adoption of responsible government, its effect on the federal judiciary has been profound. The separation of judicial power is said to be 'pure or strict',[2] in the sense that it precludes not only the exercise of federal judicial power by any institution that is not a court within the meaning of the judicature chapter of the Constitution, but that it also prohibits a federal court from exercising power that is not federal judicial power. Thus understood it provides the principal explanation for several doctrines already encountered in earlier chapters: the inability of federal courts to give advisory opinions and the conceptualisation of Commonwealth tribunals as part of the executive branch.

The separation of judicial power also is regularly invoked, with mixed success, to assist to resolve issues that in other constitutional systems would be treated as questions about constitutional rights. It thus adds to the interest of Australia as a case study of the way in which the

---

[1] *New South Wales v Commonwealth* (*Wheat* case) (1915) 20 CLR 54, 90.
[2] *R v Trade Practices Tribunal; Ex parte Tasmanian Breweries Pty Ltd* (1970) 123 CLR 361, 389.

organisation of power in an entrenched constitution can play some role in rights protection, not only through the establishment of healthy institutions, which themselves are rights conscious, but also by operating as a constitutional constraint on the exercise of power in a manner that, as a by-product, has some rights protecting effect.

The evidence for the separation of powers in the Commonwealth Constitution is the dedication of its first three chapters to the legislature, the executive and the judicature respectively. Notably, the first section in each of these chapters makes a statement about the conferral of power on the institution with which the chapter deals. The principal evidence for the extent of the separation of judicial power is the specification in chapter III of the jurisdiction exercisable by federal courts. These provisions were necessitated by the decision of the framers of the Constitution to divide jurisdiction between the Commonwealth and the States for federal purposes. Nevertheless, they have been held to be an 'exhaustive statement of the manner in which the judicial power of the Commonwealth . . . may be vested', as a 'negative' implication of the detailed affirmative vesting of power.[3] Famously, as the doctrine developed, other indications to the contrary in the Constitution were dismissed.[4]

In its present form the separation of judicial power is vulnerable to criticism on the grounds of its impact on the flexibility of institutional design.[5] In the absence of constitutional rights protection, it has also emerged as the principal battleground for competing visions of the Constitution as an instrument that merely empowers the institutions of government and as an instrument that also constrains them. The attempts of the Court to accommodate the resulting pressures have given rise to a complex jurisprudence, with considerable uncertainty at the margins.

As it operates in the Commonwealth sphere, the separation of judicial power is interdependent with judicial independence and the rule

---

[3] *R v Kirby; Ex parte Boilermakers' Society of Australia* (*Boilermakers'* case) (1956) 94 CLR 254, 270; cf KM Hayne, '"Concerning Judicial Method"—Fifty Years On' (2006) 32 *Monash Law Review* 223, 226, describing the 'central step' in this conclusion as 'founded wholly in the text' of the Constitution.

[4] F Wheeler, 'Original Intent and the Doctrine of Separation of Powers in Australia' (1996) 7 *Public Law Review* 96.

[5] A Mason, 'A New Perspective on Separation of Powers' (1996) 82 *Canberra Bulletin of Public Administration* 1.

of law. Restrictions placed by the doctrine on the powers of the legislature and the executive to interfere with the exercise of judicial power complement other more specific mechanisms for the protection of judicial independence. Conversely, the impartiality of the federal judiciary equips it for the role of arbiter of the Constitution and serves to justify its separation from other branches.[6] These qualities also underpin the rule of law, understood to involve the application of the law through a process in which the parties have confidence. The rule of law is not the exclusive preserve of the courts. Nevertheless, in Australia, doctrinal developments have associated it so closely with the role of the courts that it is convenient to deal with it in this context, although detailed consideration of the ways in which the principle is used is postponed to the end of the chapter.

B. Checks and Balances

However strict a separation of powers, it is never absolute. Mutual checks and balances between the institutions of government are necessary in the interests of accountability and efficiency, as well as the effective disaggregation of power. Thus, it is a common constitutional arrangement for one or both of the legislature and executive to be empowered to appoint and remove judges and to fund and structure the courts, which for their part interpret and apply the laws, including the Constitution, in proceedings to which the other organs of state may be parties. Within a single polity, such checks and balances develop a dynamic of their own over time. One of the challenges for institutional design is to tailor the checks and balances to ensure that no branch intrudes further than is appropriate into the functions of the others.

The design of the judicature is complicated further in a federalised state. As a generalisation, most federations have either a single court hierarchy, which may or may not be regionalised at the lower levels, or a dual court system, with multiple court hierarchies.[7] The former administers the whole law and is relatively straightforward for litigants to use but consciously breaks the nexus between the courts and the other

---

[6] See *Boilermakers'* case, n 3, 276.

[7] B Opeskin, 'Cross-vesting of Jurisdiction' in B Opeskin and F Wheeler (eds), *The Australian Federal Judicial System* (Melbourne, Vic, Melbourne University Press, 2000) 299, 301–04.

institutions of at least one sphere of government. The latter preserves the institutional integrity of each polity, but at the cost of significant jurisdictional complexity. In comparative terms, the Australian judicature is a hybrid, the consequences of which can be examined through the prism of checks and balances. The authority to adjudicate is divided for federal purposes, creating the concepts of federal and State jurisdiction. The pre-existing colonial court hierarchies are left in place by the Commonwealth Constitution, which creates the High Court in which federal jurisdiction is vested and authorises the Parliament to create other federal courts. But this essentially dualist court structure is modified in two ways. Although it is essentially a federal court, divorced from the institutions of the State sphere of government, the High Court is a court of final appeal on matters arising in State as well as federal jurisdiction. And the Constitution empowers the Commonwealth to confer federal jurisdiction on State courts, coupled with only limited power to prescribe the manner of its exercise, rather than relying on courts of its own.

The flexibility inherent in the design of the judicature has proved useful, although with hindsight it lacks a foundation in principle, which is the source of some instability. In the immediate aftermath of federation both the appellate jurisdiction of the High Court and the 'autochthonous expedient'[8] of the exercise of federal jurisdiction by State courts were rationalised as features of the Constitution that were 'more national, and less distinctively federal' in character, made acceptable by '[c]onfidence in the integrity and impartiality of the Bench'.[9] This view was persuasive to the extent that the Commonwealth relied largely on State courts for the exercise of federal jurisdiction for more than 70 years.

Even during this period, however, Owen Dixon made his much-quoted observation that 'it would not have been beyond the wit of man' to establish a single court system that was 'neither Commonwealth nor State', pointing to the High Court as a step along that road.[10] And in

---

[8]   *Boilermakers'* case, n 3, 268.

[9]   J Quick and RR Garran, *Annotated Constitution of the Australian Commonwealth* (Sydney, NSW, Angus and Robertson, 1901) 804; see also 737. The authors here use the term 'national' to refer to features in which the 'duality of national and provincial interests' is not recognised: 339.

[10]   O Dixon, *Royal Commission on the Constitution of the Commonwealth: Report of Proceedings and Minutes of Evidence,* (Canberra, NSW, Government Printer, 1929) 794.

the course of the 1970s, in a move in the opposite direction, the latent dualism of the system began to emerge. The Federal Court of Australia was established, initially with a relatively limited federal jurisdiction that progressively expanded, on the basis of arguments about the need for federal judges to interpret federal laws and for the Commonwealth 'to be able to be sued and to sue in its own courts'.[11] The Commonwealth committed itself by statute to consultation with State Attorneys in making appointments to the High Court[12]: a relatively minor concession, which nonetheless reflects a desire on the part of the States to have some greater ownership of the Court. And attempts from the 1970s to investigate the possibility of the establishment of a single system of appellate courts foundered on several of the most critical issues for the relationship between courts and the other branches of government: the mechanisms for the appointment and removal of judges and the funding of courts.

In the most recent phase of reflection on the character of the Australian judicature, the High Court has described it as 'integrated'; a development that also is linked to the emergence of the concept of a single Australian common law. The unsettled line of authority built on this description, which is outlined in part 3, is testimony to its failure adequately to take the hybrid character of the Australian judicature into account. Nor is the description consistent with the reasoning of the court on other related issues. In *Re Wakim,* for example, two Justices rejected an argument that States might confer their jurisdiction on federal courts, by reference to 'the very nature of the judicial power' as ' "the power which every sovereign authority must of necessity have to decide controversies between its subjects, or between itself and its subjects"'.[13]

The design of the Australian judicature necessitates a more extended treatment of arrangements in the State sphere than in the earlier chapters on the legislature and the executive. First, in a sense, State courts are part of a national judicial system, from which certain consequences now flow under the Commonwealth Constitution. The national character of the judicature seems likely to be further enhanced over time by policy

---

[11] R French, 'Federal Courts Created by Parliament' in Opeskin and Wheeler, n 7, 123, 149–50, quoting Attorney-General Murphy.

[12] High Court of Australia Act 1979 (Cth), s 6.

[13] *Re Wakim* (1999) 198 CLR 511, 573, Gummow and Hayne JJ, quoting *Huddart Parker & Co Pty Ltd v Moorehead* (1909) 8 CLR 330, 357.

co-ordination between governments.[14] Secondly, however, because State courts are established pursuant to State Constitutions, in which there is no formal separation of judicial power, the rules that govern their structure and operation are significantly different and merit consideration for that reason.

C. Territories

This chapter provides an opportunity to note in passing another curiosity of Australian constitutional arrangements: the position of the self-governing territories. The federal rationale for the Constitution for a long time underpinned a view that Commonwealth power to make laws for the territories under section 122 of the Constitution, was unaffected by most of the constraints that applied to Commonwealth legislation that operated in the States.[15] This approach precluded the operation in the territories of the few provisions in the Constitution with rights-type effect. Relevantly for present purposes, it also affected the application in the territories of the provisions of chapter III of the Constitution, including the separation of judicial power. In recent decades the territories power has gradually been accommodated to the rest of the Constitution, although the process is far from complete and is complicated by the disparate characteristics of the territories themselves.[16] As far as chapter III is concerned, the general effect of these developments has been to assimilate the position of the territories to the position of the States, as outlined below in part three.

---

[14] Some proposals to this effect are examined in Senate Legal and Constitutional Affairs Committee, *Australia's Judicial System and the Role of Judges,* 7 December 2009, ch.5.

[15] *Northern Territory v GPAO* (1998) 196 CLR 553, 614–21.

[16] G Carney, *The Constitutional Systems of the Australian States and Territories* (Cambridge, CUP 2006) ch.10.6–10.8; on the territories generally, see chs 11–12.

II. COMMONWEALTH

A. Courts and Judges

i. Federal Courts

The Constitution provides for the judicial power of the Commonwealth to be vested in three categories of courts: the High Court; other federal courts, and State courts. Sections 75 and 76 identify nine heads of federal jurisdiction that may be conferred on such courts, some of which are defined by reference to subject-matter and some by reference to the character of the parties.

Until well into the second half of the twentieth century, the Commonwealth established courts of its own only in the highly specialised areas of bankruptcy and industrial relations. Most federal jurisdiction was exercised by State courts, although some of the more sensitive federal matters could be heard only in the High Court in the exercise of its original jurisdiction. A federal court hierarchy began to emerge in the 1970s, with the establishment of a Family Court and the more generalist Federal Court.[17] In the first decade of the twenty-first century, most federal jurisdiction in civil matters is exercisable by federal courts, although some is held concurrently with State courts, which also exercise jurisdiction under most federal criminal law.[18]

The development of a hierarchy of Commonwealth courts from the 1970s created the possibility, hitherto avoided, that legal disputes might raise issues that could satisfactorily be resolved only by two separate court systems. Typically, these were disputes that raised claims under both federal statutes and the common law. The doctrinal response was a principle that enabled a federal court to resolve all the legal claims raised by a 'matter' over which it had jurisdiction, including claims under State law, which were said to fall within its 'accrued' jurisdiction.[19] In 1988, in a more sweeping legislative response, the Commonwealth and each State and territory enacted complementary legislation to 'cross-vest' enough

---

[17] Family Law Act 1975 (Cth); Federal Court of Australia Act 1976 (Cth): see also the Federal Magistrates Act 1999 (Cth) establishing the Federal Magistrates Service.

[18] Judiciary Act 1903 s 39B(1A)(c).

[19] Eg *Philip Morris Inc v Adam P Brown Male Fashions Pty Ltd* (1981) 148 CLR 457; L Zines, 'Federal, Associated and Accrued Jurisdiction' in Opeskin and Wheeler, n 7, 265, 290 ff.

of their jurisdiction in each other's courts to enable participating courts to dispose of all litigation of which they were properly seized.[20] Doubts about the validity of the scheme were realised in 1999, when the High Court invalidated that aspect of it that enabled federal courts to exercise State jurisdiction, pointing to the exhaustive character of the provisions of chapter III.[21] *Wakim* confirmed that federal courts are confined to the exercise of federal jurisdiction, subject to the useful but limited reach of the concept of accrued jurisdiction.

ii. Judicial Independence

Judicial independence assists to preserve the integrity of the process offered by the state for the resolution of legal disputes. The perception of judicial independence is necessary to foster the willingness of litigants to submit their disputes to the judicial process and to accept the outcome. Both derive some protection from the separation of judicial power, which is examined in the next section. This section outlines the more specific constitutional, legal and conventional means on which the Australian constitutional system relies for this purpose.

As a generalisation, a culture of respect for judicial independence provides effective protection for it at the point of individual decision. As far as is known, attempts by parties, including the state, to directly influence the outcome of particular decisions by improper means are extremely rare in Australia, if indeed they occur at all. Once a decision has been delivered moreover, however unpopular it may be, it is invariably given effect, subject to the possibility of appeal. A tendency in recent years for politicians and media commentators to publicly attack the outcome of particular cases operates as a form of indirect pressure on courts and has caused some disquiet for its impact on their independence.[22] The solution, such as it is, is examined later in this section, as part of a more general question about how and by whom actions of the courts should be explained and defended.

The position of individual federal judges receives more formal protection. The Constitution entrenches, with some modifications, the mecha-

---

[20] Jurisdiction of Courts (Cross-vesting) Act 1987 (Cth) and corresponding State Acts; see also Opeskin, n 7, 314–16.

[21] *Re Wakim* (1999) 198 CLR 511.

[22] S Parker, 'The Independence of the Judiciary', Opeskin and Wheeler, n 7, 62, 85–87.

nisms for safeguarding judicial independence that have been associated with common law constitutionalism since the Act of Settlement 1700. Section 72 requires federal judges to be appointed by the Governor-General in Council; guarantees the maintenance of their remuneration during their time in office; gives them tenure, which in the case of the High Court is for a term expiring at the age of 70;[23] and protects them from removal other than by a process that involves both the Governor-General in Council and both Houses of the Parliament 'praying for . . . removal on the grounds of proved misbehaviour or incapacity'. Section 72 also assists to define a federal court for the purposes of the separation of judicial power, as a body the members of which must hold office in accordance with its requirements.[24] The section precludes the use of acting or temporary federal judges and protects the tenure of judges even if the court to which they belong is abolished.

Section 72 is a useful, but insufficient safeguard for the appointment, remuneration and tenure of judges, and its procedures have been supplemented in various ways.

The first concerns the appointment of judges. With very few exceptions, Australian judges, including Justices of the High Court, are appointed from a practising bar, sometimes via a lower court. Power to appoint lies solely with the executive branch and there is still strong support for this process. While it creates obvious potential for partisan appointments and there is occasional concern about particular appointments, in practice the results have been considered broadly satisfactory, in terms of both impartiality and quality, if not representation. Modest changes have been made in recent years to make the procedure somewhat more inclusive and transparent through advertisement of some judicial vacancies and publication of appointment criteria.[25]

Secondly, judicial remuneration is no longer adequately protected by preserving its value in monetary terms. In an attempt to protect both real value and relative value vis-à-vis other public sector office

---

[23] The original requirement for life tenure was altered by referendum in 1977: Constitution Alteration (Retirement of Judges). The tenure of judges of other courts may be set by legislation, with the age of 70 as the default provision, which also applies to Federal Court judges.

[24] *Boilermakers'* shows, however, that a body established in accordance with s 72 nevertheless is not a court if it exercises a preponderance of non-judicial power: (1956) 94 CLR 254.

[25] These are summarised in Senate Standing Committee on Legal and Constitutional Affairs, *Australia's Judicial System and the Role of Judges* (7 December 2009) ch3.

holders, federal judicial salaries are subject to annual review by an independent Remuneration Tribunal.[26] This model has worked reasonably well, although reconciling the maintenance of judicial salary levels with the political pressures to restrain public sector remuneration remains an ongoing problem.

The traditional mechanism for the removal of judges following an address by both Houses of Parliament under section 72 raises issues of another kind. It serves the important purpose of protecting judges against arbitrary dismissal well. On the other hand, it is too blunt an instrument to be useful for dealing with complaints against the judiciary in all but the most egregious cases, and may complicate the establishment of a body to deal with complaints of a lesser kind, along lines already developed in some States.[27] As formulated in section 72, moreover, the precise requirements of the procedure are unclear. On the one occasion when the section was invoked, uncertainty about both the meaning of 'misbehaviour' and the manner in which it might be 'proved' in the highly charged party political atmosphere of the Senate became apparent, although the questions thus raised were never finally resolved.[28] A recommendation by the Constitutional Commission in 1988 to alter the Constitution to require a 'Judicial Tribunal' to inquire into the allegations before proceedings are taken in the Parliament has not been implemented.[29]

At the federal level in Australia, the independence of a court as a whole is enhanced by the substantial administrative autonomy enjoyed by each court in managing its own global budget and administering its own affairs.[30] Since the latter part of the twentieth century, however, there has been intermittent concern about a threat from another source, in the form of new levels of public criticism of the judiciary, fuelled by the high profile of particular cases and a degree of significant tension between the executive and the courts. An assumption that the Attorney-General would defend the judiciary from criticism was shaken, when the

---

[26]   Remuneration Tribunal Act 1973 (Cth), sections 7(5A),(5B),(5C).

[27]   Senate Legal and Constitutional Affairs Committee, *Australia's Judicial System and the Role of Judges*, n 25. ch.7.

[28]   EM Campbell and HP Lee, *The Australian Judiciary* (Cambridge, CUP, 2001) 102–03, 108–09.

[29]   Constitutional Commission, *Final Report, 1988* (Canberra, NSW, AGPS, 1988) 402.

[30]   High Court of Australia Act 1979 (Cth), Part III; Federal Court of Australia Act 1976 (Cth), Part IIA; Family Law Act 1975 (Cth) Part IVA.

then Attorney observed that it was unrealistic to expect the holder of high elected office to play such a role.[31]

The anxiety caused by this plain-speaking receded after a subsequent Attorney accepted his 'obligation . . . to defend the institution of the judiciary from politically-motivated attacks'.[32] In the interim, however, the courts themselves had become more adept at self-help. Chief Justices typically play more of a public role, albeit with caution; several courts have appointed media officers; courts occasionally issue a more accessible public explanation of a high profile decision; and a Judicial Conference of Australia, formed in 1993, has assumed the obligation of 'informing the community about the proper role of the judiciary' and 'communicating with the other arms of government'.

iii. Personal Designata

Collectively, federal judges hold a variety of positions on tribunals and other law-related bodies, including the Administrative Appeals Tribunal (AAT).[33] In the past, federal judges have also been appointed to perform a range of non-judicial functions, including the issue of interception warrants. Judges may be sought after for such positions on account of their perceived impartiality as well as their experience and skills. On the other hand, appointments of this kind may jeopardise the actual or perceived capacity of judges to perform their judicial role.

Federal judges necessarily undertake such functions in their personal capacity and not in their capacity as members of a court, which would directly run foul of the principle in the *Boilermakers'* case. Even so, in recent decades the practice has come under increasing challenge, in the course of which constitutional limitations have been identified, prompting greater caution in its use. In brief, a judge must have an option to accept such a function or not and the function must be compatible with judicial office. A function may be incompatible if it physically occupies too much judicial time, if it impairs the capacity of a judge to perform judicial functions with integrity or if it impairs the integrity of the judiciary as an institution by, for example, jeopardising public confidence in

---

[31] D Williams, 'The Role of the Attorney-General' (2002) 13 *Public Law Review* 252.

[32] R McClelland, 'Interview' (2008) *New South Wales Bar News* 61, 64.

[33] The *Annual Report 2007–2008* of the Federal Court identified 25 such appointments to seven tribunals and other law-related bodies at 30 June 2008.

it.[34] These limitations are best understood as products of a wider doctrine flowing from the separation of judicial power, which precludes other branches from acting so as to impair the exercise of the judicial function,[35] although it also has been ascribed to 'the principle underlying the *Boilermakers'* case or to inconsistency with section 72.[36]

B. Separation of Judicial Power

i. Evolution of the Doctrine

It was widely if not universally assumed from the outset that the Commonwealth Constitution provided for a separation of judicial power of some kind.[37] Because the evidence lay primarily in the structure of the Constitution, however, albeit informed by an understanding of the Constitution of the United States, the nature and extent of the separation were equivocal. By contrast with other principles on which the Constitution rests, moreover, there was relatively little discussion during the Conventions about the separation of powers, the constitutional purposes it might serve and the form it should take in a constitutional system that, in important respects, differed from that of the United States. The purposes of the separation of judicial power in Australia have since been elaborated in judicial reasons in terms of liberty, institutional efficacy, due process and judicial independence; the last as a means to the protection of other constitutional values including federalism, individual rights and the rule of law.[38]

---

[34] *Grollo v Palmer* (1995) 184 CLR 348, 365. The third category originally referred directly to functions that diminish public confidence in the judiciary. The Court has subsequently rejected impairment of public confidence as a test of invalidity in the context of the conferral of 'incompatible' functions on a State court: *Fardon v Attorney-General* (2004) 223 CLR 575. The observation may in time be relevant in the present context as well, despite the 'inexact . . . analogy' between the two: 618.

[35] *Wilson v Minister for Aboriginal and Torres Strait Islander Affairs* (1996) 189 CLR 1, 22, Gaudron J; see also *Grollo v Palmer* (1995) 184 CLR 348, 392.

[36] *Hilton v Wells* (1985) 157 CLR 57, 73–74, 81.

[37] F Wheeler, 'Original Intent and the Doctrine of Separation of Powers in Australia' (1996) 7 *Public Law Review* 96, 98–99.

[38] For example, *R v Davison* (1954) 90 CLR 353, 381–82; *Attorney-General (Cth) v The Queen* (1957) 95 CLR 529, 540–41 (PC); *Grollo v Palmer* (1995) 184 CLR 348, 392–94; *Albarran v Companies Board* (2007) 231 CLR 350, 368–70.

Within two decades after federation it was settled that the judicial power of the Commonwealth could be exercised only by the High Court, a federal court established in compliance with chapter III of the Constitution or a State court.[39] It was not until 1957, however, that it became clear that, conversely, neither the High Court nor another federal court may exercise any other type of power. *Boilermakers'* upheld a challenge to the admixture of non-judicial arbitration powers and judicial enforcement and contempt powers in a single body, by invalidating the latter.[40] The body in question, the Commonwealth Court of Conciliation and Arbitration, was constituted in accordance with section 72 but lacked the character of a court because its primary function was arbitration. An immediate effect of the decision was to distance 'the administration of justice according to law' from the controversial activities of the Arbitration Court at a time of industrial unrest.[41]

The separation of judicial power is not absolute, in the sense that the *Boilermakers'* majority accepted that functions that are 'incidental or ancillary' to judicial power may also be exercised by courts. As the doctrine developed, it also was established that it does not preclude the power of the Parliament to punish for contempt under section 49 of the Constitution[42] or trial by courts martial under the defence power in a way that performs a disciplinary role and is integrated into the military chain of command.[43] Both of these historical practices were rationalised, however, as not involving an exercise of the judicial power of the Commonwealth. To that extent, they are not 'exceptions' in the strict sense.

Such qualifications aside, the separation of judicial power under the Commonwealth Constitution draws a brightish line between federal courts and other institutions, which encompasses the powers that they

---

[39] *Waterside Workers' Federation of Australia v JW Alexander Ltd* (1918) 25 CLR 434.

[40] *R v Kirby; Ex parte Boilermakers' Society of Australia* (*Boilermakers'* case) (1956) 94 CLR 254; on appeal to the Privy Council as *Attorney-General (Cth) v The Queen* (1957) 95 CLR 529.

[41] F Wheeler 'The *Boilermakers* case', in HP Lee and G Winterton (eds), *Australian Constitutional Landmarks* (Cambridge, CUP, 2003) 160; the quotation is from remarks by Sir Owen Dixon on his swearing-in as Chief Justice: (1952) 85 CLR xi, xvi.

[42] *R v Richards; Ex parte Fitzpatrick & Browne* (1955) 92 CLR 157.

[43] In *Lane v Morrison* (2009) 239 CLR 230 an attempt to enhance the quality of military justice through the establishment of a permanent military court, independent of the chain of command, was invalidated as an attempt to confer federal judicial power on a body that was not a Chapter III court.

respectively exercise. While dissatisfaction with the extent of the separation in its new form rumbled on for some time after *Boilermakers* was decided, it has now become a foundational tenet of the Commonwealth Constitution.[44]

ii. Nature of Judicial Power

The form of the Australian separation doctrine requires judicial power to be distinguishable from non-judicial power. This is a notoriously difficult exercise and judicial power has never been exhaustively defined in a way that enables outcomes to be reliably predicted in the many marginal cases that arise.

There are core characteristics of judicial power, which draw on a common law understanding of the role that courts typically perform. On the basis of these, judicial power involves a binding resolution of legal rights, duties and other questions, pursuant to sovereign authority, by reference to existing law.[45] As explained in chapter three, questions that arise in federal jurisdiction must also satisfy the constitutional requirement for a 'matter', reinforcing the need for an exercise of judicial power to take place in a context that provides a concrete setting for it.

In practice, however, reliance on these characteristics encounters standard difficulties. In the first place, not all the functions historically exercised by common law courts, including Australian courts at the time of federation, have characteristics of this kind. An order effecting a voluntary sequestration in bankruptcy is one example; rules of court are another.[46] By definition, many such functions might be 'treated from another point of view', as Dixon CJ put it in *Davison,* and entrusted to another type of body instead. Secondly, at least some of the functions performed by bodies that are not courts satisfy some, if not all, of the characteristics of judicial power. Many tribunals and administrators, for example, make determinations of the rights or status of people by reference to existing legal criteria, which in practice are likely to be final, although they lack the binding and conclusive character associated with

---

[44] *R v Joske; Ex parte Australian Building Construction Employees & Builders' Labourers Federation* (1974) 130 CLR 87.
[45] For an early formulation, see *Huddart Parker & Co Pty Ltd v Moorehead* (1909) 8 CLR 330.
[46] For these and others see *R v Davison* (1954) 90 CLR 353, 369.

judicial power.[47] Thus, in this sense, also, there is a degree of overlap between judicial and non-judicial power. These difficulties increased over the course of the twentieth century, as the Commonwealth exercised its legislative power, and specially its commercial powers to the full, using the burgeoning techniques of the contemporary regulatory state.[48]

To meet these difficulties, the substantive characteristics of judicial power have been supplemented by two others, which have regard to context. One accepts that historical use may assist to determine whether a function is judicial or not. According to the second, all else being equal, a function might take the character of the body to which it has been given, on the basis of assumptions about parliamentary intention. These two factors, and in particular the latter, have introduced considerable flexibility into the separation of judicial power, with consequences that are examined below.

iii. Extent of Separation

The Australian approach to the separation of judicial power relies primarily on definition to determine the power that the respective organs of government constitutionally may exercise. This type of 'definitional' analysis[49] can be contrasted with a 'functionalist' approach, which protects only the 'core functions' of each institution, enabling flexibility at the margin, where the purposes to be served by the separation of powers are not at risk.[50] Functionalism effectively was rejected by the majority in *Boilermakers*, although the reasoning of the minority Justices would have accepted variants of it.

There are signs, however, that a type of functionalism has emerged as a by-product of the definition of judicial power, in the course of resolving the problem of functions that have a 'double aspect'. It will

---

[47] On the meaning and effect of a conclusive or binding decision see *Brandy v Human Rights and Equal Opportunity Commission* (1995) 183 CLR 245.

[48] For consideration of the significance of the 'modern regulatory state' in this context see *White v Director of Military Prosecutions* (2007) 231 CLR 570, 595; cf 637.

[49] McHugh J in argument in *Luton v Lessels* [2001] HCA Trans 495 (11 October 2001). Strauss refers to the same idea as 'formalistic' with 'rather sharp boundaries': P Strauss, 'Formal and Functional Approaches to Separation of Powers Questions—a Foolish Inconsistency?' (1987) 72 *Cornell Law Review* 488, 489. See also J Finnis, 'Separation of Powers in the Australian Constitution' (1968) 3 *Adelaide Law Review* 159, 162–63, describing such an approach as 'Abstract'.

[50] Strauss, ibid, 489.

be recalled that one consideration that has been taken into account in characterising a function as judicial or not is the nature of the body on which it is conferred. This explicit reliance on parliamentary intention is coupled with a related assumption that Parliament intends the function to be exercised in a way that is characteristic of a body of that type.

As more marginal cases emerged, reliance on this mode of analysis in resolving questions about the separation of judicial power increased. Use of what came to be called the 'chameleon' principle[51] was offset by refinement of the idea, developed in a range of contexts, that there are certain core functions that are exclusive to the judiciary and cannot be conferred on a body of another kind. Such functions include the 'determination of criminal guilt and the trial of actions for breach of contract and for civil wrongs'.[52]

This development protected core functions to the extent of ensuring that they could be exercised only by courts, but had no necessary impact on the scope of the other functions that could be conferred on courts consistently with the *Boilermakers'* doctrine. In fact, if anything, the scope of potential judicial authority has tended to expand, under the influence of the notion that there are safeguards inherent in the judicial process that make it advantageous to confer functions on courts that would not otherwise satisfy the criteria for judicial power as long, at least, as analogous functions can be identified that were exercisable by courts in the past. Thus, in *Thomas*, a majority of the Court upheld the validity of the conferral of authority on the Federal Magistrates Court to impose interim control orders on persons who as yet had committed no offence on the application of the Australian Federal Police, for the purposes of protecting the public from terrorist acts.[53]

Counsel for the Commonwealth argued in *Thomas* that, thanks to the chameleon principle, '*Boilermakers* does not matter much anymore'.[54] The argument was repudiated strongly by the minority Justices.[55]

---

[51] The first use of the term for this purpose was by Aickin J in *R v Quinn* (1977) 138 CLR 1, 18; cf, in the United States, *Bowsher v Synar* 478 US 714, 751 (1986).

[52] *HA Bachrach Pty Ltd v Queensland* (1998) 195 CLR 547, 562; also *Albarran v Members of the Companies Auditors and Liquidators Disciplinary Board* (2007) 231 CLR 350, 358 and the cases there cited.

[53] *Thomas v Mowbray* (2007) 233 CLR 307.

[54] Ibid, 316.

[55] Kirby and Hayne JJ. See also the critique of frequent recourse to the chameleon principle by Kirby J in *Albarran* (2007) 231 CLR 350, 371–72.

Nevertheless, it points to the shift towards functionalism that has occurred, albeit without acknowledgement of doctrinal change.[56] Australian experience tends to confirm Strauss' warning that functionalism is a slippery slope, whatever its other advantages. More seriously still, because the change has been effected through the definition of judicial power, it has been accompanied by no analysis of the role that the separation of judicial power plays in the distinctive conditions of the Australian constitutional system and how this might be preserved under a different analytical framework.[57]

C. Constitutional Consequences

i. Courts and Tribunals

The separation of judicial power in the abstract form accepted in *Boilermakers* had a range of consequential effects on the Australian constitutional system. The most immediate was its impact on institutional design. Both the definition of a court in Chapter III of the Constitution and the limitation on what courts may do preclude the treatment of tribunals as a part of the judiciary and by default assign them to the executive branch. The prohibition on mingling judicial and non-judicial power, even in its watered-down state, also prevents the conferral on tribunals of powers to make binding orders, requiring recourse to the courts for this purpose. Thus, for example, a complaint to the Human Rights Commission may be handled only by conciliation, followed by the commencement of proceedings in a federal court if conciliation fails. In an attempt to minimise the resulting inconvenience, a relatively streamlined procedure for handling such proceedings has been devised, but the results continue to attract criticism in terms of cost, formality and delay.[58]

---

[56] For occasional reference to the approach as functionalist, however, see *HA Bachrach Pty Ltd v Queensland* (1998) 195 CLR 547, 562; *Albarran* (2007) 231 CLR 350, 363; and a query raised by McHugh J in *Luton v Lessels* (2002) 210 CLR 333, 336.

[57] There have been some attempts to encourage such an analysis: see for example, Kirby J in *Albarran*, ibid, 367.

[58] Human Rights Commission Act 1986 (Cth), Part IIB. For critique, see Senate Standing Committee on Legal and Constitutional Affairs, 'Effectiveness of the Sex Discrimination Act 1984 in Eliminating Discrimination and Promoting Gender Equality', December 2008, ch.6.

Even more remarkable testimony to the systemic implications of the doctrine was its impact on an organ ostensibly established and empowered by the Constitution itself. Section 101 mandates an 'Inter-State Commission, with . . . powers of adjudication and administration' in relation to the provisions of the Constitution dealing with trade and commerce.[59] This was the solution of the framers of the Constitution to the difficulty of exhaustively defining protectionism, for the purposes of the constitutionally protected freedom of trade. Within 15 years after federation, however, a majority of the High Court upheld a challenge to the validity of the conferral of judicial power on the Commission on separation of powers grounds.[60] The decision is taken to have emasculated the Commission, which ceased effective operation in 1920, apart from a brief reincarnation between 1975 and 1989. With hindsight, the relatively narrow constitutional role of the Commission was an additional and perhaps more serious source of weakness. In any event, as the example of other, active, quasi-judicial bodies shows, its failure cannot be attributed to the loss of judicial power alone. The outcome nevertheless serves both to demonstrate the dominance of the constitutional separation of judicial power and as an early indicator of its implications for institutional design.

ii. Procedural Due Process

A second important consequence of the separation of judicial power is the constitutional protection that it offers some of the attributes of procedural due process. As Fiona Wheeler has shown, there are two distinct ways in which such protection might be derived from the *Boilermakers'* doctrine.[61] First, there is no point in confining the exercise of judicial power to courts unless the courts themselves are obliged to exercise the power in a court-like way, with all that this implies in terms of an impartial determination according to law.[62] Alternatively, it might be argued that power is not relevantly judicial, so as to satisfy the constitu-

---

[59]   s 103 required appointment of Commission members for 7 years, thus effectively precluding its establishment as a chapter III court. s 73 further strengthened the Commission's claim to judicial power (to no avail) by conferring a right to appeal to the High Court from the decisions of the Commission on questions of law.

[60]   *New South Wales v Commonwealth* (*Wheat* case) (1915) 20 CLR 54.

[61]   F Wheeler, 'Due Process, Judicial Power and Chapter III in the New High Court' (2004) 32 *Federal Law Review* 205.

[62]   For example, *Polyukhovich v Commonwealth* (1991) 172 CLR 501, 607.

tional requirement that courts exercise only judicial power, unless it is exercised consistently with expectations of the curial process.[63] Each of these analyses has the similar effect of protecting attributes of the exercise of judicial power that are identified as critical to it. Writing in 2004, Wheeler was inclined to prefer the former, as a purposive analysis that avoided the labyrinthine complexities of the definition of judicial power. The increasing reliance on the chameleon principle, however, with its assumption that the distinctive mode of operation of a court enables some functions to be characterised as judicial simply because they are vested in a court, suggests that the latter may now be more plausible.

There is less agreement on which aspects of due process receive constitutional protection through the separation of judicial power. Inevitably, the starting point is common law standards for judicial procedure and in particular those that are deemed to have beneficial consequences in terms of safeguarding the 'life, liberty and property of the subject' from the exercise of arbitrary power.[64] It is now the Constitution itself as interpreted by the Court that is determinative, however. Successive judicial decisions, over a period of almost 20 years, suggest that the Constitution protects at least the core judicial role of determining facts and identifying and applying the applicable law to them in a manner that is accepted as fair and that generally promotes confidence in the administration of justice. It follows that the court itself must be impartial.[65] With only a few exceptions, hearings must be open and in public.[66] The rules of natural justice are constitutionally entrenched, at least to the extent of ensuring that parties can present their case to the court and challenge the evidence against them.[67]

There are two fields over which somewhat low-key but important battles continue to be waged. One concerns the extent to which a more general guarantee of a 'fair trial' is protected by institutional arrangements the purpose of which is to 'promote the supremacy of the law

---

[63] For example, *Harris v Caladine* (1991) 172 CLR 84, 150.

[64] *Polyukhovich,* (1991) 172 CLR 501, 606, Deane J, citing Blackstone, *Commentaries,* 17th edn, (1830) vol I, 269.

[65] See generally *Nicholas v The Queen* (1998) 193 CLR 173. On the relationship between the common law rule against bias and the Constitution see *Ebner v Official Trustee in Bankruptcy* (2000) 205 CLR 337, 368, 373.

[66] *Grollo v Palmer* (1995) 184 CLR 348, 379. For the exceptions, and the rationale for them, see F Wheeler, 'The Doctrine of Separation of Powers and Procedurally Entrenched Due Process in Australia' (1997) 23 *Monash Law Review* 248, 262.

[67] *Bass v Permanent Trustee Co Ltd* (1999) 198 CLR 334, 359.

over arbitrary power'.[68] Judicial decisions that accept, for example, that
the privilege against self-incrimination can be overridden by statute and
that statute also can alter the burden of proof, suggest that protection is
not complete, without identifying clear markers.[69]

The second contested field involves the interface between the constitutional requirement for adjudication to be left to the courts and the
constitutional authority of the Parliament to make laws that apply to
and are applied by the courts.[70] It is clear that Parliament may change the
substantive law, even when the change affects rights in issue in pending
litigation.[71] It is also clear that the Parliament may enact laws that govern
judicial procedure, of which the law of evidence is an example. It may
not do so, however, in a way that amounts to a direction to a court on
the determination of the issues before it.[72] It is not always obvious on
which side of this line legislation falls in this context. Thus in *Nicholas,*
a divided court accepted the validity of legislation that retrospectively
authorised the receipt of certain evidence obtained unlawfully as
long, at least, as the court retained discretion whether to accept it or
not.

iii. Liberty and Equality

It has sometimes been claimed that the separation of judicial power
provides a degree of protection for both liberty and equality, although
in most contexts these claims have been controversial and the jurisprudence is complex and unsettled.

It is convenient to deal first with equality. In *Leeth,* in dealing with
a challenge to the validity of legislation that effectively authorised different non-parole periods for federal offenders in different States, two
Justices would have resolved the case in favour of the applicant on the
basis of a guarantee of 'legal equality' implied from various features of

---

[68]   MH McHugh, 'Does Chapter III of the Constitution protect substantive as
well as procedural rights?' (2001) 21 *Australian Bar Review* 235, 240.

[69]   *Sorby v Commonwealth* (1983) 152 CLR 281, 308; *Milicevic v Campbell* (1975) 132
CLR 307.

[70]   P Gerangelos, 'The Separation of Powers and Legislative Intervention in
Pending Cases' (2008) 30 *Sydney Law Review* 61.

[71]   *R v Humby; Ex parte Rooney* (1973) 129 CLR 231; *Builders' Labourers Federation v
Commonwealth* (1986) 161 CLR 88.

[72]   *Nicholas v The Queen* (1998) 193 CLR 173, 185–88.

the Constitution, including the separation of judicial power.[73] Theirs was a minority view and the existence of the principle on which they based their reasoning was later expressly repudiated by a majority of the High Court, in rejecting arguments by the plaintiffs in the *Stolen Generations* case that the regulations authorising the removal of children from their parents were contrary to an implied constitutional guarantee of legal equality.[74] It may nevertheless still be arguable that protection for equality of a more procedural kind can be derived from the conception of judicial power, so as to prevent 'the conferral on courts of discretionary powers which are conditioned in such a way that they must be exercised in a discriminatory manner'.[75] While this also was a minority view in *Leeth*, it escaped express condemnation in *Kruger*, and subsequently received some support from Justice McHugh, both on and off the bench.[76]

Substantive protection for liberty, such as it is, derives from the principle that the Constitution precludes the legislature from exercising judicial power. It follows that the Parliament may not constitutionally enact a bill of attainder, in the sense of an 'enactment adjudging a specific person or . . . persons guilty of an offence'.[77] On the other hand, there is no present objection on constitutional grounds to the enactment of retrospective criminal legislation, as long as it is general in its application and leaves a court to decide whether an accused falls within its terms. Thus in *Polyukhovich*, a majority of the Court upheld the validity of legislation enacted in 1988 to provide that acts in the nature of war crimes, committed in Europe between 1939 and 1945, are offences against Australian law for which the accused could be tried, even though he was not an Australian citizen at the time the offences were deemed to have occurred.

Whether the same principle precludes legislation to authorise detention without trial is a more complicated story. In *Lim* three of the majority Justices characterised 'the involuntary detention of a citizen in

---

[73] *Leeth v Commonwealth* (1992) 174 CLR 455, 486–87, Deane and Toohey JJ; cf the different reasoning of Gaudron J, who found the flaw in the legislative direction to the courts to treat persons unequally: 501–02.

[74] *Kruger v Commonwealth* (1997) 190 CLR 1.

[75] Ibid, 112, Gaudron CJ; cf her definition of judicial power in *Nicholas* (1998) 193 CLR 173, 208–09.

[76] McHugh, n 63, 251-2; see also his reasons in *Cameron v The Queen* (2002) 209 CLR 339, 352-3; cf *Putland v The Queen* (2004) 218 CLR 174. See generally the discussion in Wheeler, 'Due Process' (2004), n 61.

[77] *Polyukhovich v Commonwealth* (1991) 172 CLR 501, 535.

custody of the State' as 'penal or punitive', existing 'only as an incident of the exclusively judicial function of adjudging and punishing criminal guilt'.[78] Even they acknowledged the existence of 'exceptional cases', however, including the detention of those with mental illness or infectious diseases or for custody pending trial.

The possibility that the range of exceptions was wider still caused the fourth majority Justice, Gaudron J, to treat the utility of this line of reasoning with scepticism.[79] She has been proved correct. The requirement that detention be 'punitive' before the function in question is characterised as judicial rendered the principle inapplicable to aboriginal children compulsorily taken into care in the circumstances examined in *Kruger*. It has given rise to a series of unedifying cases probing the circumstances, if any, in which the detention of 'unlawful non-citizens' in immigration detention centres, might fall foul of the separation of judicial power. It seems that it will not do so, as long as the purpose of the detention is 'reasonably necessary' to achieve some 'legitimate, non-punitive object', irrespective of the conditions in the centres, the age of the detainees, or the length of the period for which detention might occur.[80] More recently, yet another 'exceptional' case was identified, for detention of an Australian citizen pending extradition to another country for the trial of offences alleged against him without any examination in Australia of the validity of the charges.[81] And to compound the obscurity of the underlying principle further, in *Thomas* the High Court accepted that the Commonwealth Parliament could authorise courts, also, to deprive citizens of their liberty for non-punitive purposes, including preventative detention.[82] No doubt the principle remains important as a backstop against the flagrant use of arbitrary power, but its practical application has proved to be limited.

---

[78] *Chu Kheng Lim v Minister for Immigration* (1992) 176 CLR 1, 27, Brennan, Deane and Dawson JJ.

[79] Ibid, 55; see also her reasons in *Kruger* (1996) 190 CLR 1, 110.

[80] *Behrooz v Secretary, Department of Immigration and Multicultural and Indigenous Affairs* (2004) 219 CLR 486; *Minister for Immigration and Multicultural and Indigenous Affairs* (2004) 219 CLR 365; *Al-Kateb v Godwin* (2004) 219 CLR 562. The quotation is from the reasons of McHugh J in *Lim*, cited in *Al-Kateb* at 610.

[81] *Vasiljkovic v The Commonwealth* (2006) 227 CLR 614.

[82] *Thomas v Mowbray* (2007) 233 CLR 307.

iv. Administrative Law

Finally, the separation of judicial power has been used to explain a range of distinctive developments in Australian administrative law.[83] Because the doctrine is deemed to preclude non-judicial bodies from making final decisions about the scope of their own authority, it reinforces the constitutional protection for judicial review of executive action, at least in the federal sphere.[84] This development is linked to the rule of law and is taken up again in that context later; for present purposes, however, it should be noted that it has caused Australia to preserve the distinction between jurisdictional error, which must remain reviewable by courts and non-jurisdictional error, which need not, in sharp contrast to other common law jurisdictions.[85] In somewhat similar vein, the effective rejection for Australia of the notion that courts should defer to agency interpretation of statutes, as in the United States, has been attributed to Australian constitutional design,[86] although as Taggart has argued, its conceptual roots lie in the somewhat different institutional balance between Parliament and courts that is associated with common law constitutionalism in the British tradition.[87]

Viewed from the other end of the telescope, however, the separation of judicial power can be used not only to protect the authority of courts but also to constrain it. Of course, any argument that the doctrine confines the courts to the exercise of judicial power, understood as inhibiting their capacity to consider policy or to make law, has implications not only for administrative law, but for the style of Australian adjudication more generally.[88] In relation to administrative law, moreover, it is hard to separate the influence of the separation of judicial power on the scope of judicial review from that of other factors, including the institutionalisation of merits review through the establishment of the

---

[83] For a thoughtful, but highly sceptical, analysis, see M Taggart, ' "Australian Exceptionalism" in Judicial Review' (2008) 36 *Federal Law Review* 1.

[84] *Plaintiff S157/2002 v Commonwealth* (2003) 211 CLR 476.

[85] JJ Spigelman, 'The Centrality of Jurisdictional Error' (2010) 21 *Public Law Review* 77.

[86] The authority is *Corporation of the City of Enfield v Development Assessment Commission* (2000) 199 CLR 135; for the link with the Constitution see M Gleeson, 'Outcome, Process and the Rule of Law' (2006) 65 *Australian Journal of Public Administration* 5, 12.

[87] Ibid, 10–11.

[88] D Heydon, 'Judicial Activism and the Death of the Rule of Law' (2003) 23 *Australian Bar Review* 110.

Administrative Appeals Tribunal in 1975, along lines that also were dictated by the separation of powers. Granted the challenge of isolating cause and effect, it nevertheless is worth noting that the grounds of judicial review in Australia are relatively restrained, by comparison with comparable common law jurisdictions elsewhere, and that it has sometimes been claimed that the explanation lies in the constitutional separation of judicial power.[89]

III. STATES

A. Courts and Judges

i. *State Constitutional Framework*

Each State has its own court hierarchy, albeit with the possibility of final appeal to the High Court. Each State court hierarchy includes a Supreme Court at the apex and at least two levels of inferior courts. Some States also have specialist courts, to deal with, for example, land and environment disputes. Four States have established a Court of Appeal, as a distinct division of the Supreme Court.[90]

State Constitutions and legislation are the starting point for examining the legal framework for State court systems although, as the next section shows, they are now overlaid to a significant degree by Commonwealth constitutional principles.

In fact, the State constitutional framework for State court systems is patchy. Much is left to State legislation, which also deals with courts in a fragmented way. While all States except Tasmania make some reference to courts in their Constitutions, most of them are highly selective in doing so, typically dealing primarily with the sensitive questions of the tenure and removal of judges, leaving other matters to the statutes establishing individual courts.

More significantly still, constitutional provisions dealing with State courts are subject to a special alteration procedure only in New South Wales, where approval by referendum is required and in Victoria, where alteration requires absolute parliamentary majorities.[91] The prevail-

---

[89] B Selway QC, 'The Principle Behind Common Law Judicial Review of Administrative Action—The Search Continues' (2002) 30 *Federal Law Review* 217.

[90] New South Wales, Victoria, Queensland and Western Australia. On the structure of the Court of Appeal see, for example, Constitution Act 1975 (Vic), s 75A.

[91] Constitution Act 1902 (NSW), s 7B; Constitution Act 1975 (Vic), s 18(2AA)(b).

ing narrow understanding of the extent to which States can entrench their constitutions also suggests that the attempt to do so in these two States may be ineffective. The narrow view of State entrenching powers may, of course, help to explain the thin coverage of court systems in State Constitutions. As argued earlier in chapter two, however, the narrow view is unsatisfactory in principle and, as a dispensable relic of Australia's colonial past, may not survive careful re-examination by the High Court if and when an opportunity arises.

On the assumption that entrenchment is effective, it provides the judiciary in the two States in which it occurs with some State constitutional protection. In New South Wales it protects judges against arbitrary removal; in Victoria, significantly more fulsome protection is provided, in the form of a legal framework for the Supreme Court, which also encompasses its jurisdiction. It neither case, however, does the State Constitution entrench a separation of judicial power. Not only do State Constitutions lack the structural features of the Commonwealth Constitution from which the separation of powers has been inferred, but neither Constitution confers State judicial power on the judiciary in terms from which a negative implication might be drawn, precluding the mingling of judicial and non-judicial power.[92]

It follows that the constitutional rules applicable to State courts are considerably less stringent that those for the federal court system, as far as State Constitutions are concerned. State Parliaments can confer non-judicial power on courts and judicial power on bodies that are not necessarily courts; appoint acting or temporary judges; appoint judges to non-judicial posts. And they do. Thus, in all States the Chief Justice of the Supreme Court performs the role of Governor when the latter is unavailable, either formally as Lieutenant-Governor or otherwise.[93] The use of acting judges has reached 'significant' proportions: it has been estimated, for example, that 21.1 per cent of the judges in New South Wales were acting judges in 2003.[94] The intermingling of State judicial and non-judicial power is habitual and unattended by any concern about

---

[92] *Kable v Director of Public Prosecutions (NSW)* (1996) 189 CLR 1, 77–80; also *City of Collingwood v Victoria (No 2)* [1994] 1 VR 652.

[93] Carney, n 16, 271.

[94] See the statistics cited by Kirby J in *Forge v Australian Securities and Investment Commission* (2006) 228 CLR 45, 97–104. While counsel for the Commonwealth accepted these figures, their significance was disputed, in the absence of evidence about the volume of judicial work undertaken by acting judges.

the constitutional validity of the practice from the standpoint of State constitutional law.

ii. State Constitutional Standards

While State judicial systems typically lack State constitutional protection, they do not, for this reason alone, lack constitutional standards. In these circumstances, and leaving aside for the moment the impact of the Commonwealth Constitution, State courts are in the same position as courts in any other common law jurisdiction where the Constitution is uncontrolled. In other words, in the Australian States as, for example, in the United Kingdom and New Zealand, the standards applicable to the court systems rely on a familiar combination of legislation, constitutional convention, legislative and executive restraint and the principles of the common law applied by independent courts, which in this case include the High Court.

The result is considerably greater flexibility in institutional design in the State than in the Commonwealth sphere. This has been useful for polities whose practices in this regard were set before federation and that rely on adjudication for purposes that are even less easily pigeon-holed than those of their Commonwealth counterpart. Such flexibility also lends itself to experimentation as evidenced by, for example, the introduction of a Judicial Commission in New South Wales, with both educative and complaint-handling functions.[95] Experimentation can erode as well as enhance standards, however and maintenance of the integrity of State judicial systems requires vigilance. The increasing use of acting judges, for example, has been vigorously criticised by the legal profession and more subtly by the judges themselves and remains a subject of considerable unease.[96]

Nevertheless, as a generalisation, the conventions of judicial independence are broadly respected and the broad contours of a separation of judicial power are maintained. Protection for the tenure and remuneration of State judges is included in legislation, if it is not in the State Constitution, and while it is vulnerable to alteration, the proprieties

---

[95] Judicial Officers Act 1986 (NSW).
[96] See for example the Declaration of Principles of Judicial Independence by the Eight State and Territory Chief Justices of Australia, 1997, referred to in the Australian Bar Association, Charter of Judicial Independence, 2004.

are generally observed. State court systems also attract common law principles that govern the judicial process, in a way that tends to maintain standards. Thus the High Court has held that a State criminal trial should be adjourned if in the view of the judge it is likely to be unfair because, for example, the accused is unrepresented.[97] In similar vein, it has been held that it may be a 'miscarriage of justice' for a judge to be asleep or inattentive during a jury trial, causing a conviction to be set aside and the matter to be reheard.[98]

B. State Courts and the Australian Judicature

i. *Repositories of Federal Jurisdiction*

The power of the Commonwealth Parliament to confer federal jurisdiction on a State court is a distinctive feature of the Australian judicature. It was exercised shortly after federation, in sections 38 and 39 of the Judiciary Act 1903 (Cth), which confer most federal jurisdiction on State courts in a way that also removes from those courts any State jurisdiction that they may have possessed in relation to the same matters.[99] State courts continue to exercise substantial federal jurisdiction, although federal courts now have exclusive jurisdiction in a range of areas, including Commonwealth administrative law.

The obligation for State courts to exercise federal jurisdiction flows directly from the Constitution and there is no necessity for State consent. The quid pro quo, however, is that the Commonwealth has only limited power to structure the exercise of federal jurisdiction by State courts. Under section 79 the Commonwealth Parliament may prescribe the number of judges by which federal jurisdiction is exercised and it has incidental power to do whatever is necessary to effectuate these specific grants. Otherwise, however, it cannot affect the constitution

---

[97] *Dietrich v R* (1992) 177 CLR 292. Delay so serious that it would 'bring the administration of justice into disrepute' may also justify a permanent stay: *Jago v District Court of New South Wales* (1989) 168 CLR 23, 34.

[98] *Cesan v R* (2008) 236 CLR 358, 389.

[99] State jurisdiction in the areas of federal jurisdiction is overridden also by the Constitution itself: *Felton v Mulligan* (1971) 124 CLR 367, 373. This line of reasoning also precludes the exercise of State jurisdiction in an area of federal jurisdiction by a body that is not a State court: *Commonwealth of Australia v Anti-Discrimination Tribunal (Tasmania)* (2008) 169 FCR 85, 138.

or organisation of State courts and must, as the saying goes, 'take State courts as it finds them'.[100]

ii. Impact of Integration

To the extent that the Commonwealth Constitution deals with State courts, it necessarily overrides law and practice to the contrary in the State sphere. Thus, to take an obvious example, the right of appeal to the High Court from the 'Supreme Court of any State' under section 73 requires, in a roundabout way, the retention of State Supreme Courts. As the final part of this chapter shows, section 73 acquired new significance in 2010, when the High Court held that the Supreme Courts to which the section refers must comply with constitutional standards that include a 'supervisory jurisdiction' to enforce 'the limits on the exercise of State executive and judicial power'.[101]

Other institutional links between the federal and State court hierarchies have provided a rationale for another Commonwealth constitutional constraint on State court systems. What now is described as the *Kable* principle was sparked by a challenge to the validity of New South Wales legislation that authorised the continuing detention of a named person after his sentence had been served, on the ground that he was a potential danger to the community.[102] The legislative scheme involved the Supreme Court, by empowering it to make a detention order that was renewable every six months, if it was satisfied of certain matters, including that it was 'appropriate . . . that the person be held in custody'.

A majority of the High Court invalidated the legislation on Commonwealth constitutional grounds. In doing so, they drew conclusions from what now came to be described as the 'integrated' nature of the Australian court system under which, inter alia, State courts exercise federal jurisdiction that, when exercised by federal courts, is subject to all the safeguards of a strict separation of judicial power. While the actual holding in *Kable* was not clear-cut, it is now understood to stand for the proposition that a State may not confer a function on a court

---

[100] *Federated Sawmill, Timberyard & General Woodworkers' Employees' Association v Alexander* (1912) 15 CLR 308, 313; *Russell v Russell* (1976) 134 CLR 495; *Fardon v Attorney-General (Qld)* (2004) 223 CLR 575, 599–600.

[101] *Kirk v Industrial Court of New South Wales* (2010) 239 CLR 531.

[102] *Kable v Director of Public Prosecutions (NSW)* (1996) 189 CLR 1.

that 'substantially impairs its institutional integrity'.[103] It does not apply
the Commonwealth separation of judicial power to State courts, but
precludes their treatment in a way that is 'incompatible' with their role
as repositories of federal jurisdiction. The legislation in *Kable* was incompatible, partly because of its ad hominem application, but partly also
because of aspects of the procedure prescribed for the court, described
by Gaudron J as the 'antithesis' of the judicial process.[104]

By 2010 the *Kable* principle had been used again only once to invalidate State legislation; sparked this time by details of a scheme for the
'conscription' of the Supreme Court in making restraining orders under
criminal assets recovery legislation.[105] By contrast, despite *Kable,* the
Court upheld both an arrangement whereby the salary of the Chief
Magistrate of the Northern Territory was set only for two years by executive determination and the extensive use of acting judges at all levels
of the court system in New South Wales.[106] More significantly still, in
Fardon it upheld the validity of Queensland legislation empowering the
Supreme Court to make orders for preventative detention, distinguishing *Kable* on the grounds that the legislation in this case applied to a class
of persons and that the procedure to be followed by the court was better
adapted to the judicial process.[107] On the other hand, in several instances
reliance on the *Kable* principle has encouraged the Court to interpret
challenged legislation in a way that diminishes its implications for the
integrity of judicial process.[108] And in *International Finance Trust* Heydon
J drew attention to another 'extremely beneficial' effect of the doctrine,
as an incentive for the 'inclusion within otherwise draconian legislation
of certain objective and reasonable safeguards for the liberty and the
property of persons affected by that legislation'.[109]

---

[103] *Baker v The Queen* (2004) 223 CLR 513, 519.

[104] (1996) 189 CLR 1, 106.

[105] *International Finance Trust Company Ltd v New South Wales Crime Commission*
(2009) 240 CLR 319, 362.

[106] *North Australian Legal Aid v Bradley* (2004) 218 CLR 146; *Forge v Australian
Securities and Investment Commission* (2006) 228 CLR 45.

[107] *Fardon v Attorney-General (Qld)* (2005) 223 CLR 575, 614–17, identifying the
distinguishing procedural features of the legislation.

[108] *Baker v The Queen* (2004) 223 CLR 513; *Gypsy Jokers Motorcycle Club Incorporated v
Commissioner of Police* (2008) 234 CLR 532; *K-Generation Pty Ltd v Liquor Licensing Court*
(2009) 237 CLR 501; *Bakewell v The Queen* (2009) 238 CLR 287.

[109] (2009) 240 CLR 319, 379.

The challenge is to identify a general standard for the Australian court system, which also makes allowance for differences in the court systems of the several States within a judicature that is 'integrated, but not . . . unitary'.[110] So far this has been accomplished by focusing attention on the 'defining characteristics' of a court, which distinguish it from other public bodies.[111] At this point, however, the *Kable* jurisprudence intersects with the question of the definition of a State court. *Kable* requires the States to maintain the integrity of their courts, because of their role in the Australian judicature, as potential repositories of federal jurisdiction. In *Kable* itself, the consequence of failing to meet the requisite standards in relation to the State Supreme Court was invalidation of the offending State legislation. An alternative analysis, however, at least below the level of the Supreme Court, is to deny a body the character of a court and thus the right to exercise federal—but not necessarily State- judicial power. In *K-Generation*, two intervening States tried to take advantage of the potential circularity in the definition of a court by arguing that the Licensing Court whose powers were the subject of challenge in the case was not a court for the purposes of Chapter III of the Commonwealth Constitution. The argument was repudiated, on the ground that a State may not establish a body that meets the constitutional description of a court, while depriving it of the 'minimum characteristics of institutional independence and impartiality'.[112]

But on one view, the latter also help to define a court. *K-Generation* thus highlights one other limitation on Commonwealth constitutional protection of the integrity of State judicial process as presently conceived: that State judicial power can be conferred on a body that is not a court and exercised in a way that is free of the standards that the Commonwealth Constitution is now understood to impose.

IV. RULE OF LAW

A. General Conception

The rule of law has played an important role in Australian constitutionalism from the time New South Wales began to shed its character

---

[110] *Forge v Australian Securities and Investment Commission* (2006) 228 CLR 45, 65.
[111] Ibid, 76.
[112] *K-Generation* (2009) 237 CLR 501, 544.

as a penal colony to become a 'free society'.[113] By the latter part of the twentieth century, it had become a defining feature of the Australian constitutional system, as an indispensable component of an institutional approach to constitutional law. This section outlines the general conception of the rule of law, as it applies in both spheres of government. The next section concludes the chapter with a reflection on the interdependence of the Commonwealth Constitution and the rule of law.

The Australian conception of the rule of law is recognisably in the common law tradition as articulated by AV Dicey at the turn of the twentieth century.[114] Thus, at the very least, the rule of law assumes that punishment by the state takes place pursuant to law, which in turn is administered by independent courts, rather than as an exercise of arbitrary power; and that public officials, like everyone else, are subject to ordinary law, in ordinary courts. Equally, while the Australian Constitution leaves considerable supremacy to Parliament, it is tempered by the Diceyan assumption that once a law is enacted it falls to interpretation by the courts, influenced by 'the general spirit of the common law'.[115]

The similarities should not be overstated. The conception of the rule of law continued to evolve over the course of the twentieth century in Australia as elsewhere. In particular, it is now a commonplace that a developed system of administrative law, which in addition may involve the use of specialist tribunals, enhances, rather than detracts from the rule of law. The proposition that officials are subject to law has been lent greater verisimilitude by the weakening of the presumption of executive immunity from statute; the removal of procedural impediments to legal action against governments; and the expansion of judicial review to decisions taken pursuant to inherent executive power or by a head of state.[116] The development of a 'working hypothesis' that Parliament does not intend to abrogate rights unless it states its intention with 'irresistible clearness'

---

[113] D Neal, *The Rule of Law in a Penal Colony* (Cambridge, CUP, 1991) xii.

[114] According to van Caenegem, in this part of his theory Dicey drew on the work of DE Hearn, first Dean of the Melbourne Law Faculty: RC van Caenegem, *An Historical Introduction Western Constitutional Law* (Cambridge, CUP, 1995) 16.

[115] AV Dicey, *Introduction to the Study of the Law of the Constitution*, 8th edn (London, Macmillan, 1915) 120, 273.

[116] See respectively: *Bropho v Western Australia* (1990) 171 CLR 1; the various authorities cited in M Leeming, 'The Liability of the Government under the Constitution' (1998) 17 *Australian Bar Review* 215; *Minister of Arts, Heritage and Environment v Peko-Wallsend* (1987) 15 FCR 274; *FAI Insurances v Winneke* (1982) 151 CLR 342.

has strengthened the principles of statutory interpretation and is itself an attribute of the contemporary rule of law.[117]

Even so, however, the Australian conception of the rule of law remains essentially procedural rather than substantive and thin rather than thick. It is not offended by the absence of enforceable guarantees of rights or by failure to comply domestically with international law.[118] It co-exists with doctrines that accept the retrospectivity of legislation.[119] As the then Chief Justice Gleeson explained in his sixth Boyer lecture, at the core of the Australian conception of the rule of law is 'the impartial administration of justice' to which both citizens and government look to enforce legal claims that are derived from positive law.[120]

B. Constitution and the Rule of Law

i. *An assumption of the Constitution*

At one level, the linkages between the Constitution and the rule of law are obvious. To the extent that the separation of judicial power as encapsulated in chapter III of the Constitution protects judicial independence and the integrity of the judicial process it also enhances the rule of law. But there are statements in the case law that encourage speculation that the rule of law may have deeper constitutional significance in a way that gives it more substantive effect. The starting point in this regard is the *Communist Party* case in which, in the course of invalidating legislation to dissolve the Communist Party of Australia that purported authoritatively to assert the constitutional facts on which its validity relied, Dixon J observed that the rule of law was an 'assumption' of the Constitution.[121] This passage was quoted in *Kartinyeri* where, dealing with the potential for discriminatory use of the 'races' power, Gummow and Hayne JJ

---

[117] *Electrolux Home Products Pty Ltd v Australian Workers' Union* (2004) 221 CLR 309, 329.

[118] See for example the position of the majority Justices in *Al-Kateb v Godwin* (2004) 219 CLR 562; and cf Lord Bingham, 'The Rule of Law' (2007) 66 *Cambridge Law Journal* 67.

[119] *Polyukhovich v Commonwealth* (1991) 172 CLR 501.

[120] M Gleeson, 'The Judiciary' in *Rule of Law and the Constitution* (ABC, Boyer Lectures, 2000).

[121] *Australian Communist Party v Commonwealth* (1951) 83 CLR 1. See generally G Winterton, 'The *Communist Party* case' in HP Lee and G Winterton (eds), *Australian Constitutional Landmarks* (Cambridge, CUP, 2003) 108.

added that 'the occasion has yet to arise for consideration of all that may follow' from the idea of the rule of law as a constitutional assumption.[122] It was used again in *Plaintiff S157/2002,* not only in the context of construing an ouster clause, which is considered below, but also in rejecting the possibility, raised in argument by the Commonwealth, that the Parliament might delegate to the Minister 'the power to exercise a totally open-ended discretion as to what aliens can and what aliens cannot come to and stay in Australia'.[123]

So far, these remarks have proved to be much less open-ended than at first glance they appear. The only additional ways in which it is possible to say with any degree of certainty that the rule of law is given effect by the Constitution are as follows. First, and most obviously, the Constitution adds to the body of law by reference to which the rule of law operates. Secondly, the Constitution gives the courts both the authority and the responsibility to enforce the Constitution; at the very least, the *Communist Party* case stands for this.[124] Thirdly, chapter III entrenches the supervisory jurisdiction of the High Court and the State Supreme Courts. To this extent, Australia offers a rather old-fashioned example of the contemporary phenomenon of the constitutionalisation of administrative law. The next section considers this function in more detail.

ii. *Safeguarding Judicial Review*

The Constitution entrenches judicial review of the lawfulness of Commonwealth action through the heads of jurisdiction conferred on the High Court in section 75. Two are relevant in particular. The first is section 75(iii), which gives the Court jurisdiction in matters in which the Commonwealth is a party. The second is section 75(v), which confers jurisdiction over matters in which 'a writ of Mandamus or prohibition or an injunction is sought against an officer of the Commonwealth'. The protective effect of these paragraphs is reinforced by the separation of judicial power, to the extent that it prevents a body that is not a court finally determining the scope of its own authority.

---

[122] *Kartinyeri v Commonwealth* (1998) 195 CLR 337.

[123] *Plaintiff S157/2002 v Commonwealth* (2003) 211 CLR 476, 512–13.

[124] Winterton, n 121, 127. See also *APLA Limited v Legal Services Commission* (2005) 224 CLR 322, 351–52, describing the rule of law as an 'assumption on which the Constitution depends for its efficacy'; cf *Thomas v Mowbray* (2007) 233 CLR 307.

Between them, sections 75 (iii) and (v) ensure that the High Court has authority in its original jurisdiction to enforce the Constitution against or on behalf of the Commonwealth, even in the highly unlikely event that it is not invested with the general constitutional review jurisdiction pursuant to section 76(i). In addition, it appears that section 77(iii) removes the general procedural immunity from suit in contract and tort that the Commonwealth might otherwise have had.[125] It may be noted in passing that the references to the 'Commonwealth' and the 'States' in section 75 and elsewhere in the Constitution have avoided uncertainty about the extent to which the respective polities are juristic persons that are subject to suit and to that extent serve the rule of law as well.[126] Finally, and importantly, section 75 limits the effect of legislation that attempts to oust the jurisdiction of the Court to examine the lawfulness of Commonwealth action.

It does so by conferring jurisdiction on the Court to issue some of what originally were prerogative and equitable remedies against 'officers of the Commonwealth'.[127] The remedies themselves are now termed 'constitutional' and they draw meaning from their constitutional context in the same way as other constitutional expressions.[128] An 'officer of the Commonwealth' has been generously construed to include all those who hold a Commonwealth 'office', even when exercising power under State legislation.[129] One consequence of a prolonged struggle spanning the turn of the present century between the government and the courts over judicial review of decisions under the migration legislation was to confirm what in any event seems obvious enough on the face of the section: that, to some degree at least, it precludes ouster of the jurisdiction of the High Court.[130] This 'entrenched minimum provision of judicial review' extends at least to errors of 'sufficient gravity' to be characterised by the Court as jurisdictional in kind.[131] The section does not directly protect

---

[125]   *Commonwealth v Mewett* (1997) 191 CLR 471.

[126]   *Bank of New South Wales v Commonwealth (Bank Nationalisation)* (1948) 76 CLR 1, 363.

[127]   Despite its omission from the section, certiorari issues are ancillary to the other 'constitutional' writs: *Plaintiff S157/2002,* n 123, 507.

[128]   *Re Refugee Tribunal; Ex parte Aala* (2000) 204 CLR 82.

[129]   *Re Cram; Ex parte NSW Colliery Proprietors' Association Ltd* (1987) 163 CLR 117. State judges do not fall within the phrase, in yet another illustration of the duality of the court systems: *R v Murray & Cormie* (1916) 22 CLR 437.

[130]   See *Plaintiff S157/2002*, n 123 above.

[131]   Ibid, 513–16.

the jurisdiction of other federal courts although it may affect them indirectly where, for example, an ouster clause with application to all courts is read down to preserve its constitutionality.[132]

Self-evidently, section 75(v) does not protect the jurisdiction of State courts to review the lawfulness of State executive action. Until 2010, attempts by States to oust the jurisdiction of their courts were handled through techniques of statutory interpretation that discouraged, without invalidating, State ouster clauses.[133] As long as this situation prevailed, therefore, quite different rules applied to ouster clauses in the Commonwealth and State spheres.

As is evident from this chapter, there has been a growing tendency for the rules applicable to the federal and State court systems to converge, not withstanding their different constitutional settings. And so it has been with ouster clauses. In the seminal case of *Kirk*[134] the High Court held that the provision for appeals to the High Court from State Supreme Courts in section 73 of the Constitution requires the States to maintain Supreme Courts which, in order to satisfy the Commonwealth constitutional description, must have a supervisory jurisdiction over the State executive and State courts. Thus understood, section 73 effectively entrenches the same 'minimum provision' for judicial review as is protected in the High Court by section 75(v).

Kirk brings together many themes of this chapter: the progressive if complex integration of the federal and State judiciaries; the concept of the unity of Australian law; insistence on the role of independent courts in the Australian constitutional system. Consistently also with the established approach to constitutional interpretation, both *Plaintiff S157/2002* and *Kirk* purport to rely on constitutional text and structure avoiding, once again, overt reliance on the rule of law. The reasoning in both cases, nevertheless, is influenced by rule of law considerations. Their effect is to significantly reinforce it.

---

[132] *Plaintiff S157/2002,* n 123, 511; cf. *MZXOT v Minister for Immigration and Citizenship* (2008) 233 CLR 601.

[133] *R v Hickman; Ex parte Fox and Clinton* (1945) 70 CLR 598.

[134] *Kirk v Industrial Court of New South Wales* (2010) 239 CLR 531.

SELECTED READING

Aronson, M, Dyer, B, Groves, M, *Judicial Review of Administrative Action*, 4th edn (Sydney, NSW, Thomson Reuters, 2009)

Campbell, EM and Lee, HP, *The Australian Judiciary* (Cambridge, CUP, 2001)

Cowen, Z and Zines, L, *Federal Jurisdiction in Australia*, 3rd edn (Annandale, NSW, The Federation Press, 2002)

Crawford, J and Opeskin, B (eds), *Australian Courts of Law*, 4th edn (South Melbourne, Vic, OUP, 2004)

Gleeson, M, *The Rule of Law and the Constitution*, Boyer Lectures 2000

Opeskin, B and Wheeler, F (eds), *The Australian Federal Judicial System* (Melbourne, Vic, Melbourne University Press, 2000)

Senate Standing Committee on Legal and Constitutional Affairs, *Inquiry into Australia's Judicial System and the Role of Judges*, 2009

Wheeler, F, 'The *Boilermakers* case' in HP Lee and G Winterton (eds), *Australian Constitutional Landmarks* (Cambridge, CUP, 2003)

Winterton, G, 'The *Communist Party* case' in HP Lee and G Winterton (eds), *Australian Constitutional Landmarks* (Cambridge, CUP, 2003) 108

7

Federalism

———◆◆◆———

Principle – Power and Authority – Social and Economic Union – Co-operation

I. PRINCIPLE

A. Significance

i. *Federalism and the Constitution*

FEDERALISM IS CENTRAL to the Australian Constitution. Without federalism, the six Australian colonies would not have come together in a single political system at the end of the nineteenth century. The Constitution on which they agreed was designed to establish and protect the autonomy of two spheres of government that federalism requires. The Constitution was essential to Australian federalism, but the converse also was true: federalism provided the rationale for a written, entrenched Constitution, given overriding effect through judicial review. Absent the desire to establish a federal form of government, the Australians may not have felt any need for a Constitution that functioned as fundamental law.

Federalism permeates the written Constitution. The first three chapters divide legislative, executive and judicial competence between the Commonwealth and the States. Other provisions strengthen union through guarantees of internal mobility that assume the federal division of the territory. The few express rights protecting provisions apply only within the sphere of authority of the Commonwealth, leaving the States to determine their own standards. And significantly, as earlier chapters have shown, the framework for the institutions of Commonwealth government also reflects the federal structure of the state: in the design of the Senate; in the guarantee of minimum State representation in the House of Representatives; in the prohibition against federal electorates straddling State boundaries; and in the requirement for the approval of proposals for constitutional change by the people organised in States as well as by the people organised nationally.

ii. Form of the Federation

Were it not for the complication of colonial status, Australia would be an almost classic model of a federation that is formed by bringing together a number of formerly autonomous polities. Typical of a federation formed in this way, Australia has strong federal features. The six powerful States predated the Commonwealth as political communities. While the Constitution transformed them, formally, into the Original States of a new federation, it presumed their existence and preserved their structure and powers, subject to the agreed demands of federal union. The States are conceived as equals for constitutional purposes, despite disparities in wealth and population size. The Commonwealth has no constitutional authority to direct the States in the performance of their own functions.

As a further by-product of the manner in which the federation was formed, the Commonwealth and each State has its own set of institutions to exercise its allocated authority. The dualism of the institutional arrangements in the Australian federation further reinforces the autonomy of the respective orders of government. Equally importantly from the standpoint of other constitutional principles, however, it dictates the lines of democratic accountability from each government through its Parliament to its people, so that, in effect, each jurisdiction has a democratic ecosystem of its own. The co-operative exercise of power that is a hallmark of contemporary federations has profound implications for this institutional structure that are considered further in part four.

iii. Checks and Balances

By dividing and therefore limiting power, federalism provides one of the checks and balances of the Australian Constitution. This is not its primary justification, but it adds to the significance of federalism in the Australian constitutional context. Its role in this regard is greater still if two of the other checks and balances in the Commonwealth sphere, the Senate and the High Court of Australia, are understood also to be linked to the federal character of the polity: the former, most obviously, as a federal chamber and the latter as the judicial guardian of a federal constitution.

Considered as a check and balance, the federal division of power is a blunt instrument, with somewhat random effect. Sometimes, however, it operates to restrain excess of power, with rights-protecting effect. The Commonwealth can override State legislation that infringes human rights commitments under any international instrument to which Australia is a party.[1] And the federal division of power also constrains the Commonwealth in ways that sometimes protect constitutional values other than federalism itself. Thus in 1951, Commonwealth legislation that sought to outlaw the Australian Communist Party was held to be invalid, for want of adequate legislative power.[2]

The effectiveness of federalism as a check and balance is weakened but not necessarily eliminated altogether when Parliaments take collective action. The point is illustrated by a reference of power by the States to the Commonwealth in 2003 to enhance its capacity to make laws with respect to terrorist acts.[3] The reference was designed to overcome any shortfall in Commonwealth power of the kind exposed in the *Communist Party* case. Nevertheless, reputedly, the scope of the legislation enacted with the support of the reference was watered down in important respects that included the removal of 'shoot-to-kill' authority, as a by-product of the involvement of multiple governments.[4]

---

[1] Human Rights (Sexual Conduct) Act 1994 (Cth), overriding ss. 122, 123 of the Criminal Code (Tas) in reliance on Article 17 of the International Covenant on Civil and Political Rights. Its effect was confirmed in *Croome v Tasmania* (1997) 191 CLR 119.

[2] *Australian Communist Party v Commonwealth* (1951) 83 CLR 1; see also *Davis v Commonwealth* (1988) 166 CLR 79.

[3] Terrorism (Commonwealth Powers) Act 2003 (Vic). In the event, the Commonwealth legislation was upheld without relying on the reference: *Thomas v Mowbray* (2007) 233 CLR 307.

[4] A Lynch, 'Don't Lie Back and Think of England' (2005) *Human Rights Defender* 10, describing how the Chief Minister for the ACT made the Anti-Terrorism (No.2) Bill 2005 available electronically, thus providing an opening for public debate.

B. Countervailing Forces

i. *National Identity*

Despite its centrality to the written Constitution, the influence of federalism in the Australian constitutional system has been weakened over time by a range of other forces, including the rise of national identity, the combination of federalism with responsible government and the pragmatism that characterises the Australian approach to constitutional questions.

Any federation that is formed by bringing together distinct polities hopes for the development of a sense of national identity in order to strengthen the new union.[5] In Australia's case, the process was given early impetus by participation in the First World War.[6] National identity has been fostered by the homogeneity of a small and relatively mobile population, which also has been a catalyst for a corresponding decline in the sense of belonging to a particular State. In the latter decades of the twentieth century rapid development of the national economy, in response to international economic competition, became a further force for identification with the country as a whole.

These developments in turn have influenced judicial understanding of the character and purpose of the Constitution. In the immediate aftermath of the First World War the terminology of federal 'compact' was abandoned in favour of characterisation of the Constitution as a 'political compact of the whole of the people of Australia'.[7] This paved the way for a view of the Constitution articulated in *Pape* as a framework for national government, federally organised, under arrangements in which the Commonwealth enjoys 'comparative superiority' and which is

---

[5] In relation to Australia see J Quick and RR Garran, *Annotated Constitution of the Australian Commonwealth* (Sydney, NSW, Angus and Robertson, 1901), 340–41 : 'the nation will arise like a bridegroom coming forth from his chamber'. In less florid mode and only slightly later see observations of the first High Court in *Commissioners of Taxation (NSW) v Baxter* (1907) 4 CLR 1087, 1108.

[6] For the 'uniquely' distinctive character of Australian patriotism, however, see M Richardson, *Once a Jolly Swagman* (Melbourne, Vic, MUP, 2006) 170–71, describing it as 'sardonic, complicated, subtle and pervasive'.

[7] *Amalgamated Society of Engineers v Adelaide Steamship Co Ltd* (*Engineers'* case) (1920) 28 CLR 129, 142. For the terminology of compact see, for example, *Australian Boot Trade Employees Federation v Whybrow & Co* (1910) 10 CLR 266, 291.

no 'mere aggregation of the federating colonies'.[8] The shift draws on a version of the constitutional story that was present from the outset but that has grown in the telling, in that the Constitution was deliberately written, not only to enable the nation to evolve but to enable post-constitutional independence to be absorbed.

This perception of the Constitution underpins the interpretive method of the High Court. It has particular consequences for the federal division of powers but affects decisions on other federal questions as well, including economic union and the rules of choice of law. While the initial change was attributed, with unusual candour, to the emergence of 'national identity'[9] particular interpretive approaches more commonly are justified in technical terms informed by this constitutional understanding. Thus decisions that tend to expand the scope of central power and authority may be justified variously as the consequence of an approach to a federal division of power that leaves the States with only an unexpressed residue of power; as a corollary of the supremacy of Commonwealth law over inconsistent State law; or by reference to the Commonwealth as the heir to the authority of the imperial power in relation to Australia as independence was achieved.

ii. Responsible Government

A second feature of the Australian constitutional system that competes with the federal principle is the combination of federalism with responsible government, hailed by the *Boilermakers'* majority in 1956 as '[p]robably the most striking achievement' of the framers of the Constitution.[10] The framers themselves had been troubled from the outset, however, about whether the two were compatible. Their concern was that a powerful Senate, which at the time they accepted as indispensable to federalism, was incompatible with a system of responsible government under which the executive depended on the confidence of the House of Representatives.[11] This particular apprehension was realised in 1975, when the Governor-General dismissed a Prime Minister who retained the confidence of the House but was unable to obtain supply

---

[8] *Pape v Federal Commissioner of Taxation* (2009) 238 CLR 1, 85.

[9] For example, *Victoria v Commonwealth (Payroll Tax case)* (1971) 122 CLR 353, 397; *New South Wales v Commonwealth (Workchoices case)* (2006) 229 CLR 1, 193.

[10] *R v Kirby; Ex parte Boilermakers' Society of Australia* (1956) 94 CLR 254, 275.

[11] Quick and Garran, n 5. 127.

from the Senate, challenging the traditional understanding of responsible government. Aspects of this dramatic event are examined in chapters four and five.

But with hindsight it is possible to see that there are other ways as well in which these two sets of constitutional principles are in tension. Responsible government tends to concentrate power and to place a premium on speed and efficiency, tempered by regular elections. Federalism involves limited government and values diversity and pluralism, including pluralism in electoral choice. And while the written Constitution is overwhelmingly federal in character, responsible government has been claimed as 'the central feature of the Australian constitutional system'.[12] The outcome of the resulting clash of principle is an approach to constitutional interpretation that tends to favour central power without abandoning federal limits altogether.

Latent in responsible government, however, is a challenge to the institution of judicial review itself, either generally or in relation to the federal division of power. One version of this challenge parallels the influential argument of Herbert Wechsler in the United States, adapted to the different Australian institutional setting.[13] On this view, the courts should defer to a decision of the Commonwealth Parliament about the constitutional limits of its own powers because, at the end of the day, the governments of both the Commonwealth and the States are 'formally answerable to a unified Crown and . . . politically answerable to a unified . . . people', through the institution of responsible government.[14] The argument is underpinned by characterisation of federation as a means to 'enlarge . . . self-government'.[15] It also relies on the continued existence of the States, in order to contribute to the 'political interplay' on which, on this account, their responsibilities depend.

---

[12] *See Boilermakers' case,* n 10, 294. See also the quotation from Lord Haldane in the *Engineers'* case, n 7 at 147, in which the High Court, at least temporarily, abandoned federal implications: 'This bill is permeated through and through with the spirit of the greatest institution which exists in the Empire . . . I mean the institution of responsible government'.

[13] S Gageler, 'Beyond the text: A vision of the structure and function of the Constitution' (2009) 32 *Australian Bar Review* 138; H Weschler, 'The Political Safeguards of Federalism: The Role of the States in the Composition and Selection of the National Government' (1954) 54 *Columbia Law Review* 543.

[14] Gageler, ibid, 147.

[15] Ibid, 145, quoting the preliminary resolutions of the National Australasian Convention, 1897.

This is not a familiar way of thinking about Australian constitutionalism and is contrary to High Court observations about its own role. Given the way in which politics is played in Australia, it also overstates the checks on central power that can realistically be expected without an effective constitutional legal framework. At least from the standpoint of federalism, however, it is broadly—although not completely—consistent with the outcomes of a century of litigation, as the author has observed.

iii. Constitutional Pragmatism

A third and somewhat more speculative influence on the operation of the federal principle in Australia is the pragmatism that affects thinking about most constitutional issues. It may causally be linked to the influence of utilitarianism on early Australian constitutional ideas, to which reference was made in chapter one.

Hollander and Patapan have type-cast what they term 'pragmatic federalism' as 'problem-defined and problem driven'.[16] On their account, pragmatism not only affects policy-makers and courts in dealing with questions of federalism, but also channels public debate. As they observe, an approach to decision-making that is driven by consideration of concrete problems has potential advantages in terms of tackling immediate needs with relative speed and effectiveness. But it has longer term consequences for constitutional development that are less beneficial. In adopting particular solutions to particular problems, little attention is paid to flow-on consequences for the operation of the system of government. The result is that many decisions of a broader constitutional kind in effect are made by default; the progressive widening of the federal fiscal imbalance is only one of many important examples. The problem is compounded by the reluctance of the courts to engage with the values of federalism. The observations of Kirby J in the *Workchoices* case about the contribution of federalism to the protection of freedom 'in an age when the pressures of law, economics and technology tend to pull in the opposite direction' are a rare exception.[17]

---

[16] R Hollander and H Patapan, 'Pragmatic Federalism from Hawke to Howard' (2007) 66 *Australian Journal of Public Administration* 280, 291.

[17] *New South Wales v Commonwealth* (2006) 229 CLR 1, 229.

C. The State of Australian Federalism

i. Federation Without Federalism

One consequence of the various forces outlined in the preceding part is that Australia has a weak federal culture and that Australians, taken collectively, are ambivalent about their federal form of government. The position should not be overstated. In Australia, as elsewhere, there is a range of views on federalism. Attachment to devolution and choice tends to strengthen with distance from the national capital. History, geography, the federalisation of much private as well as public activity and the gravitational pull of the status quo give federalism deeper roots in Australia than sometimes may be supposed. There are inefficiencies in government from the centre, in a country that is geographically large and diverse. Nevertheless, complaints that Australia is 'over-governed' are common and the first decade of the twenty-first century was marked by unusually insistent calls for federalism reform.

At times, opposition to federalism spills over into calls for it to be abandoned.[18] Typically, the alternative suggested is a radical restructuring, to reduce the three spheres of Commonwealth, State and local government to two, either by abolishing the States or by reconfiguring State and local government as a single, regional tier, which might, but probably would not, be a partner in a new federation.[19] Given the extent to which a federal system built around a relatively small number of States pervades the institutions of constitutional government in Australia, such suggestions are impracticable, absent the will and the capacity to revise the entire Constitution, of which there are no signs.[20]

For the foreseeable future, therefore, Australia is likely to remain a federation, albeit one with a limited commitment to the federal principle itself. Parts two and three examine its operation more closely, from a doctrinal point of view. As in earlier chapters, both parts focus on relations between the Commonwealth and the States as the orders of

---

[18] G Greenwood, *The Future of Australian Federalism* (Melbourne, Vic, MUP, 1946).

[19] For a range of such proposals, see W Hudson and AJ Brown (eds), *Restructuring Australia: Regionalism, Republicanism and Reform of the Nation-State,* (Annandale, NSW, Federation Press, 2004).

[20] But cf the proposal of Tony Abbott MP, subsequently elected Leader of the Opposition, for a constitutional amendment to give the Commonwealth power to generally override State law: *Battlelines* (Melbourne, Vic, MUP, 2009).

government that enjoy constitutional autonomy. The two mainland territories function for most purposes as constituent units of the federation but are not subject to the federal constitutional framework.

ii. Form and Substance

The various pressures on Australian federalism manifest themselves in the way in which the federation operates in practice. The point was made earlier that judicial review has been centripetal in its overall effect, although the High Court continues to acknowledge its obligation to apply federal constitutional norms and its decisions are not all one way. More significantly still for present purposes, a vast network of co-operative arrangements between governments, underpinned by a fiscal imbalance in favour of the Commonwealth, has not only shifted the centre of gravity of the federation but has begun to affect its essential design. Thus, it might be said that Australian federalism has not only evolved from a co-ordinate to a co-operative (or even coercive or organic) form but that, despite the dualism of the constitutional structure of the federation, it now operates in many respects as an integrated model in which policies are formulated by the Commonwealth but implemented by the States and territories.[21] I return to this possibility at the end of the chapter, following closer examination of the nature and extent of co-operation.

II. POWER AND AUTHORITY

A. Model for Allocation of Power

i. Vertical, Partially Enumerated, Concurrent

The Constitution divides power between the Commonwealth and the States vertically, in the sense that the allocation of both executive and judicial power broadly follows that of legislative power. The division of executive power for federal purposes is examined in chapter five and the distinction between federal and State jurisdiction in chapter six.

[21] On co-ordinated, co-operative and organic federalism see G Sawer, *Modern Federalism* (Carlton, Pitman, 1976) 98; for the distinction between dual and integrated federalism see C Saunders, 'Legislative, Executive and Judicial Institutions: A Synthesis' in K Leroy and C Saunders (eds), *Legislative, Executive and Judicial Governance in Federal Countries* (Kingston, McGill-Queen's University Press, 2006).

Legislative power is divided by enumerating the powers of the Commonwealth Parliament in sections 51 and 52, effectively leaving the residue to the Parliaments of the States through the operation of section 107. Section 51 lists 40 heads of power 'with respect to' which the Commonwealth may legislate, subject to the rest of the Constitution. All are succinctly expressed, giving rise to a range of interpretive issues.

One large group of powers is broadly commercial in character: those dealing with interstate and overseas trade and commerce (i); postal telephonic and other services (v); banking (xiii); insurance (xiv); weights and measures (xv); bankruptcy (xvii); copyright (xviii); corporations (xx); and industrial disputes (xxxv) are examples. Another group is inherently national in nature: these include defence (vi); quarantine (ix); immigration (xxvii); and external affairs (xxix). A smattering of powers are more social in their orientation: marriage (xxi); divorce (xxii); the provision of a range of social welfare benefits (xxiii, xxiiiA); and, perhaps, the race power (xxiv).

Section 107 leaves State Parliaments with all their existing powers except those exclusively vested in the Commonwealth or otherwise withdrawn from them by the Constitution. The powers in section 51 are not expressed to be exclusive and so for the most part are concurrent, in the sense that they can be exercised by both the Commonwealth and the States.[22] By contrast, the few powers listed in section 52 are expressed to be exclusive. The most important of these is the power to impose duties of customs and excise. This model makes it difficult to categorically list the powers of the States. As a generalisation, however, the States are responsible for civil and criminal law, on-shore natural resources and most of the service areas of government including education, health, transport, housing and infrastructure and planning.

ii. Inconsistency and Conflict

Concurrency makes it necessary to decide which law prevails when two orders of government exercise the same power. In Australia, as in most federations in which this issue arises, Commonwealth law is supreme. Under section 109, in the event of inconsistency the Commonwealth law prevails and the State law is invalid, 'to the extent of the inconsist-

---

[22]   But cf the powers over defence (vi) and currency (xii), effectively made exclusive by sections 114 and 115 respectively.

ency'. Invalidity is understood to make the State law inoperative, so that it revives if the inconsistency is removed.[23]

The most important of many questions raised by this section is the meaning of inconsistency itself. It has long since been established that inconsistency may arise indirectly as well as directly, where a Commonwealth law manifests an intention to cover an entire legislative field and the State law purports to intrude upon it.[24] It is established also that two laws may be directly inconsistent even when it is theoretically possible to obey them both: a State law that denies a right created by a Commonwealth law is an example. The variety of ways in which the laws of different jurisdictions in the same polity may come into conflict, however, makes it impracticable to categorise exhaustively the circumstances in which a State law might 'alter, impair, or detract from' the operation of a Commonwealth law so as to attract section 109.[25] It is also presently uncertain to what extent inconsistency can be grounded in the practical effect, as opposed to the legal operation of the laws.[26]

Section 109 was once characterised by a Justice of the High Court as an express constitutional guarantee 'against being subjected to inconsistent demands by contemporaneously valid laws'.[27] This view has been accepted since, and analysis often turns on the centrality of the section. Parliament may deny an intention to cover the field in order to save the application of State laws but the latter will be invalid nevertheless, by virtue of section 109, if direct inconsistency is found. Parliament can evince an intention to cover a legislative field and thereby attract section 109 but it may not legislate directly to oust State law.[28] Most strikingly of all, the Parliament cannot legislate retrospectively to deny an intention to cover the field if there was an inconsistency between two Acts as they originally stood within the terms of section 109.[29]

---

[23] *Western Australia v Commonwealth* (*Native Title Act* case) (1995) 183 CLR 373, 464.
[24] *R v McLean* (1930) 43 CLR 472, 483, Dixon J, also noting that the doctrine does not apply if the State law deals with a different subject.
[25] *Victoria v Commonwealth* (1937) 58 CLR 618, 630; *Telstra v Worthing* (1999) 197 CLR 61.
[26] *APLA Ltd v Legal Services Commissioner (NSW)* (2005) 224 CLR 322.
[27] *Street v Queensland Bar Association* (1989) 168 CLR 461, 522; *Dickson v The Queen* [2010] HCA 30.
[28] *Wenn v Attorney-General (Vic)* (1948) 77 CLR 84, 120. There is a fine line between the two, particularly where the Commonwealth law is deregulatory: *New South Wales v Commonwealth* (*Workchoices* case) (2006) 229 CLR 1, 166.
[29] *University of Wollongong v Metwally* (1984) 158 CLR 447.

B. Legislative Power

i. Principles of Interpretation

As recounted in chapter three, 1920 was a turning point in constitutional interpretation. In the *Engineers'* case, the High Court repudiated earlier approaches to the interpretation and application of Commonwealth legislative powers that had relied on two implications drawn from the federal character of the Constitution. The first assumed that the 'instrumentalities' of each order of government were largely immune from the laws of others. The second required ambiguities in the meaning or scope of Commonwealth power to be resolved by reference to powers notionally reserved to the States by section 107 as well as contextually, by reference to other heads of power. In their place, the High Court adopted a new interpretive approach, more closely aligned with the principles of statutory interpretation.[30]

In practice, the interpretive challenge proved more complex. Textual ambiguities, changing circumstances and novel applications of powers became catalysts for the development of a range of techniques to assist in resolving the two central questions that regularly arose: how to determine the meaning of a power and how to establish whether a challenged law was one 'with respect to' a head or heads of power. For both these purposes, nevertheless, *Engineers'* remains the foundation case. Typically, the Court interprets each head of power in isolation from the others.[31] And it invariably rejects argument about the scope of Commonwealth power that involves consideration of the power of the States.[32] The result has been the consistent expansion of the reach of Commonwealth power. Certain heads of power have proved particularly adaptable to creative use: taxation, corporations and external affairs. Ironically, however, in view of the role of the commerce clause in the United States, the interstate trade and commerce power is not amongst them. The High Court has so far interpreted section 51(i) so as

---

[30] *Amalgamated Society of Engineers v Adelaide Steamship Co Ltd* (*Engineers'* case) (1920) 28 CLR 129, 152.

[31] The categories of possible exceptions are examined in L Zines, *The High Court and the Constitution*, 5th edn (Annandale, NSW, Federation Press, 2008) 32.

[32] State power was taken into account in determining whether a law was supported by the incidental power in *Gazzo v Comptroller of Stamps (Vic)* (1981) 149 CLR 227; the status of this approach is no longer clear.

to maintain the distinction between interstate and intrastate trade unless the two are physically intertwined.[33]

By contrast, the notion that each order of government is protected to some degree from the exercise of power by the other has re-entered Australian jurisprudence, albeit in new forms. This development is less noteworthy as far as the Commonwealth is concerned. Ever since *Engineers'*, it has been accepted that Commonwealth power exercised pursuant to statute is likely to be protected from State legislation by the operation of section 109 and that Commonwealth action in the exercise of what once was the prerogative is protected directly by the Constitution. In these circumstances the challenge has been, rather, to ensure that Commonwealth action is subject to general State law, consistently with the rule of law. While the doctrine is not entirely stable, this has now been achieved. State law may not impair the 'capacities' of the Commonwealth but it can regulate activities, such as leasing property, in which the Commonwealth chooses to engage.[34]

The limitation on Commonwealth power vis-à-vis the States, on the other hand, is a departure from *Engineers'*. Over a period of more than half a century, the High Court has developed a doctrine that, as now formulated, precludes Commonwealth legislation that impairs the capacity of States to 'function effectually as independent units'.[35] This deliberately vague principle may, depending on the circumstances, be infringed either by a Commonwealth law of general application that impinges on the capacity of a State to function as a government or by a Commonwealth law that singles out and places a special burden on one or more States. Its justification draws on an understanding of 'the conception of a central government and a number of State governments separately organised' as '[t]he foundation of the Constitution' which 'predicates their continued existence as independent entities'.[36] The principle has been applied on one or other of these bases to invalidate

[33] *Airlines of New South Wales Pty Ltd v New South Wales (No 2)* (1965) 113 CR 54; cf *Attorney-General (WA) v Australian National Airlines Commission* (1976) 138 CLR 492. Cf *Betfair Pty Ltd v Western Australia* (2008) 234 CLR 418, 476.

[34] *Re Residential Tenancies Tribunal (NSW); Ex parte Defence Housing Authority* (1997) 190 CLR 410, 427, 438–39.

[35] *Austin v Commonwealth* (2003) 215 CLR 185, 217, Gleeson CJ, citing Dawson J in *Queensland Electricity Commission v Commonwealth* (1985) 159 CLR 192, 260.

[36] *Melbourne Corporation v Commonwealth* (1947) 74 CLR 31, 82, Dixon J. Tellingly, the quote continues by describing the States as 'bodies politic whose existence and nature are independent of the powers allocated to them'.

Commonwealth laws that limited the range of banks that States and their authorities could use;[37] applied special rules to the settlement of industrial disputes involving the electricity authorities of Queensland;[38] placed a tax surcharge on the pension entitlements of New South Wales judges in a manner construed to interfere with decisions of the States about the remuneration of their own judges;[39] and imposed a similar surcharge on the retirement benefits of former members of the Parliament of South Australia.[40]

ii. Meaning

A host of questions about the meaning of individual heads of power have arisen in the past and continue to do so, generally prompted by the particular context in which the power is used. Examples, the answer to all of which is yes, include the following. Is an incorporated football club a 'trading corporation'? Can a child born in Australia be an 'alien'? Does a power with respect to 'external affairs' authorise the Commonwealth to prohibit development in a world heritage area? Can plant breeders' rights be protected by a power over 'patents of inventions'?

Consistently with *Engineers*, Australian courts answer such questions by applying common law techniques for the interpretation of statutes, unaffected by concern for the scope of State power and overlaid by consideration of the character of the Constitution as 'an instrument of government meant to endure and conferring powers expressed in general propositions wide enough to be capable of flexible application'.[41] The primary tools are text, context and previous authority. Context is understood broadly, to include 'any . . . circumstance that could rationally assist understanding of meaning', although, oddly, in determining the meaning of a section 51 power, it excludes the context of the rest of section 51 itself, as another casualty of rejection of the reserved powers doctrine. Historical conditions at the time the Constitution was written are relevant, but not determinative.[42]

One technique by which powers can be adapted to new conditions is the distinction drawn by the Court connotation and denotation.

[37]   Ibid.
[38]   *Queensland Electricity Commission v Commonwealth* (1985) 159 CLR 192.
[39]   *Austin v Commonwealth* (2003) 215 CLR 185.
[40]   *Clarke v Commissioner of Taxation* (2009) 240 CLR 272.
[41]   *Australian National Airways Pty Ltd v Commonwealth* (1945) 71 CLR 29, 81.
[42]   *Singh v Commonwealth* (2004) 222 CLR 322, 331–38.

As explained in chapter three, the former identifies the essential characteristics of a term, which are unchangeable, without constitutional amendment, while its denotation is apt to pick up a range of phenomena that share these characteristics. Views may differ on where the boundary between the two lies in relation to particular terms. Nevertheless, this reasoning has played a role in extending the coverage of Commonwealth power to aviation, new forms of intellectual property, a wider range of industrial disputes, and radio and television broadcasting.

Commonwealth legislation generally survives claims that it does not fall within the subject-matter of a power. This is not invariably the case, however. In one famous instance in 1990, for example, the Court held that the power to make laws with respect to categories of corporations 'formed within the limits of the Commonwealth' did not support legislation for the formation of corporations and thus precluded the Commonwealth from unilaterally enacting a national corporations law.[43]

iii. Characterisation

The analytical process by which the Court decides whether a challenged law is one 'with respect to' a head of power lies at the heart of the process of 'characterisation'. In some cases it is straightforward. The Quarantine Act 1908 is intuitively a law with respect to quarantine; the Bankruptcy Act 1966 is a law with respect to bankruptcy. The difficulty arises where a power is used more creatively, to produce outcomes not suggested by the terms of the power and otherwise beyond the Commonwealth's reach. Again, the point is best made by examples in which Commonwealth laws were upheld. Can the corporations power be used to regulate workplace relations between incorporated employers and their employees? Can the taxation power be used to tax employers who do not spend a specified minimum on training and thus, in effect, to require them to do so? Can the trade and commerce power be used to prohibit the exportation of mineral sands so as to discourage their mining in Queensland?

These outcomes are the consequence of a series of interlocking principles. First, with the exception of defence, Commonwealth powers are not considered to be purposive.[44] There is thus limited opportunity

---

[43] *New South Wales v Commonwealth* (1990) 169 CLR 482.

[44] There also are elements of purpose in determining whether a law implements a treaty or can be supported as an exercise of an incidental power to effectuate the substantive grant of power: Zines, n 31, 60–65.

for proportionality analysis, even in the form of the mild inquiry typically found in Australian jurisprudence as to whether a law is 'appropriate and adapted' to a legitimate end.[45] Assessment of whether a law is one 'with respect to' a head of power generally depends instead on whether there is a 'sufficient connection' between the law and the subject-matter of the power, of a legal or, perhaps, practical nature. A connection will exist if the law operates directly on the subject-matter of the power. All the examples in the previous paragraph are explained on this basis. Depending on the circumstances, even an indirect connection may be sufficient to sustain the validity of a law as an exercise of a power. In *Workchoices*, for example, legislation authorising and regulating the registration of associations of employers and employees for the purpose of the new industrial relations regime was upheld as an exercise of the corporations power.[46] If a law can be characterised in several ways it is immaterial that some fall outside Commonwealth power as long as one falls within it. No consideration is given in these circumstances to the real or dominant character of the law.

The manner in which legislative power is divided in Australia, coupled with the interpretive techniques developed by the Court, has expanded the reach of Commonwealth power and encouraged constitutional adventurism on the part of government and Parliament. At the same time, however, the insistence by the Court that there are justiciable limits, which occasionally are transgressed, makes it difficult to predict with certainty in advance whether some of the more adventurous legislation lies within the limits of Commonwealth power or not. These forces have combined to produce a drafting style in which the operation of Commonwealth Acts is expressed as dependent on the ambit of Commonwealth power, throwing the onus on those potentially affected by them to have a view on complex questions of constitutional law in order to determine their own course of action.

The legislation challenged in the *Workchoices* case provides a simple example. The Act applied primarily to employers who were 'constitutional corporations'.[47] This shorthand term refers to the categories of 'foreign

---

[45] *Thomas v Mowbray* (2007) 233 CLR 307.
[46] *New South Wales v Commonwealth* (2006) 229 CLR 1; cf *Re Dingjan; Ex parte Wagner* (1995) 183 CLR 323.
[47] Workplace Relations Amendment (Work Choices) Act 2005 (Cth) s 6(1)(a). A more complex example was the Water Act 2007 (Cth), which relied on a smorgasbord of Commonwealth powers, including trade and commerce, posts and telegraphs,

... trading or financial' corporations that fall within Commonwealth power under section 51(xx). The boundaries of the category of 'trading corporation' in particular, are unclear. It thus fell to corporations at the margins of this category, of which the Aboriginal Legal Service of Western Australia was an example, to determine for themselves, not always correctly, whether to comply with Commonwealth or State law.[48] The problem of this drafting style is compounded when the power provides an incomplete and thus not entirely rational basis for the legislation, as often is the case when the corporations power is engaged.

C. Fiscal Power

i. Fiscal Framework

On the face of the Constitution, fiscal powers are divided between the Commonwealth and the States in the same way as other powers. This allocation is consistent with the original understanding of the Australian federation as one in which each sphere of government would have sub-stantial autonomy over its own affairs. But Commonwealth fiscal powers also have been subject to the same interpretive principles as other pow-ers, with the same expansive effect. As a result, over the century since the Constitution was promulgated, the fiscal capacity of the Commonwealth has grown to the point where it collects 85 per cent of all taxation, but is responsible for only half the expenditure on government services.[49] The Commonwealth's financial dominance in turn has enabled it to further enlarge its authority, through grants and direct spending, where its own legislative powers fall short.

Section 51(ii) confers power with respect to 'taxation' on the Commonwealth. As a matter of law, the States retain their pre-federation power to impose taxation as well, diminished only by the loss of the power to impose duties of customs and excise under section 90.

---

meteorological observations, quarantine, weights and measures, corporations and external affairs, before supporting State references were made.

[48] *Aboriginal Legal Service of WA (Inc) v Lawrence (No.2)* (2008) 252 ALR 136; in which it was held that the ALS was not a trading corporation and that an employee could bring a claim for wrongful dismissal under State law. By early 2010, the point had been raised in litigation in at least nine other cases, with mixed results.

[49] Government of Victoria, *Strategy and Outlook, 2009–2010,* Budget Paper No. 2, 82.

These general taxation powers of the Commonwealth and the States are understood as powers to tax for their respective purposes, thus precluding inconsistency, as long as the understanding holds.[50]

The de facto hegemony of the Commonwealth in relation to taxation has three primary causes. The first is the expansion of the definition of duties of excise to include, effectively, all taxes on goods. The second is the de facto transfer to the Commonwealth of power to impose income tax, in the wake of the Second World War. And the third is the gradual abandonment by the States of some of their other, lesser, taxes as a condition of Commonwealth general revenue support.

Each of these developments is examined more fully in the next section. The scale of the fiscal imbalance, however, creates a need for revenue redistribution, which can conveniently be noted here. The limited provision for revenue redistribution made by the framers of the Constitution in order to cover the expected shortfall in State revenues following the withdrawal of duties of customs and excise duties proved ineffective within the first decade after federation.[51] As a result, the Constitution barely deals with revenue redistribution at all. Revenue transfers from the Commonwealth to the States depend entirely on political decisions, given effect through a power to make grants to the States that was included in the Constitution as an afterthought, as section 96. The arrangements currently in place entitle the States to the proceeds of the Commonwealth's Goods and Services Tax (GST). A proportion of this is now proposed to be 'dedicated' to health and hospital services in each jurisdiction, in the most recent illustration of the fragility of the fiscal position of the States.[52]

General revenue grants are divided between the States in the light of recommendations of a statutory Commonwealth Grants Commission (CGC), first established in 1933, after a long period of dissatisfaction with funding arrangements on the part of the financially weaker States.[53] While the CGC has a highly complex methodology, its general mandate

---

[50]   *Victoria v Commonwealth (Second Uniform Income Tax* case) (1957) 99 CLR 575, 614.

[51]   Section 94; the requirement for the Commonwealth to pay 'surplus revenue' to the States has been consistently circumvented by the appropriation of any surplus to trust funds, in a practice upheld by the High Court in *New South Wales v Commonwealth* (1908) 7 CLR 179.

[52]   National Health and Hospitals Network Agreement 2010, to which all States except WA were parties in August 2010.

[53]   Commonwealth Grants Commission *Equality in Diversity*, 2nd edn (Canberra, NSW, AGPS, 1995).

is to apply fiscal equalisation principles, which in Australia seek to enable each State 'by reasonable effort, to function at a standard not appreciably below the standards of other States'.[54] On the relativities applicable in 2010–11, Western Australia was projected to receive the lowest per capita share (.68) and Tasmania the highest (1.6).[55]

ii. Taxation Power

The Commonwealth has a general power to legislate for taxation, as long as it does not 'discriminate between States or parts of States'. Subject to section 114, which prevents the Commonwealth and the States imposing taxes 'on' each other's property, the Commonwealth can tax the States. In 2010, the principal Commonwealth taxes were personal and corporate income taxation, goods and services tax and other sales taxes, customs and excise duties, fringe benefits taxes and resource rent taxes.[56]

The effective scope for State taxation raises more complex questions of constitutional law. Section 90 prevents the States imposing taxes in the nature of duties of customs and excise. Customs duties are taxes on goods entering or leaving a jurisdiction. The meaning of excise duties was contested for almost 100 years after federation. In 1997 a narrow majority of the Court fixed the definition at its widest point, on the basis of an assumption that the purpose of section 90 was to give the Commonwealth 'real control of the taxation of commodities'.[57] *Ha* established that a duty of excise is an 'inland' tax on any step in dealing with goods up to, but possibly not including, literal consumption. Its effect was to remove all taxes on goods, including sales taxation, from the purview of State taxation. It is something of an irony, in the circumstances, that the arrangements for the distribution of GST revenues to the States require them to approve any change in the rate and base of the tax, although admittedly the requirement itself is non-justiciable.[58]

[54] Commonwealth Grants Commission Act 1973 (Cth) s 5(1).

[55] Commonwealth Government, *Australia's Federal Relations 2010–2011*, Budget Paper No. 3, Part 3.

[56] Commonwealth Government, *Budget Strategy and Outlook 2010–2011*, Budget Paper No. 1, Part 5.

[57] *Parton v Milk Board* (1949) 80 CLR 229, 260, quoted in *Ha v New South Wales* (1997) 189 CLR 465, 507.

[58] A New State Tax System (Managing the GST Rate and Base) Act 1999 (Cth) s 11; Intergovernmental Agreement on Federal Financial Relations, Schedule A, A.13.

In terms of the Constitution, both levels of government can impose income tax and did so on the eve of the Second World War. In 1942, however, a series of Commonwealth Acts effectively forced the States out of the field.[59] An immediate challenge to the legislation failed; and while a subsequent challenge partly succeeded the political complexity of reimposing income tax field deterred the States from doing so, leaving the Commonwealth with a monopoly over a second, major tax source.[60]

The *Uniform Tax* cases accepted that grants to the States could be made on condition that they refrained from imposing certain taxes. The technique has subsequently been used to further restrict the range of taxes that the States impose. Most recently, in the Federal Financial Relations Agreement 2009, the States agreed to abolish financial institutions duties, a range of stamp duties, bed taxes and debits taxes by 2013.

One consequence of these developments is that the States impose only a small range of relatively minor taxes: payroll tax, land tax, duties on conveyances, gambling taxes and car taxes. The implications for the system of government more generally of progressively withdrawing responsibility to impose taxation from the States are more difficult to calculate. On any view they obscure clear lines of accountability from both the Commonwealth and the States to their Parliaments and to voters for moneys raised and spent. The 2009 overhaul of federal financial relations that purports to tackle this problem through the way in which revenue transfers are handled is likely to be too little too late.[61] More significantly still, the fiscal imbalance has weakened the vitality of the State sphere of government, with results that are now being felt.

iii. Borrowing

Government borrowing was a potential factor in the federal financial settlement from the outset because of the levels of colonial debt. Even so, however, the original premise of the Constitution was that each order

---

[59] C Saunders, 'The Uniform Income Tax Cases' in HP Lee and G Winterton (eds), *Australian Constitutional Landmarks* (Cambridge, CUP, 2003).

[60] *South Australia v Commonwealth* (*First Uniform Tax* case) (1942) 65 CLR 373; *Victoria v Commonwealth* (*Second Uniform Tax* case) (1957) 99 CLR 575.

[61] Commonwealth Government, *Australia's Federal Relations* Budget Paper No. 3, 2009–2010, 160, explaining that the 'new centrally administered payment arrangements' are intended to help 'reinforce that State agencies are primarily accountable to their own Parliament and public for their service delivery performance'.

of government would be responsible for its own borrowings and for its own debts.

This assumption was disturbed in 1928 when, after many years of negotiation, the Constitution was amended to provide a framework for intergovernmental agreements about State debt. Section 105A is a unique provision, which not only authorises agreements but provides that they are binding notwithstanding anything to the contrary in the Australian Constitutions. For decades, the Agreement made under this section authorised the Commonwealth to borrow on behalf of all governments in accordance with the decisions of an intergovernmental Loan Council, in which the Commonwealth had a weighted vote. Erosion of this system through 'off-program' borrowings led, in the 1990s, to a new Agreement that left each jurisdiction free to borrow on its own behalf, made compliance with Loan Council allocations voluntary, and relied on transparency to ensure responsible borrowing, reinforced by the discipline of the ratings agencies. The global financial crisis of 2008–9 prompted a further change whereby the Commonwealth made a guarantee available for State borrowing. In early 2010, however, the government announced that the guarantee would close for new issues of securities at the end of 2010.[62] On the assumption that this occurs, it is unlikely that the provision of a guarantee on this occasion will have a lasting impact on the division of borrowing authority.

iv. Spending

Consistently with the vertical division of power in the Australian federation, the Commonwealth administers its own legislation and spends money for its own purposes. As in the United States and Canada, however, a more difficult issue concerns its capacity to spend for other purposes. In Australia, this issue derives additional practical significance from the vast fiscal imbalance in favour of the Commonwealth, while major expenditure responsibilities remain with the States.

Unlike these other two federations, the Commonwealth Constitution includes an express power to spend through grants to the States. Under section 96, the 'Parliament may grant financial assistance to any State on

---

[62] Australian Government 'The Guarantee of State and Territory Borrowing', http://www.stateguarantee.gov.au/ (viewed 4 August 2010). Neither the Guarantee of State and Territory Borrowing Appropriation Act 2009, nor the Deed of Guarantee itself are time-limited.

such terms and conditions as the Parliament thinks fit'. Subject to the Constitution, there are no limits to the conditions that the Parliament may impose.[63] In particular, grants can be made on condition that a State exercises its powers in a particular way or that it refrains from exercising a power. A State is not compelled to accept a grant, although given the fiscal imbalance, refusal is rare.

The use of section 96 to make general revenue grants to the States was considered earlier. At least an equivalent amount also is paid by the Commonwealth to the States each year for particular purposes, often on detailed conditions, including requirements for Commonwealth approval of programs or projects. Some rationalisation of these in 2009 is part of the story of intergovernmental co-operation and is examined in the final part of this chapter. For the moment, it is sufficient to note that, through the mechanism of conditional grants, the Commonwealth exercises extensive de facto control over most areas of State responsibility that involve significant levels of expenditure.

The presence of section 96 in the Constitution may have inhibited the development of a more general power of the Commonwealth to spend for purposes beyond its substantive legislative powers other than through grants to the States. It is now established that its legal authority to do so, such as it is, depends on the breadth of the executive power. As explained in chapter five, the executive power in section 61 of the Constitution parallels the legislative powers of the Commonwealth and also gives it 'a capacity to engage in enterprises and activities peculiarly adapted to the government of a nation . . . which cannot otherwise be carried on for the benefit of the nation'.[64] This test originally was propounded in a challenge to the validity of Commonwealth expenditure on regional development, in 1975. While the challenge failed, the outcome was equivocal for the scope of the power to spend.[65] By the time the next challenge was mounted, in 2009, Commonwealth use of an assumed spending power had grown exponentially.

But the decision in *Pape* was equally equivocal.[66] While four of the seven Justices upheld the validity of the payment of 'tax bonuses' as part

[63] For confirmation of the impact of express constitutional limits see *ICM Agriculture Pty Ltd v Commonwealth* (2009) 240 CLR 140.

[64] *Victoria v Commonwealth and Hayden* (*AAP* case) (1975) 134 CLR 397.

[65] C Saunders, 'The sources and scope of Commonwealth power to spend' (2009) 20 *Public Law Review* 256.

[66] *Pape v Federal Commissioner of Taxation* (2009) 238 CLR 1.

of an economic stimulus package by reference to the executive power the reasoning of one of these, French CJ, was closer to that of the minority Justices on the doctrine to be applied. If these positions hold in a future case, his views are likely to be determinative. Possibly deliberately, however, his observations in *Pape* itself have little predictive value. While noting that the executive power must be 'capable of serving the proper purposes of a national government' he also warned that these 'exigencies . . . cannot be invoked to set aside' the federal distribution of powers or the separation of powers.[67] He raised, without resolving, the question of the extent to which the 'nationhood' dimension of the executive power provides a constitutional base for existing Commonwealth expenditure programs.[68] This awaits another case.

Two more radical suggestions about the scope of the spending power were made by the other three Justices in *Pape*. One was that there might be a link between an unlimited taxation power and the scope of the spending power. The other was that the Commonwealth executive might in some way have inherited the unlimited spending power of the United Kingdom in relation to Australia, when independence was achieved.[69] Both are minority views, obliquely expressed. It is too early to tell whether they will ultimately have an influence on this aspect of constitutional law.

III. SOCIAL AND ECONOMIC UNION

A. Constitutional Framework

Most federations seek to consolidate union while also legitimising difference. The Commonwelath Constitution places particular emphasis on economic union in the form of internal free trade and, to a lesser extent, on the internal mobility of people. The key provisions to these ends are the guarantee of the 'absolute' freedom of interstate trade, commerce and intercourse in section 92 and an enigmatic prohibition of discrimination on grounds of State residence in section 117. Inevitably, these represent only the minimum requirements for social and economic union, both of which have deepened in a myriad of ways that are independent of the constitutional mandates. Since 1992, for example, the States and territories

---

[67] Ibid, 60.
[68] Ibid, 23.
[69] Ibid, Gummow, Crennan and Bell JJ, at 89–90.

have been bound to recognise each other's standards for goods and occupations under co-operative mutual recognition legislation.[70]

Social and economic union in a federation cannot entirely eradicate the relevance of State boundaries as geographic markers of the authority of the States. There are natural incidents of membership of a State as a democratic community and the responsibility of States to act in the interests of their people, within the limits of their constitutional authority, is part of the raison d'être of federalism. How and where the line is drawn between the requirements of union and legitimate State action is a critical question, the final answer to which falls to the High Court, now unaided by the Inter-State Commission.[71]

Economic and social union is more likely to be threatened by State than by Commonwealth action. Nevertheless, the Constitution also places some constraints on the Commonwealth. Section 92 now binds the Commonwealth although, as the notion of free trade has evolved, Commonwealth action is unlikely to infringe it.[72] Several other sections place specific restrictions on the Commonwealth. The taxation power must be exercised 'so as not to discriminate between States or parts of States'; bounties must be uniform; and 'no Commonwealth law or regulation of trade, commerce, or revenue' may give preference to one State or any part thereof over another State or any part thereof'.[73] These provisions have been a mixed blessing. They prevent the Commonwealth from playing favourites between States, if it was otherwise minded to do so, or from eroding economic union in ways that depend on State boundaries. But they also inhibit national economic policies that are sensitive to the different needs of States. In practice, they have been interpreted narrowly. As matters presently stand, for example, they have no effect on the allocation of State grants.[74]

[70] Mutual Recognition Act 1992 (Cth) and supporting State legislation; Mutual Recognition Agreement 1992; a parallel scheme also involves New Zealand.

[71] As described in ch.6, the adjudicatory function of the Commission, designed for this purpose by the framers, fell foul of the separation of powers in 1915: *New South Wales v Commonwealth* (1915) 20 CLR 54.

[72] *Cole v Whitfield* (1988) 165 CLR 360. The Commonwealth probably is subject also to section 117, although the issue has not yet clearly arisen for decision: see *Street v Queensland Bar Association* (1989) 168 CLR 461.

[73] Constitution sections 51(ii) and (iii) and 99 respectively; see generally A Simpson, 'The High Court's Conception of Discrimination: Origins, Applications and Implications' (2007) 29 *Sydney Law Review* 263.

[74] *Deputy Federal Commissioner of Taxation (NSW) v WR Moran Pty Ltd* (1939) 61 CLR 735.

B. Freedom of Trade, Commerce and Intercourse

Section 92 requires 'trade, commerce, and intercourse among the States' to be 'absolutely free'. The most difficult of the various interpretive questions to which this apparently simple proposition gives rise is the nature and extent of the freedom that it guarantees. In the mid twentieth century it was understood to create a right, subject only to reasonable regulation, to trade across State borders. As long as this doctrine prevailed, it precluded nationalisation of industries that otherwise fell within Commonwealth power, including aviation and banking.[75] In 1988, however, the increasing incoherence of this approach prompted a fundamental revision of the understanding of the section by reference to its purpose in the Constitution. A unanimous Court accepted that, as far as trade and commerce were concerned, the section was directed to the elimination of discriminatory burdens of a protectionist kind.[76] The reference to interstate intercourse, by contrast, continued to provide more general protection for freedom of mobility.

Section 92 is most difficult to apply when State action appears to be directed to a legitimate goal but nevertheless has an impact on interstate trade. *Cole v Whitfield* illustrates the problem. A Tasmanian law that prohibited the possession of crayfish below a certain size, ostensibly in order to protect the Tasmanian crayfish stock, was held not to be relevantly discriminatory and protectionist in its application to crayfish caught in other parts of Australia where different environmental conditions justified a lower minimum size.[77] By contrast, two years later, in *Castlemaine Tooheys,* a non-discriminatory deposit requirement for non-refillable bottles which on the face of the legislation was non-discriminatory, was held invalid on the ground that it placed a discriminatory burden on out-of-state brewers. A State law enacted for the 'well-being' of its people could burden interstate trade, but only if its discriminatory impact was 'incidental' and not 'disproportionate' to the achievement of a legitimate goal.[78]

It now appears that this formulation was too generous. *Betfair* involved a challenge to Western Australian legislation in its application

---

[75] *Australian National Airways Pty Ltd v Commonwealth* (1945) 71 CLR 29; *Bank of New South Wales v Commonwealth* (1948) 76 CLR 1.
[76] *Cole v Whitfield* (1988) 165 CLR 360.
[77] Ibid, 409; cf *Betfair Pty Ltd v Western Australia* (2008) 234 CLR 418, 477.
[78] *Castlemaine Tooheys v South Australia* (1990) 169 CLR 436, 473.

to an internet betting exchange that was licensed in Tasmania.[79] The legislation sought to neutralise the impact of internet betting on the gambling revenues of the State in two ways. First, it was made an offence for punters in Western Australia to bet through a betting exchange. This provision would also have applied to any betting exchange within the State and thus was on the face of it neutral. Secondly, the legislation prohibited a betting exchange from making a WA race field available without State approval. Both sections were held invalid: the latter as a direct burden on interstate trade and both because of their tendency to protect the gaming industry in Western Australia from competition offered through the 'new economy'.

Following *Betfair,* claims that a legitimate objective justifies State legislation must show that the impact on interstate trade is 'reasonably necessary'.[80] While the Court clearly was sceptical about the 'neutral' objectives claimed for this legislation it held that, in any event, the legislation was not appropriate and adapted to achieving them in the relevant sense. In the long run, the broader ramifications of the case may stem from the terms in which the Court characterises the 'legal and economic milieu' in which section 92 now operates: the significance of the national market as an expression of 'national unity', the impact of 'internet-dependent businesses' on the relevance of geographical boundaries and, somewhat more surprisingly, the endorsement through intergovernmental agreement of the value of competition. In the face of these developments, the reasons suggest, the concepts of both 'the people of' a State and their 'localised well-being' are in flux.

Meanwhile, a separate line of authority has begun to tease out the vexed relationship between freedom of intercourse and freedom of trade. It is clear that no law may have as its purpose the restriction of movement across State borders.[81] A more difficult question is the validity of a law enacted for another purpose that also burdens interstate intercourse. The prevailing view appears to be that such a law will be valid as long as the burden is no greater than 'reasonably required'.[82] At the very least, this suggests a weakening of the idea in *Cole v Whitfield* that freedom of intercourse is a personal freedom.[83] On the other hand,

---

[79]   *Betfair Pty Ltd v Western Australia* (2008) 234 CLR 418.
[80]   Ibid, 477.
[81]   *Gratwick v Johnson* (1945) 70 CLR 1.
[82]   *APLA Limited v Legal Services Commissioner* (2005) 224 CLR 322, 393.
[83]   Zines, n 31, 191, 193.

it brings the tests for the two limbs of the section closer together, particularly in the wake of *Betfair*. To the extent that a difference remains, a law that can be characterised by reference to both trade and commerce and to intercourse is likely to be subject to the tests for the former.[84]

C. Freedom of Mobility

Section 117 also provides a mobility right of a kind. As noted in chapter one, the section is all that survived of an attempt to introduce into the Constitution a version of the Fourteenth Amendment to the Constitution of the United States, as a means of highlighting the significance of belonging to the new Australian community.

The section provides that 'A subject of the Queen, resident in any State, shall not be subject in any other State to any disability or discrimination which would not be equally applicable to him if he were . . . resident in such other State'. For more than 80 years it was interpreted formalistically, so that it was triggered only when residence was, literally, the criterion for discrimination. This changed in 1989 when, in *Street*, the Court held that rules of admission to the Queensland Bar that required applicants to reside in Queensland and to cease practice in other States could not constitutionally apply to an applicant resident in New South Wales.[85] In finding relevant discrimination, the Court compared the actual situation of the plaintiff with his position had he been a resident of Queensland. The reasoning in *Street* suggests that the section has other significant applications: for example, in relation to university admission policies that favour school leavers from the home State.

As with section 92, there is a question whether and to what extent section 117 leaves room for State legislation that recognises the rights of State residents and confers discrete benefits on them. The right to vote in State elections is an obvious case. The provision of State services, funded by contributions from State residents, is a more difficult example, although endorsed by several Justices in *Street*.[86] The attitude towards the

---

[84] *APLA Ltd v Legal Services Commissioner (NSW)* (2005) 224 CLR 322, 390.

[85] *Street v Queensland Bar Association* (1989) 168 CLR 461.

[86] (1989) 168 CLR 461, 492, 528, 546, 572. The issue was potentially raised in the context of State no-fault accident compensation schemes in *Sweedman v Transport Accident Commission* (2006) 226 CLR 363 but avoided; for a critique see Zines, n 31, 577–78.

broadly comparable issue in *Betfair* suggests that such questions are more likely to be determined through analysis of the concept of discrimination in section 117 than by reference to a protected sphere for State action.

IV. CO-OPERATION

A. Co-operation and the Constitution

Intergovernmental co-operation plays a highly significant role in the practical operation of the Australian federation. Australia is not unique in this respect: collaboration between jurisdictions is a feature of all federations, although in some it is more clearly anticipated in constitutional design.[87] In Australia as elsewhere the forms that co-operation takes affect and are affected by the rest of the institutional structure of government. Features of the Australian system that have a bearing on intergovernmental co-operation include parliamentary government in a form that enables substantial executive control; the rule of law, understood in terms of the availability of judicial review of the lawfulness of executive action; and a federation in which each order of government has a complete set of institutions and administers its own legislation even in areas of concurrent legislative power.

There has been debate in Australia about whether the Australian federation has a 'co-operative' character that affects constitutional interpretation. Early cases established that co-operation is no bar to validity as long as each jurisdiction acts within constitutional limits.[88] But towards the end of the 1990s, in *Wakim,* the Court rejected argument that the co-operative character of the federation might cure deficiencies in power in the context of intergovernmental schemes.[89] It followed that State jurisdiction could not be conferred on federal courts in order to ensure the uniform interpretation of co-operative companies legislation, because chapter III is understood as an exhaustive statement of the jurisdiction that federal courts may exercise. Doubts raised by the reasoning in *Wakim* about the validity of schemes that confer State

---

[87]   C Saunders, 'Comparative Conclusions' in K Leroy and C Saunders, *Legislative, Executive and Judicial Governance in Federal Countries* (Montreal and Kingston, McGill-Queen's University Press, 2006) 344.

[88]   *R v Duncan; Ex parte Australian Iron and Steel Pty Ltd* (1983) 158 CLR 1.

[89]   *Re Wakim* (1999) 198 CLR 511.

executive authority on other Commonwealth institutions subsequently were confirmed, at least in part, in *Hughes*.[90]

The angst that greeted these decisions is a reflection of how far assumptions about Australian federalism, grounded in practice, have departed from the text and structure of the Constitution itself. Intergovernmental co-operation in one form or another affects almost every aspect of government in Australia. Co-operation is critical for dealing with major national challenges for which the Constitution makes inadequate provision of which the environment, including management of scarce water resources, is an example. Co-operative arrangements have a profound effect on the ways in which regulation occurs and governments allocate resources. On the other hand, the Constitution establishes a federation with a remarkable degree of institutional dualism, on which the accountability systems for both levels of government are built.[91] And while there are a few co-operative mechanisms in the Constitution itself, they assume the underlying dualism of the federation as well and are broadly compatible with it.[92]

The debate on the place of intergovernmental co-operation in the Australian constitutional system is not over yet. There are unresolved questions about the meaning of sections of the Constitution that have a bearing on the nature and extent of co-operation. Apart from the executive power to spend, which has been considered already, these include the effects of reliance on the executive power, coupled with the incidental legislative power, in support of co-operative schemes and the operation of the Commonwealth power to make laws on matters referred by the States. There are intermittent proposals to amend the Constitution to overturn the effects of *Wakim* and *Hughes* or more generally to facilitate, or mandate, intergovernmental co-operation.[93] And in 2009 there was a radical overhaul of intergovernmental relations under the rubric of the COAG Reform Agenda, directed primarily to the efficacy of co-operation, but with inevitable constitutional consequences. The key features of these changes are examined in the next section.

---

[90] *R v Hughes* (2000) 202 CLR 535.
[91] *Australian Securities and Investment Commission v Edensor Nominees Pty Ltd* (2001) 204 CLR 559, 572.
[92] In particular, sections 51(xxxvii), 77(iii), 96, 105A, 119, 120.
[93] These are canvassed in House of Representatives, Standing Committee on Legal and Constitutional Affairs, *Inquiry into Constitutional Reform*, 2008, ch.4.

B. Instruments of Co-operation

i. Ministerial Councils

The driving force for the intergovernmental relations system in Australia is a network of more than 40 ministerial councils, with the Council of Australian Governments (COAG) at its apex. In addition to their membership of COAG, the heads of government also are members of a Treaties Council, established to consider international treaties of particular significance to the States. Below the level of the heads of government there are councils for most areas of State governmental activity. Most councils include the Commonwealth as well as the States and Territories but the leaders of the latter also meet separately in a Council for the Australian Federation.

Councils meet at least once a year. They generally take decisions by consensus, although sometimes other voting rules apply. They are usually, although not always, serviced by a secretariat based in the corresponding Commonwealth department. Councils set their own agendas which, in principle, are supposed to be confined to matters that are of national concern. They play critical roles in approving legislation for enactment under schemes designed to secure uniformity; making governance decisions in relation to joint administrative agencies; and, sometimes, considering the conditions on which funding will be made available by the Commonwealth to the States. The control that Australian governments exercise over their respective parliaments ensures that decisions taken in ministerial councils are likely to be readily implemented in practice and justifies description of the process as 'executive federalism'.

The ministerial council system cuts across the lines of accountability that responsible government assumes. It also obscures the decision-making process to a degree that makes it difficult to pinpoint the causes of underperformance. The transjurisdictional character of a ministerial council complicates judicial review; an attempt by the Tasmanian Wilderness Society to challenge the authority to borrow to build a dam in a world heritage area failed, for example, because the Loan Council was not an 'authority of the Commonwealth' for the purposes of the Australian Heritage Commission Act 1975 (Cth).[94]

---

[94] *Tasmanian Wilderness Society v Fraser* (1982) 153 CLR 270.

Successive waves of reform have sought to tackle these problems with a degree of success, although so far the changes operate almost entirely within the confines of the executive branch and there is more to be done. There is now a Compendium of Ministerial Councils, which can be found on-line and which includes information about the composition, role and decision-making procedures of each council, with varying degrees of generality.[95] The Compendium requires councils to report annually and to distribute their minutes to the Department of the Prime Minister and Cabinet; there is no requirement to report to the equivalent departments in the States, however, nor to the Parliaments. The procedures of councils are adapted to the proprieties of collective decision-making by Cabinets, at least in theory by, for example, requiring agendas to be circulated in time for Cabinets to determine the position of their ministers on key items. It is still relatively rare for Councils to be empowered by legislation, although the practice is increasing, without any clear framework of principle for it.[96]

ii. Agreements

Australian governments regularly enter into agreements with each other to achieve joint outcomes. Some, although not all, are signed formally on behalf of all participating governments. The most significant are signed by heads of government. Agreements may establish a supervising ministerial council; prescribe the steps towards the enactment of uniform legislation; lay down procedures for the operations of a shared administrative agency; and commit governments to the expenditure of funds. They involve an exercise of executive power and, with the notable exception of agreements about borrowing made under section 105A, are subject to any constraints in the Commonwealth Constitution.[97] They are generally assumed not to be intended to create legally enforceable obligations although this depends ultimately on the terms of an agreement, including the character of the undertakings.[98]

---

[95] Council of Australian Governments, *Commonwealth-State Ministerial Councils Compendium* 2009, http://www.coag.gov.au/ministerial_councils/docs/compendium.pdf (viewed 5 August 2010).

[96] Eg Safe Work Australia Act 2008 (Cth).

[97] C Saunders, 'Intergovernmental agreements and the executive power' (2005) 16 *Public Law Review* 294.

[98] *South Australia v Commonwealth* (1962) 108 CLR 130. Relevantly, National Partnership Agreements made under the auspices of the 2009 Intergovernmental

While agreements are not law, they may function as soft law binding governments to act, if only politically. In some cases they also affect the operation of legislation. They are rarely scheduled to legislation, however and they are not systematically made available in other ways. There is a list of agreements on the COAG website; even if this is understood as confined to COAG level agreements, however, it is incomplete and there are also many more agreements executed at ministerial or agency levels. As with ministerial councils, attempts are being made to deal with the range of accountability problems that arise; as with ministerial councils also, there is more to be done.[99]

iii. References

Intergovernmental arrangements in Australia often aim at uniformity and use a variety of mechanisms to achieve it. The choice of mechanism depends on the depth of uniformity required. One mechanism that sought to achieve deep uniformity of the texts, administration and interpretation of State law in order to simulate the effect of an exercise of Commonwealth power in a process known as 'federalisation'[100] was restricted by the decisions in *Wakim* and *Hughes*. Another, which secures deep uniformity in a much more straightforward fashion, is provided by the Constitution itself. Section 51(xxxvii) empowers the Commonwealth Parliament to make laws on 'matters' referred to it by the Parliaments of one or more States 'but so that the law shall extend only to States by whose Parliaments the matter is referred, or which otherwise adopt the law'. An exercise of the power results in legislation that is genuinely federal law, with the usual attributes of it.

Famously, the States have been reluctant to refer power to the Commonwealth. Following the decisions in *Wakim* and *Hughes*, however, significant references were made in the areas of corporations, antiterrorism and industrial relations law and recourse to this mechanism is likely to be more frequent. Some of the State concerns that initially

---

Agreement on Federal Financial Relations prescribe procedures for the resolution of disputes through COAG.

[99] See for example the still relatively unsophisticated procedures for publishing and tabling the Agreement associated with the Work Safe Australia Act 2008 (Cth), s 71.

[100] Commonwealth, House of Representatives, *Debates* (8 November 1990) p 3663 ff (Attorney-General Duffy).

inhibited references have been resolved by judicial decision. It is clear, for example, that a 'matter' can be referred subject to conditions and that a condition may make a reference terminable.[101] Others are more difficult to resolve, however, including the potential for the Court to construe a referred matter broadly, thus exacerbating the impact on existing State law of Commonwealth legislation enacted pursuant to a reference.

The States have developed increasingly sophisticated techniques for minimising such concerns, in the referring legislation or in supporting agreements. One is to refer a matter in the form of the text of agreed legislation for enactment by the Commonwealth Parliament. But this technique merely postpones the problem if, as sometimes is the case, the States agree also to refer sufficient authority to enable the Commonwealth to amend the legislation from time to time. In *Thomas,* three Justices held that Commonwealth legislation that purported to restrict the use of a reference to amend anti-terrorism legislation, (itself based on a reference), by requiring the prior agreement of a majority of State governments, was ineffective.[102] The extent of the use of the reference power in future is likely to depend on the resolution of questions of this kind.

iv. COAG Reform Agenda

In the course of the early 1990s, COAG agreed to arrangements to enhance Australia's economic competitiveness through co-operation.[103] The drivers included a series of competition policy payments from the Commonwealth to the States, to mark progress in implementing the agreed changes, as assessed by a National Competition Council. In 2006, this technique was adapted to underpin co-operation in a wide range of other areas. In 2008, a non-statutory COAG Reform Council was established to monitor performance of this wider agenda, which now was described as designed to 'boost productivity, workforce participation and geographic mobility, and support wider objectives of better services for the community, social inclusion, closing the gap on Indigenous disadvantage and environmental sustainability'.

[101] *R v Public Vehicles Licensing Tribunal (Tas); Ex part Australian National Airways Pty Ltd* (1964) 113 CLR 207.

[102] *Thomas v Mowbray* (2007) 233 CLR 307 .

[103] Productivity Commission, *Review of National Competition Policy Reforms,* February 2005.

In 2009 these arrangements were overlaid by the Federal Financial Relations Agreement, as a comprehensive framework for grants from the Commonwealth to the States, which also would enhance the reform agenda. Under the Agreement, general revenue grants to the States continue to be determined by reference to the proceeds of the Commonwealth GST. Conditional payments are now divided into two broad categories, however: National Specific Purpose Payments, for use in the broadly defined areas of healthcare, education, skills, disability, housing and indigenous affairs and National Partnership Payments in connection with more specific programs, ranging from early household education to a seamless national economy and from social housing to preventative health.[104]

Many advantages are claimed for this new approach: that it has rationalised a large number of existing conditional grant programs; that it provides a focus on outcomes rather than imposing predetermined conditions that constrain State action; and that it enhances accountability by clarifying the roles of each level of government and providing for regular performance monitoring by the COAG Reform Council. But scrutiny of the agreements and the minimal supporting legislation suggests that they even further transfer authority from Parliaments to governments acting pursuant to agreements, 'implementation plans' and one-line appropriations. Despite protestations to the contrary, they will also enhance the effective authority of the Commonwealth at the expense of the States, unless there is genuine collaboration between governments in the development of the strategies, outcomes and benchmarks around which each of the programs revolves.

C. Integration Without Structure

These latest developments in intergovernmental co-operation further consolidate a trend that has been developing for some time. The very structure of the Australian federation is changing, in practice although not in law, in the sense that, increasingly, policy is made by the Commonwealth leaving policy implementation to the States. In this regard, the emphasis on 'services' in the contradictory statement of principle in the Federal Financial Relations Agreement is telling:

---

[104] Details are available on the COAG website: http://www.coag.gov.au/about_coag/index.cfm (viewed 5 August 2010).

. . . the States . . . have primary responsibility for many of the service sectors covered by the National Agreements. . . . The primacy of State . . . responsibility in the delivery of services in these sectors is implicit in the Constitution of the Commonwealth of Australia and it is not the intention of the Parties to alter the Constitutional responsibility or accountability of the Commonwealth [and] States.[105]

Elsewhere, such a model would be described as integrated federalism.[106] Germany is the paradigm case: a federation in which the Lander have constitutional authority to administer federal laws and a constitutional say in federal legislation through the representation of their governments in the Bundesrat. But in Australia the shift is taking place within the confines of an old Constitution that has none of the safeguards of a deliberately integrated federation and is based on different assumptions about how accountability is achieved. This style of integrated federalism operates through executive, rather than legislative institutions and through executive action, rather than legislation. It provides no guaranteed sphere of autonomy within which State decisions are made, even at the level of service delivery. Measures to provide different mechanisms for accountability are likely to be rendered less effective, if they are not foiled altogether, by the complexity of the arrangements and the inherently opaque character of activities confined to the executive branch. In an Australian constitutional setting, the concentration of power in a federation that is integrated de facto removes one of the few institutional checks and balances and diminishes opportunities for policy and electoral competition. These are issues not merely for federalism, but for Australian democracy and the rule of law.

SELECTED READING

Aroney, N, *The Constitution of the Federal Commonwealth* (Cambridge, CUP, 2009)

Council of Australian Governments, *Commonwealth-State Ministerial Councils Compendium,* 2009

Crommelin, M, 'Federalism' in PD Finn (ed), *Essays on Law and Government, Vol. 1* (Sydney, NSW, Law Book Co. Ltd, 1995) 168

[105] Clause 6. References to the Territories are omitted in the interests of clarity.

[106] TO Hueglin and A Fenna, *Comparative Federalism: A Systematic Inquiry* (Ontario, Broadview Press Ltd, 2006) 235.

Painter, M, *Collaborative Federalism* (Cambridge, CUP, 1998)

Parkin, A and Anderson, G, 'The Howard Government, Regulatory Federalism and the Transformation of Commonwealth-State Relations' (2007) 42 *Australian Journal of Political Science* 295

Saunders, C, 'Constitutional Structure and Australian Federalism' in P Cane (ed), *Centenary Essays for the High Court of Australia* (Sydney, NSW, Butterworths, 2004) 174

Sawer, G, *Modern Federalism* (Carlton, Vic, Pitman, 1976)

Twomey, A and Withers, G, 'Australia's Federal Future', Federalist Paper 1, April 2007.

Zines, L, *The High Court and the Constitution*, 5th edn (Annandale, NSW, Federation Press, 2008)

8

Rights and Freedoms

———◦◦———

Principle – Beyond the Formal Constitution – Constitutional Rights – Rights Instruments

I. PRINCIPLE

A. Last but not least?

IT IS UNUSUAL, in the twenty-first century, for a book about a national constitutional system to leave the chapter on rights to the last. The reason for doing so in this case should now be evident, however. Unlike other 'modern legal systems' Australia has no 'formally enacted bill of rights'.[1] With a few exceptions, the Australian Constitution provides no explicit protection for rights at all. Rights therefore do not arise as a constitutional issue in Australia in the same way as in other comparable countries. Rather, as the last four chapters have shown, rights protection is dependent on institutional arrangements in ways that cannot fully be appreciated until the institutions themselves are understood.

The purpose of this chapter is to draw these threads together in a single account that also examines the few express rights-type provisions in the Australian Constitution. To this end, part two deals with rights protection beyond the written Constitution and part three with constitutional rights. Part four examines the history of bills of rights in Australia: past attempts to introduce a rights instrument in some form; the legislative bills of rights currently in place in the Australian Capital Territory (ACT) and Victoria; and the presently doubtful prospects for a rights instrument in the Commonwealth sphere.

---

[1] Cf J Waldron, 'Refining the Question about Judges' Moral Capacity' (2009) 7 *International Journal of Constitutional Law* 69, 71.

Several themes run through this chapter, each of which is explored further in the sections below. One is the hybrid character of the Australian approach to rights protection, which pursues a form of political constitutionalism within a formal constitutional framework that accepts the legitimacy of judicial review for other purposes. The second is the impact of internationalisation on Australian constitutional law. Both themes reveal Australia to be grappling with problems that are similar to those in countries elsewhere. Both also show that, at least in some respects, the Australian response is distinctive.

As in some other chapters, it is necessary at particular points to distinguish the position in the Commonwealth and State spheres. This is most obviously so in relation to the express rights in the Commonwealth Constitution, which apply to the Commonwealth alone although, as earlier chapters have shown, the application of implied rights to the States is a more complicated story. In addition, dependence on institutions for rights protection makes a degree of variation between jurisdictions inevitable, although it is mitigated by the doctrine of a single common law and the growing significance of international rights standards. Finally, at the very least, Victoria and the ACT require separate treatment, as the only jurisdictions with general rights instruments. The variation in minimum rights standards between Australian jurisdictions is another distinctive feature of Australian constitutional law.

There is a question whether the distinctive approach to rights protection in Australia reflects different preferences in institutional design or different attitudes to rights. The answer may be both. There is a strong and so far prevalent view in Australia that governments and parliaments, rather than courts, should determine whether and how to comply with rights standards, at least in the enactment of legislation. This position typically is attributed to considerations either of institutional competence, broadly defined to include concern about the politicisation of the judiciary or of democratic legitimacy, often described, somewhat implausibly in the circumstances, in terms of parliamentary sovereignty.[2] It applies to all the standard categories of rights: political, civil, social, economic, cultural and environmental. It is nurtured by Australia's reasonable rights record.

---

[2] National Human Rights Consultation Report, 2009, ch.13, (hereafter NHRC Report).

On the other hand, considerations of rights in Australia are readily trumped by other public policy goals unless, at least, their impact on rights is egregious. Australia's rights record is not nearly as good as it should be, considering Australia's favourable political, economic and social circumstances. Much of the media response to the modest recommendations of the 2009 report of the National Consultation on Rights was startling in its hostility: one respected columnist described the thrust of the report as 'downgrading . . . the public and national interest'.[3] It would be going too far to characterise the Australian position as one of rights scepticism. But it would be fair to describe Australia as a state in which rights tend to be viewed from a systemic or collective perspective so that the outcome on any question in which rights are in the balance is never pre-ordained.[4]

B. The Platypus

In 2008, the genome sequencing of the platypus showed that its hybrid characteristics can partly be explained by the point at which it diverged from the rest of the mammalian line, preserving features that others have lost and developing unique characteristics of its own.[5]

Rights protection in Australia, to which the platypus is native, also exhibits hybrid characteristics. These can be explained as the consequence of the superimposition of a written entrenched Constitution along US lines on uncodified constitutional institutions, principles and practices derived largely from the British constitutional tradition. At the risk of straining the metaphor too far, there is a sense in which Australia diverged from the British constitutional mainstream in 1901 when the Commonwealth Constitution was put in place. The two traditions were reconciled at the time by confining the Constitution to institutional arrangements and leaving rights to elected institutions and the common law. Australia was hardly unique in this respect; Canada had taken the same course even earlier. But Canada and the United Kingdom

---

[3] P Kelly, 'Human rights report poisoned chalice', *The Weekend Australian* October 10–11, 2009, 14.

[4] In this respect, the Australian position is close to that of R Bellamy, *Political Constitutionalism* (Cambridge, CUP, 2007) 29–35.

[5] US Department of Health and Human Services, 'Duck-Billed Platypus Genome Sequence Published', *NIH News,* 7 May 2008.

subsequently converged again in the latter decades of the twentieth century, strengthening rights protection in ways that left the last word to Parliament and so, to that extent, preserved its sovereignty. By contrast Australia has retained the features of the original compromise largely intact, at least as far as outward appearances are concerned.

Over time, however, each of these strands of Australia's constitutional makeup has influenced the evolution of the other. Chapters four and six have already shown how the incorporation of institutions in a written constitution can provide some protection for the rights associated with them in order to protect the integrity of the institutions themselves, with particular reference to the rights to vote, political communication and aspects of due process. Conversely, the assumption that rights protection can and should be left to elected institutions and independent courts applying common law principles has affected the interpretation and operation of the written Constitution. The few rights that are expressed in or implied from the written Constitution typically are interpreted narrowly. Conceptually, they are viewed as limits on power, held only against the state. The institutional focus of the written Constitution has made adherence to legalism more plausible as an interpretive method than it might otherwise have been. Ironically, it has also enabled the courts to eschew explicit recourse to concepts of deference, as long as questions of law are engaged. These by-products of the current arrangements have embedded them further, feeding apprehension about the institutional consequences of the adoption of a wide-ranging rights instrument.

C. International Overlay

It is trite that the phenomenon of internationalisation has affected traditional assumptions about the authority of states and their exclusive relationship with their citizens. International human rights law provides influential benchmarks for an extraordinarily wide range of existing and emerging rights. Compliance with such standards is often a factor in international relations, in contexts ranging from the conditions on which aid is granted to threats of international intervention. International human rights institutions provide avenues to which people can take individual grievances, subject to prior acceptance of these procedures by the states concerned.

Australia is not immune from these developments. It was a founding member of the United Nations and one of a small group of countries that drafted the Universal Declaration on Human Rights. It is a
party to most international human rights instruments. It has acceded to
protocols that enable Australians to take complaints about rights
infringements directly to the relevant international body. The rights
instruments that have been enacted in the ACT and Victoria draw largely
on international human rights standards and authorise international law
to be taken into account in their interpretation.[6] International human
rights commitments may affect the interpretation of Australian legislation, the development of the Australian common law and the procedural
obligations imposed on government by administrative law, in ways that
are described in the next part.

Despite all this, the impact of international human rights law on
Australian domestic law is limited. International law does not have direct
effect in Australian law. Australian adherence to international human
rights treaties is only occasionally followed by legislation to incorporate
them into domestic law. A range of international human rights instruments is scheduled to the legislation constituting the Australian Human
Rights Commission, but it is clear that this does not make them directly
applicable.[7]

The mismatch between Australia's international human rights commitments and their legislative incorporation into Australian law is generally justified on the basis that human rights in Australia are protected
in a variety of ways, of which specific implementing legislation is only
one. In a common core document prepared for the purposes of reports
to treaty bodies in 2006 the government identified these as Australia's
'strong democratic institutions', the Constitution, the common law
and existing legislative measures.[8] That document also made a familiar
claim that governments do not enter into international commitments on
behalf of Australia unless they are satisfied that Australian law is already
compliant. Repeated criticisms of international bodies show that there
is a shortfall, however. Complaints to the United Nations Human Rights

---

[6] Human Rights Act 2004 (ACT), s 31; Charter of Human Rights and
Responsibilities Act 2006 (Vic) s 32(2).
    [7] Australian Human Rights Commission Act 1986 (Cth) schedules 1–5; *Dietrich v
R* (1992) 177 CLR 292.
    [8] Australia, *Common Core Document incorporating the Fifth Report under the ICCPR and
the Fourth Report under the ICESC*, June 2006, 20.

Committee by Australian citizens under the first optional protocol to the ICCPR, for example, are upheld often enough to demonstrate that there is a problem of some kind, although Australia disputes some of the conclusions of the Committee.[9] In its final conclusions on Australia's Fifth Periodic Report in 2009 the Committee drew attention to a range of ongoing human rights infringements, including Australia's failure to give effect to many of its Views on individual communications.[10] The Committee also reiterated earlier concerns about the lack of a 'comprehensive legal framework' for the protection of international human rights commitments.

Australian caution about the domestic effect of international human rights can be seen as a subset of a more general suspicion of formal rights protection, exacerbated by a degree of defensiveness over sovereignty. The role of international law in human rights protection in Australia nevertheless is more complex than it might at first appear. In the absence of a domestic rights instrument, Australians tend to have recourse to the international bill of rights, if only for political purposes, when the limited opportunities for legal argument fail. Furthermore, as the final part shows, the need to comply with international human rights norms has become part of the Australian debate about the future of rights protection.

II. BEYOND THE FORMAL CONSTITUTION

A. Parliament and Government

i. Respect and Restraint

In the absence of constitutionalised rights, an exercise of legislative power by either the Commonwealth or a State Parliament can override rights and freedoms. The potential for legislative power to be used in this

---

[9] A list of recent communications can be found at Attorney-General's Department, *Human rights communications,* http://www.ag.gov.au/www/agd/agd.nsf/Page/Human_rights_and_anti-discriminationCommunications (viewed 6 August 2010).

[10] United Nations, *Concluding Observations of the Human Rights Committee: Australia* CCPR/C/AUS/CO/5, 7 May 2009, pointing to, for example, the Intervention in the Northern Territory, homelessness, extradition to countries where there is a risk of torture, excessive use of force in law enforcement, mandatory immigration detention and the impact of anti-terrorism legislation.

way is affected by constitutional constraints associated with federalism, separation of powers and representative democracy. In the scheme of things, however, these limitations are relatively insignificant. As a generalisation, as far as rights are concerned, Australian Parliaments have plenary power. Attempts to argue that some rights are so deeply embedded in the 'democratic system of government and the common law' that they could not be overturned by legislation have proved unavailing.[11] In *Kable* such an argument was met by a response from Dawson J that the 'doctrine of parliamentary sovereignty is . . . as deeply rooted as any in the common law'.[12] This remains the mainstream view.

The view that rights are adequately protected through the institution of Parliament is explained and defended in several ways. One, echoing Dicey, points to the representative character of Parliament. An observation made by Harrison Moore in 1902 that the rights of individuals are 'sufficiently secured' under the Australian Constitution 'by ensuring, as far as possible, to each a share, and an equal share, in political power', continues to be influential.[13] A variation on this account stresses the significance of the combination of parliamentary democracy with responsible government 'where Ministers sit in Parliament, can be questioned, and give answers, and the government itself may be turned out, if parliament feels that it is doing things which violate the proper rights of individuals'.[14] Both versions are reinforced and complemented by the distinctive features of Australian electoral democracy that were identified in earlier chapters: short parliamentary terms; the efficiency of the electoral process; and the requirement for all electors to vote.

The view that the political process can be relied on to respect rights is more persuasive in relation to the rights of the majority than in relation to those of minorities, especially unpopular minorities, or of those with no present stake in the Australian political community. The point could be illustrated readily enough by reference to, for example, Indigenous Australians, refugee claimants, terrorism suspects or people involved in the criminal justice system. Even from the standpoint of the majority, however, this is a somewhat romantic view. Parliaments meet infrequently and pass large volumes of legislation at the behest of the executive

---

[11] *Durham Holdings v New South Wales* (2001) 205 CLR 399.

[12] *Kable v Director of Public Prosecutions (NSW)* (1996) 189 CLR 51.

[13] H Moore, *The Constitution of the Australian Commonwealth* (London, John Murray, 1902) 329.

[14] J Howard, 'Proposed Charter of Rights', Menzies Lecture, August 2009.

government. Elected representatives have only a general appreciation of rights standards, which attract attention only in the most obvious cases. It is highly unlikely that an Australian government would be 'turned out' in mid term for any reason by a Parliament in which its supporters are in a majority and there is no evidence to suggest that lack of regard for rights would be particularly persuasive in this context. Infringement of rights by legislation in any event may be difficult to detect in the absence of a concrete case.[15] Rights also may be infringed by executive, rather than legislative action, in the exercise of broad and general powers conferred by statute or, sometimes, in reliance on inherent executive power.

Recent research has cast light on how the legislative process deals with questions of rights in practice and to what effect.[16] It shows that at least until the advent of legislative protection for rights in the ACT and Victoria, there was little requirement for the systemic consideration of rights by government or bureaucracy during the policy-making phase in any Australian jurisdiction. Equally, there was little systemic consideration of rights issues in any of the Parliaments, with the important but limited exceptions of committees specifically charged with the scrutiny of bills or delegated legislation by reference to human rights standards. Thus the Senate has Standing Committees on both Scrutiny of Bills and Regulations and Ordinances with responsibilities for examining all proposed and delegated legislation by reference to criteria that include 'undue trespass on personal rights and liberties'. There is a link here with the Australian penchant for bicameralism, in the sense that such committees are more likely to be effective where, as in the case of the Commonwealth Parliament, they are drawn from and report to a House in which the government typically lacks a majority.

Even so, the results are patchy from the standpoint of rights. In practice the Senate committees take a relatively narrow range of rights into account for the purposes of this term of reference.[17] And consensus within the committees is achieved at cost to the depth of their inqui-

---

[15] *Davis v Commonwealth* (1988) 166 CLR 79 is an example.

[16] S Evans and C Evans, 'Australian Parliaments and the Protection of Human Rights' *Senate Occasional Lecture Series 2006–2007*.

[17] In its report covering the parliamentary term 2004-2007, for example, the 'rights and liberties' to which the Committee had regard were retrospectivity, the privilege against self-incrimination, reversal of the onus of proof, strict liability, search and seizure, legal professional privilege, privative clauses, jury trial and voting rights: Senate Standing Committee on the Scrutiny of Bills, *The Work of the Committee during the 41st Parliament* 2008.

ries. The Regulations and Ordinances Committee draws a distinction between 'technical legislative scrutiny' and 'policy merits', steering clear of the latter in order to focus on 'non-partisan principles of personal rights'.[18] Reports of the Scrutiny of Bills Committee are cast at a level of generality that the Evans' research suggest may be a function of both the limited time available to the committee and the difficulty of reaching an agreed view. Adverse reports from a committee are not necessarily considered by the Senate in any event. Preliminary research results covering the three year period 2001–2003 suggested that approximately 10–15 per cent of laws enacted by the Commonwealth Parliament each year burdened rights recognised in the International Covenant on Civil and Political Rights alone and that between one half and one third of these escaped any form of attention during the parliamentary process.[19]

In 2008 the Commonwealth Government appointed a committee to conduct an Australia-wide 'consultation' on how Australia might better protect and promote human rights, short of constitutional entrenchment. As described in the final part of this chapter, a cautious report from the committee received an even more cautious response from the government. If implemented, the proposed new *Human Rights Framework* nevertheless would enhance parliamentary scrutiny of new legislation by reference to international human rights standards and to that extent would affect the overview given in this section.

ii. Protection and Fulfilment of Rights

Rights protection involves more than restraining the infringement of rights by state institutions. Positive action also may be needed, to identify new rights, to protect rights holders against third parties, to provide effective mechanisms for the realisation of rights and, in some cases, to ensure the fulfilment of rights. These broader dimensions of rights protection apply to all categories of rights, but are critical for social, economic, environmental and, often, cultural rights. They are peculiarly suited to action by the elected branches of government. All Australian Parliaments are active in rights protection in these ways, although they may not always conceive their actions in these terms.

[18] Senate Standing Committee on Regulations and Ordinances, *Introduction* http://www.aph.gov.au/Senate/committee/regord_ctte/cominfo.htm (viewed 6 August 2010).
[19] Evans and Evans, n 16, 26–28.

Three points should be made, to convey an impression of this aspect of the Australian constitutional system.

The first is that there is legislation of all Australian Parliaments recognising and giving effect to particular rights, some of which are new or emerging rights. The rationale for this deserves some attention. Under constitutional arrangements in which the starting point is assumed to be that citizens have liberty to the extent that it is not limited by law the enumeration of rights is problematic. Over time, however, litigation over this core principle has given rise to a body of rights that are recognised by the common law. In the absence of constitutional or legislative rights protection and in circumstances in which international human rights commitments do not have direct domestic effect common law rights constitute the sole source of rights. But the rights thus developed are necessarily incomplete, in consequence both of the historic values of the common law and of the limitations of the judicial process for this purpose.

Specific, statutory rights regimes fill some of these gaps. Amongst several examples that might be given, the most striking is the body of anti-discrimination legislation. Protection against discrimination has been described as '[o]ne of the great deficiencies' of the common law.[20] Anti-discrimination legislation began to be put in place in the 1960s, marking a change in attitude towards the diversity of the Australian community, manifested also in the removal of discriminatory references to Indigenous Australians from the Constitution and the abandonment of the White Australia policy. All jurisdictions now have anti-discrimination or equal opportunity laws prohibiting discrimination on a range of grounds, including race, sex, sexual orientation, religion, disability and age. While there are other specific statutory rights regimes, of which information privacy is an example, the legislative focus on discrimination is testimony to a particular deficiency in rights protection under earlier law.[21]

The second point relates to the scheme of specific legislative rights regimes. Typically, they have horizontal as well as vertical effect, protecting the right in issue against private as well as public action. Typically also, they provide elaborate mechanisms for investigation, public education and the handling of complaints about infringement in a way that is relatively accessible. Again, anti-discrimination law provides an instruc-

---

[20] N Rees, Katherine Lindsay, Simon Rice, *Australian Anti-Discrimination Law: Text, Cases and Materials* (Annandale, NSW, Federation Press, 2008) 1.

[21] On privacy more generally see Australian Law Reform Commission *For Your Information: Australian Privacy Law and Practice* (ALRC 108, 2008).

tive example. All Australian jurisdictions have an Anti-Discrimination Commission or its equivalent, which in the Commonwealth sphere is the Human Rights Commission. Most States also have an Anti-Discrimination Tribunal or its equivalent, for the resolution of disputes when conciliation fails. Disputes under Commonwealth legislation can finally be resolved only by a court, as a consequence of the constitutional separation of powers.

A final point of a different kind concerns extraterritorial rights protection. In the absence of a general constitutional or even legislative bill of rights, questions about the extraterritorial application of legally enforceable rights to either protect or restrain Australian citizens are less likely to arise in Australia.[22] On the other hand, questions about the obligations owed by the executive government to Australian citizens abroad are beginning to come before courts, as actions in administrative law or tort. In *Hicks v Ruddock*[23] the Federal Court refused an application by the Commonwealth to summarily dismiss a challenge by an Australian held at Guantanamo Bay to the lawfulness of the government's decision not to request his return to Australia. The court refused to accept that the action had 'no reasonable prospect of success' so as to justify dismissal. In the event, however, Hicks was returned to Australia before the litigation could proceed further. More recently, in early 2010, a Full Court of the Federal Court refused to dismiss actions in tort against the Commonwealth by another Australian who had been held overseas and who alleged that Commonwealth officers had aided and abetted his torture and inhuman treatment contrary, inter alia, to the Crimes (Torture) Act 1988.[24] Those proceedings are still underway.

B. Courts and the Common Law

Explanations of why Australia does not have a bill of rights generally point not only to parliamentary responsible government but also to the role of independent courts administering the common law. There are echoes here of Dicey's reconciliation of parliamentary sovereignty with

---

[22] Some of the developments elsewhere are canvassed in GL Neuman, 'The Extraterritorial Constitution after *Boumediene v Bush*' (2009) 82 *Southern California Law Review* 250; see also *Al-Skeini v Secretary of State for Defence* [2008] AC 153.

[23] (2007) 156 FCR 574.

[24] *Habib v Commonwealth of Australia* (2010) 183 FCR 62.

the rule of law. In any event, it is clear that references to the common law in this context include not only the application and, perhaps, further development of substantive common law principles but also the interpretation of legislation in accordance with rebuttable presumptions that had their origins in the common law.

Not all common law entitlements are recognised as rights, at least for the purposes of statutory interpretation. With statute now the most pervasive source of law it would be inappropriate for legislation to be interpreted in a way that privileges all previously existing common law doctrines, even where these can be expounded in terms of rights. 'Ordinary' common law rights are now distinguished from those 'fundamental rights, freedoms and immunities' that, typically, have a long historical pedigree in the common law.[25] With a degree of circularity, the status of a right that is 'fundamental' in this sense can often be confirmed by reference to cases that acknowledge a presumption that Parliament does not intend to override it. For obvious reasons there is no definitive list of these fundamental common law rights and freedoms although there are some influential and useful compilations, which collectively identify personal liberty, freedom of speech and movement, a fair trial, the presumption of innocence, the privilege against self-incrimination; freedom from arbitrary search and seizure, access to courts, legal professional privilege, procedural fairness, and property rights.[26]

The common law provides protection for rights that have been recognised by courts, even in the absence of statute. Under a common law understanding of executive power, even 'ordinary' common law rights generally cannot be abrogated by executive action. And the responsibility for giving effect to some rights falls on the courts themselves, in the course of adjudication. In one high profile case, for example, the High Court was urged to hold that a trial had miscarried because the accused was unrepresented in breach of his common law right to counsel.[27] While the court rejected the existence of a right in such 'absolute' terms, it accepted that an accused had a right to a fair trial or, more accurately, a right not to be tried unfairly. In the case of a trial for a serious offence,

---

[25] The distinction is drawn by McHugh J in *Gifford v Strang Stevedoring Pty Ltd* (2003) 214 CLR 269, in the context of a claimed 'right' to bring an action for psychiatric injury.

[26] JJ Spigelman, 'The Common Law Bill of Rights', 2008 McPherson Lectures 1, March 2008; *Malika Holdings Pty Ltd v Stretton* (2001) 204 CLR 290, 298; *Wentworth v New South Wales Bar Association* (1992) 176 CLR 239, 252–53.

[27] *Dietrich v R* (1992) 177 CLR 292.

this right would be likely to be breached by lack of legal representation, causing a conviction to be quashed by an appellate court if proceedings were not adjourned by the trial judge.

While the ambit of common law rights continues to be embellished through judicial decisions, the common law is an unlikely vehicle for the recognition of new substantive rights or rights that historically were not recognised in some form. Thus in *Dietrich,* in refusing to hold that the common law recognised a right to legal representation, the High Court rejected an argument that it should develop such a right by reference to international human rights instruments to which Australia is a party, at least where the position at common law is tolerably clear. Similarly, Australian courts have been cautious in responding to claims that there is a common law right to privacy or a cause of action for invasion of privacy, although the latter at least remains arguable, by analogy with existing causes of action.[28]

Fundamental rights derived from the common law have particular impact in the context of statutory interpretation. Either Commonwealth or State legislation can override common law rights. In the case of fundamental rights they must do so clearly, however, in a manner that, in Lord Hoffman's words, requires Parliament to 'squarely confront what it is doing and accept the political cost'.[29] What is now known as the 'principle of legality' is rationalised by reference to the presumed intention of Parliament and has been recognised in Australian law for more than 100 years.[30] In the current age of rights, however, it has been invoked relatively frequently and formulated in terms that raise the bar high, requiring an 'unmistakeable and unambiguous' statement by the Parliament that it has 'directed its attention to the rights and freedoms in question and has consciously decided upon abrogation or curtailment'.[31]

In the final analysis, however, this is only a rule of statutory interpretation. The presumption can be rebutted by a sufficiently determined Parliament and Australian experience suggests that the political cost of doing so will not necessarily be great. Thus in *Al-Kateb v Godwin* a

---

[28] *ABC v Lenah Game Meats* (2001) 208 CLR 199; see also the analysis of subsequent developments in *Giller v Procopets* [2008] VSCA 236.

[29] *R v Secretary of State for the Home Department; Ex parte Simms* [2000] 2 AC 115, 131.

[30] *Potter v Minahan* (1908) 7 CLR 277.

[31] *Plaintiff S157/2002 v Commonwealth* (2003) 211 CLR 476, 492, Gleeson CJ; cf French CJ in *International Finance Trust Company Ltd v New South Wales Crime Commission* (2009) 240 CLR 319, 349, warning against placing a 'counterintuitive judicial gloss' on the meaning of statutes.

majority of the High Court held that a prohibition in the migration legislation against releasing an unlawful non-citizen from detention 'otherwise than for removal or deportation' overrode the right to liberty, even
in the case of a person for whom removal was not feasible and who thus
faced indefinite administrative detention.[32] In dissent, Gleeson CJ held
that the legislation did not sufficiently directly contemplate the possibility of permanent incarceration to satisfy the principle of legality. For the
majority, by contrast, the legislation was unambiguous however 'tragic'
the case: the limits had been reached of what could be done 'under the
guise of interpretation' by a court constrained by its (own) understanding of the consequences of the separation of judicial power.[33]

C. International Human Rights

International law forms no part of the official explanation for why
Australia lacks a bill of rights. International human rights law nevertheless plays a subtle if complex role in Australian rights protection which,
although limited, may be growing. The purpose of this section is to
identify more specifically the ways in which this occurs.

It has already been noted that Australia is a party to most international human rights treaties. This fact alone has constitutional significance, because it triggers the exercise of the Commonwealth's external
affairs power (s.51 (xxix)). After an early skirmish over the validity of
the Racial Discrimination Act 1975 (Cth), the High Court accepted that
a law to implement Australia's international human rights commitments
is a law with respect to external affairs.[34] This is the power on which the
Commonwealth has relied to enact most of its anti-discrimination laws
and to override State legislation that is inconsistent with international
human rights standards. It is the power on which the Commonwealth
would rely if it were to enact national human rights legislation. It follows, further, that Commonwealth human rights legislation must adhere

---

[32] *Al-Kateb v Godwin* (2004) 219 CLR 562.

[33] In an additional insight into the dynamics of human rights protection in
Australia, following the controversy aroused by this decision, Al-Kateb was granted
a visa and a new category of visa was created to deal with persons in his position:
S Evans, 'Australia: Mandatory Administrative Detention' (2006) 4 *International
Journal of Constitutional Law* 517.

[34] *Koowarta v Bjelke-Petersen* (1982) 153 CLR 168; *Victoria v Commonwealth* (1996)
187 CLR 416.

reasonably closely to the terms of the international instrument that it purports to implement, although partial implementation is possible.

The mere existence of these international obligations also has significance in other ways. The possibility that proposed legislation might conflict with an international commitment requires some attention to be paid to the latter during the policy-making phase.[35] Participation in international human rights arrangements typically carries with it an obligation to make regular reports on progress to an international monitoring body, which inevitably is preceded by a process of internal review and some self-reflection. Optional protocols place pressure on States to enable their citizens to take allegations about infringement of rights to international bodies once domestic avenues have been exhausted and Australia has acceded to several of these. Adverse Views require response, preceded by more reflection, whether the conclusions of the international body are accepted or not.

While only some of Australia's international human rights commitments have been incorporated into Australian law, international law has indirect legal effect in several ways. It may assist in the development of a principle of common law, as *Mabo No 2* famously showed. It can be taken into account in interpreting ambiguous legislation. And there is Australian authority, which has been adopted elsewhere, that an unincorporated treaty commitment can give rise to a legitimate expectation that a decision-maker will act in accordance with the treaty, attracting an obligation to accord procedural fairness.[36]

None of these possibilities should be overstated, however. Australian courts act with 'due circumspection' in developing the common law by reference to international treaties, to avoid offering a 'backdoor means' of treaty incorporation.[37] The notion that an unincorporated treaty gives rise to a legitimate expectation of compliance was immediately repudiated by the Commonwealth government and more recently has been doubted by Justices of the High Court itself.[38] Even the precise circumstances in which a treaty can be used for statutory interpretation are unclear. In *Teoh*

---

[35] Department of the Prime Minister and Cabinet, *Legislation Handbook* (2000) 32.

[36] *Minister of State for Immigration and Ethnic Affairs v Teoh* (1995) 183 CLR 273; see generally M Aronson, B Dyer and M Groves, *Judicial Review of Administrative Action*, 4th edn (Sydney, NSW, Thomson Reuters, 2009) 443.

[37] *Minister of State for Immigration and Ethnic Affairs v Teoh* (1995) 183 CLR 273, 288.

[38] Aronson, Dyer and Groves, n 36, 438–42; *Re Minister for Immigration and Multicultural and Indigenous Affairs; Ex parte Lam* (2003) 214 CLR 1, esp. 32–34.

Mason CJ and Deane J cautiously endorsed a 'canon of construction' that favoured interpretation of statutes so as to conform with international legal obligations 'as far as the language of the legislation permits' as long, at least, as the legislation post-dates ratification of the relevant treaty.[39] Compare, however, the more sober formulation by Gleeson CJ, a mere eight years later: 'where legislation has been enacted pursuant to, or in contemplation of, the assumption of international obligations under a treaty or international convention, in cases of ambiguity a court should favour a construction which accords with Australia's obligations'.[40] Points of potential difference include the extent of the 'ambiguity' that might trigger recourse to international law and the relationship between the statute and the treaty. The underlying logic of this latter approach may help to explain the refusal of the High Court to take international law into account for the purposes of constitutional interpretation, as discussed in chapter three.

D. Assessment

It is difficult to assess the success of an approach to rights protection that is as multifaceted as that of Australia and so interdependent with its distinctive national circumstances. On the other hand, at a time when there is debate in all constitutional systems about the appropriate role of the judicial branch in determining questions that engage deeply contested values there is likely to be some curiosity about how well the Australian approach works. What follows therefore is intended to identify some principal lines of inquiry.

The most obvious criterion for evaluating the effect of any approach to rights protection is outcomes, measured in terms of compliance with generally accepted rights standards. But there are other possible criteria as well. One might focus on the extent to which the gap left by more limited judicial review is filled by public deliberation on important rights issues, which is claimed as the principal alternative to judicial determination of rights questions. Another might measure success by reference to public understanding of rights issues on which, in the end, all approaches depend in a democratic system but on which political mechanisms are more immediately reliant.

---

[39] *Teoh*, n 36 at 287.
[40] *Plaintiff S157/2002 v Commonwealth* (2003) 211 CLR 476, 492.

In terms of outcomes, the Australian approach rates relatively well. Global surveys regularly place Australia high on the list of rights-respecting countries.[41] But there are areas of significant weakness as well, to which international bodies continue to draw attention: a readiness to waive equality standards where Indigenous Australians are concerned; intrusive anti-terrorism laws; immigration detention; disproportionate law enforcement mechanisms. A similar picture emerges if attention is focused on what Waldron has described as 'watershed' rights issues: major choices that societies must make, raising questions of 'value and principle'.[42] Australia has achieved broadly consensual outcomes within accepted human rights standards on many of the issues that Waldron identifies as 'watershed' for the United States: the death penalty, abortion, religious toleration, electoral rules, and gender equality. Like many other liberal democracies it appears to be working its way towards equality on grounds of sexual orientation as well. But outcomes on other issues of international concern are far less satisfactory. These include cultural rights, including discrimination on grounds of ethnicity and aspects of law and order.

The scorecard on public deliberation is complex. Few highly contested rights issues in Australia are finally determined by courts. Instead, they are resolved through the political process and may be revisited from time to time without constitutional difficulty. For the most part resolution occurs without significant public deliberation, at least in the forum of the Parliaments, on which the justification for these arrangements relies. Whatever deliberation goes on within the executive branch rarely reaches the public sphere and it is unclear how, if at all, rights are weighed in the balance. There are other mechanisms that offer greater deliberative potential: the work of Human Rights Commissions; media investigations; and activities within civil society. If a problem is serious enough, the interaction of these institutions and other institutions may, although will not necessarily, create a synergy that leads to change. These opportunities are not negligible, but nor are they reliable. The claim for public deliberation can be put no higher than this.

Finally, as a generalisation, the Australian approach is not conducive to public understanding of the range of rights and how and why

[41] For example, Freedom House Annual Global Survey of Political Rights and Civil Liberties, 2008: www.freedomhouse.org/template.cfm?page=410&year=2008.

[42] J Waldron, 'Judges as moral reasoners' (2009) 7 *International Journal of Constitutional Law* 2, 22–23.

they deserve respect. Australian arrangements for rights protection are extraordinarily complex and opaque, even for the specialist. In the absence of a domestic rights instrument, moreover, it is almost impossible to assist public understanding of rights issues in a way that offers both breadth and depth. It may be that Australians have a certain innate understanding of rights issues. Ironically, however, it is likely to be the product as much of a derivative knowledge of the constitutional arrangements of others as of Australian history or the course of Australian public debate.

III. CONSTITUTIONAL RIGHTS

A. Relevance of the Constitution

Despite the extent of its reliance on democratic institutions for rights protection, Australia is not a classic example of political constitutionalism. The entrenched Australian Constitution, enforced through judicial review, provides some protection for some rights, both expressly and by implication. The story of the latter has been told in earlier chapters and need be recapped only briefly here. The remainder of this part deals with the few, principal examples of express rights: the requirement in section 51(xxxi) for property to be acquired on 'just terms'; the provision for trial by jury in section 80; and the protection for aspects of freedom of religion in section 116. One other contender for inclusion in this category is the prohibition in section 117 against discrimination on grounds of State residence, which plays a role in federal union and was examined earlier in that context.

In a series of decisions in the 1990s, although with roots that can be traced to earlier jurisprudence, the High Court accepted that principles that are broadly in the nature of rights and freedoms could be derived from the constitutional provisions establishing and empowering the Commonwealth Parliament and government and the federal courts. In this sense, these principles are by-products of the institutional arrangements that give effect to representative democracy, responsible government and separation of powers. Those presently identified with a reasonable degree of clarity protect freedom of political communication, prohibit arbitrary deprivation of voting rights, preclude the gross distortion of electoral boundaries, constitutionalise core aspects of the concept of a fair trial and prevent the arbitrary detention of Australian citizens. The list is unlikely to be closed.

This development was controversial, partly because constitutional rights protection is a novelty in Australian jurisprudence and partly because of the extent of the discretion apparently thus conferred on the courts. As the doctrines have evolved, however, it is apparent that these are rights with a difference, which provide only a minimum constitutionally guaranteed default position, subject to which the elected institutions retain very considerable latitude in the exercise of their powers. The Court prefers not to characterise them as rights at all, equating them instead with limits on power, as the more familiar dynamic under the Constitution.

The so-called express rights that are examined below share some of these characteristics. All are incidental to the main purposes of the Constitution. All can be portrayed as limits on power, rather than rights. All apply only to the Commonwealth.[43] It will be recalled that the prohibition against discrimination on the grounds of State residence is an exception, both because it is framed in terms of a right and because it applies to the States. Like the other express rights, however with the exception, this time, of the property right, it was subjected to a literal and restrictive interpretation until the last decade of the twentieth century. While the Court has taken a somewhat more purpose-oriented approach to these provisions since that time, their impact remains relatively confined.

B. Acquisition of Property

i. *A Power as a Right*

Section 51(xxxi) empowers the Commonwealth Parliament to make laws with respect to 'the acquisition of property on just terms from any State or person for any purpose in respect of which the Parliament has power to make laws'. It appears in the list of the concurrent legislative powers of the Parliament, to which it was added to ensure that the Commonwealth

---

[43] Earlier interpretation of these provisions as restricting the Commonwealth only when operating in the States and not in the territories is gradually being eroded: in relation to the acquisition of property, see *Wurridjal v Commonwealth* (2009) 237 CLR 309.

had powers of compulsory acquisition.[44] The clause thus has a double function as legislative power and constitutional guarantee. It has become the most far-reaching of all the express rights provisions, claimed as a 'great constitutional safeguard' demanding a 'generous interpretation'.[45]

All the critical words in section 51(xxxi) have proved ambiguous, individually and collectively. The 'property' to which section 51 (xxxi) applies extends well beyond traditional conceptions to 'every species of valuable right and interest' including, for example, a chose in action, confidential information and, although not without controversy, money.[46] An 'acquisition' requires more than an extinguishment of property rights; something, although not necessarily the same thing, must be acquired by the Commonwealth or by somebody else under Commonwealth law. Exactly what just terms require depends on the circumstances. Commonwealth legislation that may be construed to acquire property within the meaning of section51(xxxi) typically makes provision for 'reasonable compensation' under procedures that, if all else fails, involve determination by a court.

The dual character of section51(xxxi) as both a power and a right has had some noteworthy consequences. One concerns its relationship with the other heads of power. The normal rule, following *Engineers*, is that the section 51 powers are interpreted so as not to limit each other. Applied to section 51(xxxi), however, this would enable the guarantee to be easily avoided. Section 51(xxxi) consequently has become the most prominent of several exceptions to the rule, limiting the capacity of the Commonwealth to rely on other powers to acquire property. On the other hand, the characterisation techniques used by the Court to apply the heads of power has proved useful for preventing the guarantee from becoming overbroad. It applies only to laws that can be characterised as laws 'with respect to the acquisition of property other than on just terms'. It thus has no application to the exercise of powers to which the notion of 'just terms' is 'irrelevant or incongruous', of which taxation,

---

[44] J Quick and RR Garran, *Annotated Constitution of the Australian Commonwealth* (Sydney, NSW, Angus and Robertson, 1901) 640.

[45] The quotations are from *Trade Practices Commission v Tooth* (1979) 142 CLR 397, 403, and *Street v Queensland Bar Association* (1989) 168 CLR 461, 527. The authorities to this effect are collected in *ICM Agriculture Pty Ltd v Commonwealth* (2009) 240 CR 140, 212–13.

[46] The quotation is from *Minister of State for Army v Dalziel* (1944) 68 CLR 261, 290; see generally L Zines, *The High Court and the Constitution* 5th edn (Annandale, NSW: Federation Press, 2008) 579.

bankruptcy and the forfeiture of goods under customs procedures are examples.[47] A similar analysis can be used to explain decisions in which it has been held that modification of a statutory right that on one view represents 'property' does not attract the requirement for just terms pursuant to a power to make laws for the 'acquisition of property'.[48]

ii. Acquisition of Property under State Law

Self-evidently, section 51(xxxi) applies only to Commonwealth law. In practice, each State also has laws requiring compensation for the compulsory acquisition of property. But these requirements have the status only of ordinary legislation and can be overridden for particular purposes.

Intergovernmental schemes sometimes seek to take advantage of the fact that, while the Commonwealth is constitutionally obliged to provide just terms for the acquisition of property, the States are not. Cases dealing with challenges to arrangements made pursuant to the National Water Initiative 2004 suggest that this possibility is now severely restricted, if indeed it exists at all.[49] These cases in fact were decided on the basis that the substitution of a new form of license to draw groundwater under State legislation was not an acquisition of property within the meaning of section 51(xxxi). In dicta, however, a majority of the Court made it clear that the Commonwealth cannot make a grant to the States on conditions requiring the acquisition of property without just terms. Whether a grant would similarly be vitiated if the condition were merely implicit was not decided.

iii. Acquisition of Indigenous Property

Section 51(xxxi) combines with other provisions of the Constitution to provide a measure of protection for indigenous interests in land. Logically, one result of the decision in *Mabo (No.2)* that in some circumstances the common law of Australia would recognise native title was that native title interests could not be acquired under Commonwealth legislation without meeting the constitutional requirement for just terms. While

---

[47] *Mutual Pools & Staff Pty Ltd v Commonwealth* (1994) 179 CLR 155, 220.

[48] *Wurridjal v Commonwealth* (2009) 237 CLR 309, 360–61; cf *ICM Agriculture v Commonwealth* (2009) 240 CLR 140, 222–233.

[49] *ICM Agriculture Pty Ltd v Commonwealth* (2009) 240 CLR 140; *Arnold v Minister Administering the Water Management Act 2000* (2010) 240 CLR 242.

section 51(xxxi) does not apply to the States, the Racial Discrimination Act 1975 (Cth) overrode State legislation that purported to deal with the property interests of Indigenous Australians in a discriminatory way. But following negotiations between the government and indigenous leaders over how best to manage the decision in *Mabo,* the Native Title Act 1993 'wound back' the Racial Discrimination Act to allow the controlled validation of earlier discriminatory acts that had extinguished native title. In so doing it set a precedent that has been followed on other occasions for a range of less consensual purposes.[50]

Since *Mabo* was decided, moreover, more questions have arisen about the application of section 51 (xxxi) to the extinguishment of indigenous interests in land. The problem stems from the distinctiveness of the concept of native title coupled with ambivalence in the jurisprudence of the Court over the application of section 51 (xxxi) to interests derived from statute and, by extension, to interests that are 'inherently suscepti-ble of variation' and might be argued to include native title.[51] The better view is that the extinguishment of native title interests is an acquisition of property that attracts the just terms requirement.[52] Nevertheless the issue appears to remain open. In *Wurridjal* the majority accepted that the statutory lease in favour of the Commonwealth over what was effectively a fee simple interest in land held by the Aboriginal Land Trust under specific land rights legislation amounted to an acquisition of property, requiring the payment of just terms. In doing so, however, two members of the Court, with two others apparently agreeing, emphasised that the statutory fee simple in issue in this case was not 'so unstable or defeasible ... to deny any operation of section 51(xxxi)', thereby suggesting, if only by implication, that in other cases this might not be so.[53]

---

[50]   L Strelein, *Compromised Jurisprudence: Native Title Cases Since Mabo* (Canberra, NSW, Aboriginal Studies Press, 2009).

[51]   The quotation is from *Health Insurance Commission v Peverill* (1994) 179 CLR 226, 237. The link with native title was made by Gummow J in *Newcrest Mining (WA) Ltd v Commonwealth* (1997) 190 CLR 513, 613; it was footnoted, perhaps with intent, by Heydon J in *ICM Agriculture P/L v Commonwealth* (2009) 240 CLR 140, 215.

[52]   S Brennan, 'Native title and the "Acquisition of Property" under the Australian Constitution' (2004) 28 *Melbourne University Law Review* 28.

[53]   *Wurridjal v Commonwealth* (2009) 237 CLR 309, 382, 420, 464.

C. Trial by Jury

i. *The Right that isn't*

The operative words of section 80 provide that 'The trial on indictment of any offence against any law of the Commonwealth shall be by jury'. The provision is clearly adapted from Article III section 2 of the Constitution of the United States. Consistently with the original design of the Constitution, it applies only to trials under Commonwealth law. And consistently with the focus of the Commonwealth Constitution on 'the structure and relationships of government rather than individual rights or freedoms' its function has been portrayed as systemic as well as protective of individual liberty.[54] In consequence, in *Brown,* a majority of the Court refused to allow an accused to decline trial by jury, on the ground that the procedure had a role to play in the system of criminal justice.

The weakness of section 80 is evident on its face: it is mandatory only in the event of a trial on indictment and there is no constitutional obligation for a trial to be initiated in this way. For much of the twentieth century, this deficiency caused the section to be treated as an essentially procedural provision that could be evaded by providing for an offence to be triable summarily.[55] Interest in the potential of section 80 revived in the latter decades of the century, as part of the more general resurgence of interest in rights. Individual Justices, both before and since, have occasionally suggested that the section should be interpreted to require trial by jury for serious offences, identified by Deane J in *Kingswell* as those punishable by imprisonment for one year or more.[56] For the moment, however, the orthodox view of the section is that the Parliament may choose whether an offence is to be tried on indictment or not.

Criminal law in Australia is primarily a State matter, although the range of federal crimes has broadened in recent years, to deal with terrorism, the distribution of drugs and people smuggling and to incorporate

---

[54] *Brown v R* (1986) 160 CLR 171, 208.

[55] Zines, n 46, 573. For the distinction between the two forms of trial see M Chesterman, 'Criminal Trial Juries in Australia: From Penal Colonies to a Federal Democracy' (1999) 62 *Law and Contemporary Problems* 69, 73–75.

[56] *Kingswell v R* (1985) 159 CLR 264, 298–302. See also *R v Federal Court of Bankruptcy; Ex parte Lowenstein* (1938) 59 CLR 556, 580; *Li Chia Hsing v Rankin* (1978) 141 CLR 182, 198.

international legal offences into Australian law.[57] There is no constitutional guarantee of jury trial under State law although, typically, State law requires trial by jury for serious criminal offences. Typically also, jury trials under Commonwealth law take place in the State court system, where court rooms provide the necessary infrastructure for jury trials to be held. In such cases, Commonwealth legislation generally picks up and applies the procedural law of the State in which the trial is held.[58]

ii. Changing Values

However imperfect the Australian guarantee of trial by jury, it provided the catalyst for judicial reflection on the impact of changing values on the institution of trial by jury and thus became the context for a landmark case on Australian constitutional interpretation.

In *Cheatle*, the defendant was tried for an offence against Commonwealth law in South Australia where legislation allowed majority verdicts.[59] He appealed against his conviction on the ground that the Constitution required a unanimous decision by a jury of twelve persons. The High Court upheld his claim: this was the understanding of trial by jury at the time the Constitution was framed and it was also consistent with principle. In response to argument by the Crown that the standards of 1901 also produced juries comprised solely of men who satisfied property qualifications the Court distinguished between the essential and inessential features of a jury. Unanimity was an essential feature, flowing from the representative and deliberative character of a jury. But the qualifications of jurors might vary over time, depending on community standards. On this basis, by the late twentieth century, the representative character of a jury demanded, rather than precluded, the involvement of women and the abandonment of property qualifications.

From one perspective, this was no more than an application of the Court's familiar distinction between the connotation and denotation of constitutional terms. On the other hand, as Zines has observed, this was 'perhaps . . . the first time' that changes in the denotation of a term responded to contemporary values rather than to developments of a more tangible kind.[60]

---

[57] Criminal Code Act 1995 (Cth).

[58] Judiciary Act 1903 (Cth) s 79.

[59] *Cheatle v R* (1993) 177 CLR 541.

[60] See Zines, n 46 above, 574; also referring to other, lesser, departures from unanimity that have since been allowed.

D. Freedom of Religion

i. *A Precaution Against Power*

Section 116 precludes the Commonwealth from making law to establish any religion; to impose any religious observance; to prohibit the
free exercise of religion; and to impose a religious test as a requirement
for public office. Like the other provisions considered in this part, it is
framed as a limitation on power. Like the other provisions also, it applies
only to the Commonwealth. Oddly, it is included in chapter V dealing
with the States, having replaced an earlier proposal to prevent the States
prohibiting the free exercise of religion, which was rejected. The application of such a provision to the Commonwealth was intended to deflect
the possibility that the inclusion of a reference to 'Almighty God' in the
preamble to the Constitution Act in some way conferred power on the
Commonwealth with respect to religion. According to Henry Bournes
Higgins, its principal proponent, 'the power to deal with religion in every
shape and form should be clearly denied to the Federal Parliament'. The
States, on the other hand, were left with 'free and unfettered exercise of
their power over religion'.[61] Understood in this way, as Dawson J once
noted, section 116 is a federalism provision, which deals with the division
of powers between the Commonwealth and the States.[62] Nevertheless, in
its terms, it bears an obvious resemblance to Article VI section 3 and the
first amendment to the Constitution of the United States.

ii. *Religion and the State*

But there the resemblance ends. There are very few cases dealing with
the application of section 116. The foundation cases are still war-time
cases in which claims based on freedom of religion are given short shrift.
In 1943, for example, the proscription of a Jehovah's Witness group on
grounds that it promulgated views that were prejudicial to the war effort
was held not to contravene the guarantee of 'free exercise of religion',
which allowed for limitations described by one Justice as 'reasonably
necessary for the protection of the community and in the interests of
the social order'. The observation of Rich J in the same case remains

[61] Quick and Garran, n 44, 952–53.
[62] *Kruger v Commonwealth* (1997) 190 CLR 1.

broadly correct: the section is 'wide in the area of religious faith that it seeks to protect' but 'narrow in its description of the kinds of laws which it disallows'.[63] It may well be, as Zines has suggested, that the Court would adopt a more nuanced proportionality analysis to determine whether a law infringes the 'free exercise' requirement, should the issue arise again.[64] The fact that this has not happened, over a period of more than half a century, points to the relatively uncontroversial character of religion in Australian public life.

One religious issue that historically has been contentious in Australia is government funding for schools run by religious groups. Even here, however, section 116 has played virtually no role. Education is a State responsibility and the States are not subject to section 116 or to any comparable constitutional constraint on their power. A guarantee of 'religious freedom' in section 46 of the Constitution of Tasmania is not an exception for this purpose, as the provision is not entrenched and has no greater status than ordinary law. The Commonwealth in fact provides considerable funds for private schools, including those run by religious organisations, in the form of conditional grants to the States. On the one occasion on which a challenge to this practice was mounted, however, in 1981, it failed.[65] The Court accepted that, in some circumstances, a Commonwealth law granting funds to the States on condition might offend a constitutional guarantee, including section 116. But a law that provided grants to States for private schools, including religious schools, was not a 'law for establishing' a religion within the meaning of a section that, in this respect, was interpreted as purposive. There is no reason to suspect that the outcome would be any different were another such challenge to be mounted now.

---

[63] *Adelaide Company of Jehovah's Witnesses Inc v Commonwealth* (1943) 67 CLR 116, 155, Starke J; 148, Rich J. In a different context, although with implications for s 116, the Court has accepted that scientology is a religion: *Church of the New Faith v Commissioner for Pay-Roll Tax (Vic)* (1983) 154 CLR 120.

[64] Zines, n 46, 571.

[65] *Attorney-General (Vic); Ex rel. Black v Commonwealth* (1981) 146 CLR 559.

IV. RIGHTS INSTRUMENTS

A. Past

Various attempts have been made to provide more general positive rights protection at the national level in Australia, with either constitutional or legislative status. Some took place during the drafting of the Constitution. Others occurred at intervals following World War II, reflecting developments in the international sphere and in countries elsewhere.

It is commonly said that Australians rejected the idea of a constitutional bill of rights at the time when the Constitution was made. In fact, the framers of the Constitution did not specifically consider a constitutional bill of rights: an omission that may itself be telling, given their familiarity with the Constitution of the United States. As earlier chapters have noted, debate occurred over a more limited rights proposal that subsequently became section 117. In its broadest form, this would have recognised a status of Australian citizen to which 'privileges and immunities' attached, which could not be 'abridged' by any State and prohibited action by a State to 'deprive any person of life, liberty or property without due process of law, or deny to any person within its jurisdiction the equal protection of its laws'.[66] The proposal was opposed on a variety of grounds, of which faith in democratic institutions was only one. Others included its implications for federalism; the incongruity of recognising a status of citizenship under a constitutional monarchy; and, shockingly by modern standards, the undesirability of including a provision in the Constitution which might preclude discrimination on the grounds of race. The truncated form in which the section ultimately was included in the Constitution prohibits discrimination on the grounds of State residence between 'subjects of the Queen', with consequences that are explained in chapter seven.

All subsequent attempts to implement rights instruments at the national level so far have also failed. In 1944 a proposal to amend the Constitution to protect freedom of expression and to extend the guarantees of religious freedom in section 116 to the States for a period of five years as part of a post-war reconstruction program was rejected at referendum. In 1973 a bill to implement the International Covenant on Civil and Political Rights in a form that could affect both Commonwealth

[66] Official Record of the Debates of the Australasian Federal Convention, Melbourne, 8 February 1898, 667–91.

and State action lapsed in Parliament. In 1985 another proposal for a legislative bill of rights, with application only in the Commonwealth sphere, also failed in the Parliament. In 1988, proposals to amend the Constitution to extend the few express constitutional rights to the States and to require jury trial for all offences punishable by imprisonment for two or more years was rejected at referendum.[67]

In each case, the failure of the proposal depended in part on political circumstances peculiar to it. Collectively, however, the causes lie in a cocktail of concerns grounded in federalism, parliamentary sovereignty, the implications of rights protection for public policy, and the perceived consequences of expanding the authority of courts. As the response of the Commonwealth government to the report on the National Consultation on Rights demonstrates, moreover, what Hilary Charlesworth has described as Australia's 'reluctance about rights' persists.[68] The substance of this response is considered in greater detail below, in the context of the future of rights protection in Australia.

B. Present

i. *Bottom-up Rights Protection*

The introduction of legislative bills of rights by New Zealand and the United Kingdom in the 1990s demonstrated that more effective rights protection could be secured through what gradually became characterised as 'dialogue' between the branches of government without impairing the legal authority of Parliaments to have the last word. The United Kingdom experience with the Human Rights Act 1998 attracted particular attention in Australia, leading to the enactment of legislative bills of rights in the Australian Capital Territory and Victoria, in both cases after extensive public consultation.[69] It may be that similar measures will be introduced in some other States as well.[70] For a while also, it seemed that

---

[67] For these and other initiatives see National Human Rights Consultation, *Report*, September 2009, ch.10.

[68] H Charlesworth, 'The Australian Reluctance About Rights' (1993) 31 *Osgoode Hall Law Journal* 195.

[69] Human Rights Act 2004 (ACT); Charter of Human Rights and Responsibilities Act 2006 (Vic).

[70] An overview of developments in the States and territories to September 2009 is provided in National Human Rights Consultation Report, n 2, ch.10.

the introduction of rights instruments from the bottom-up in this way might lead to national rights protection. That possibility has now been rejected, at least for the time being.

Both the ACT Human Rights Act and the Victorian Charter rely on a set of interconnected features drawn from the Human Rights Act 1998 (UK). First, there is a list of protected rights, which in the case of the Australian instruments are drawn largely from the International Covenant on Civil and Political Rights (ICCPR). Public authorities are obliged to act consistently with rights; courts are authorised to interpret statutes to be rights compliant if possible; where legislation cannot be interpreted in a manner that is consistent with protected rights, courts may make a declaration to that effect; a declaration does not invalidate legislation but is intended to place public pressure on governments and Parliaments to consider legislative change; proposed new legislation must be accompanied by a statement about its compatibility with rights to ensure that rights issues are considered during the legislative process and drawn to public attention; and parliamentary committees are charged with the responsibility of scrutinising proposed legislation by reference to the protected rights standards and reporting their conclusions to their respective legislatures. Both Australian instruments also authorise the imposition of such 'reasonable limits' on rights as can be 'demonstrably justified in a free and democratic society' by reference to a range of listed criteria drawing most obviously, for this purpose, on the South African Constitution.[71]

A legislative bill of rights is a deliberately weak form of rights protection. Rightly anticipating controversy, however, policy-makers in both Australian jurisdictions caused these instruments to be weakened further than their progenitors in New Zealand and the United Kingdom.[72] The title of the Victorian Charter refers to 'responsibilities' as well as rights.[73]

---

[71] Human Rights Act 2004 (ACT), s 28; Charter of Human Rights and Responsibilities Act 2006 (Vic) s 7; Constitution of the Republic of South Africa, s 36. See also, however, the limitations clauses in the Bill of Rights Act 1990 (NZ) s 5 and the Canadian Charter of Rights and Freedoms, s 1.

[72] For detailed analysis see CM Evans and SC Evans, *Australian Bills of Rights* (Chatswood, NSW, LexisNexis Butterworths, 2008).

[73] George Williams has noted that the idea originated in the public consultations where for 'many people, responsibilities were a more powerful way of addressing community problems than what they perceived to be more individualistic conceptions of human rights: 'The Victorian Charter of Human Rights and Responsibilities: Origin and Scope' (2006) 30 *Melbourne University Law Review* 880, 892.

Only natural persons are rights holders. Both Acts restrict the authority of courts to interpret legislation in a way that is compatible with human rights 'so far as it is possible to do so' by adding a requirement for the interpretation to be consistent with the 'purpose' of the legislation in issue. Both Acts provide a broad definition of 'public authority' but exclude courts, unless acting in an 'administrative capacity', thus precluding reliance on these instruments to develop the common law. The Victorian Charter provides no clear cause of action for infringement of rights by a public authority and no discrete remedy. If the Supreme Court concludes that legislation is incompatible with protected rights, the declaration that it may make is described as a declaration of 'inconsistent interpretation', which a Parliament may find it easier to ignore. The Victorian Charter also includes a procedure whereby the Parliament may override the Charter in relation to a provision of an Act, so that neither the interpretive mechanism nor the declaration of inconsistent interpretation can be used.

Both these instruments are still new and the case law applying them is correspondingly small. Nevertheless, it is already evident that their impact on the law of the jurisdictions in which they operate is not dramatic. There is a range of possible explanations. First, there are procedural impediments to the use of the instruments, particularly in Victoria, where notice must be given to the Attorney-General when a question arises in relation to application of the Charter in either the Supreme or County Court. Secondly, predictably enough, the governments in the jurisdictions concerned take a reasonably sanguine view of the scope of the Parliament's authority to limit rights, once they have decided that legislation is needed.[74] Thirdly, the courts have adopted a somewhat cautious approach in interpreting and applying the new provisions. Thus in *Momcilovic* the Court of Appeal of the Supreme Court of Victoria held that the interpretive provision in the Victorian Charter did not create a special rule of interpretation but merely gave statutory force to existing interpretive rules, including the 'powerful' common law presumption of legality.[75]

Nevertheless, these instruments are a significant development in the Australian context. They provide structured and public avenues for the

---

[74] In Victoria, a register of statements of compatibility can be found on the website of the State Human Rights Commission: www.humanrightscommission.vic.gov. au/Home.asp (viewed 2 October 2010).

[75] *R v Momcilovic* [2010] VSCA 50 [101]. An appeal in the High Court is pending.

evaluation of legislation and government action by reference to rights. The list of protected rights is clear and accessible, with potentially beneficial educative effects in the public sector as well as in the community at large. The mere existence of statutory rights obligations has led to review of existing laws and practices and presumably operates as an ongoing constraint at least to a degree. The exchange of views between Ministers and parliamentary committees about the impact of proposed legislation on rights is salutary if occasionally frustrating.[76] Little by little, judges in these jurisdictions are becoming accustomed to rights talk. And the rights instruments have enhanced the role of human rights commissions and galvanised human rights groups in civil society, equipping them with better instruments to monitor government action.[77] Given opposition to formal rights protection in Australia, moreover, it may be no bad thing that neither instrument has had revolutionary effect.

ii. Transplantation and its Perils

By way of a postscript, it may be noted that the introduction of legislative bills of rights in Australia offer an instructive case study of the challenges of transplanting the constitutional arrangements of one jurisdiction to another. The legislative bills of rights first developed in New Zealand and the United Kingdom were designed for unitary polities with uncontrolled constitutions. In Australia, they were introduced into a federation with a rigid constitutional framework, apparently with little anticipation of the difficulties that this might present. As time has gone on, however, it has become apparent that it is impossible to implement a dialogue model in Australia that produces the same effect as in states in which parliamentary sovereignty is more of a reality.

State Constitutions are less prescriptive and more readily changed than that of the Commonwealth. The constitutional framework therefore has been less of a problem at the State level than it might have been for the Commonwealth, had a proposal for a national legislative bill of rights gone ahead. Even so, however, questions can arise about

---

[76] C Carli MP, 'Scrutiny and the Charter of Rights and Responsibilities', a paper delivered to the Australia-New Zealand Scrutiny of Legislation Conference, July 2009, http://www.aph.gov.au/Senate/sl_conference/papers/carli.htm (viewed 21 April 2010).

[77] The activities of the Human Rights Law Resource Centre in Victoria is one, particularly impressive example: http://www.hrlrc.org.au/ (viewed 6 August 2010).

the impact of a State Constitution on instruments of this kind if, for example, State Constitutions are regarded as legislation to be interpreted consistently with the Charter.[78]

The Commonwealth Constitution also has some implications for the form and operation of State legislative rights instruments. The exclusion of courts from the definition of public authority under both the Human Rights Act (ACT) and the Victorian Charter is typically justified by reference to a perceived constitutional requirement to maintain a single Australian common law. Concerns have been raised about whether a 'declaration of inconsistent interpretation' is sufficiently concrete to constitute a 'matter' that can constitutionally be determined by the High Court on appeal from the Supreme Court of a State under section 73 of the Constitution.[79] These questions are likely to be resolved, one way or another, when the High Court hears the first appeal from a Declaration under the Victorian Charter. The requirement to comply with rights in the ACT and Victoria also has presented some minor difficulties for intergovernmental schemes, which have not been resolved in favour of rights compliance. Thus the Protocol on Drafting National Uniform Legislation notes the need for uniform legislative schemes that impinge on rights to make their intention to do so 'explicit' in order to avoid the operation of the interpretation procedures in the ACT and Victoria.[80]

A range of additional constitutional issues require consideration in the context of a proposal for a Commonwealth rights instrument. The one that attracted most attention during the National Consultation on Human Rights was whether a declaration of incompatibility by a federal court would satisfy the constitutional requirements for the separation of federal judicial power. In advice to the Committee, the Solicitor-General of the Commonwealth concluded that a declaration of incompatibility would be likely to be held to be an exercise of federal judicial power. The advice was hedged around with qualifications, however: the rights in issue should be 'capable of judicial determination' thus, potentially, excluding social and economic rights; the parties to the proceedings should be bound by the declaration, requiring joinder of the Attorney-

---

[78] An argument to this effect was available in *General Television Corp v Director of Public Prosecutions* (2008) 19 VR 68, 80, but not pursued.

[79] P Tate SC, 'Protecting Rights in a Federation' (2007) 33 *Monash University Law Review* 217, 233.

[80] Parliamentary Counsel's Committee, *Protocol on Drafting National Uniform Legislation*, 3rd edn (2008) 6.15.

General as a party; the declaration should be sought only in proceedings for other relief, so as to ensure the existence of a 'matter'.[81] The Committee duly recommended, cautiously, that a Commonwealth legislative bill of rights confer authority to make declarations, but only on the High Court. It added that if declarations could not 'fairly and practicably' be restricted to this Court there should be no provision for a formal declaration at all.[82]

Different but equally difficult questions arose from the federal division of power. It is clear that the external affairs power would support Commonwealth legislation to implement international human rights treaties to which Australia is a party. The Solicitor-General advised that the legislation could apply to both levels of government and would override inconsistent State legislation. But it was not clear that it should do so. A Commonwealth legislative bill of rights could invalidate inconsistent State legislation but could not reproduce a 'dialogue' model between State governments, Parliaments and courts. At the State level, therefore, it would replace parliamentary with judicial supremacy, partly defeating the purpose of the exercise. In the end, the Committee recommended that a Commonwealth bill should bind only federal public authorities. This has its difficulties as well, however, raising the prospect of arrangements for the protection of human rights in Australia that apply to both levels of government in some parts of the country but not in others and offering only patchy implementation of Australia's international human rights commitments.

C. Future

The Australian *Human Rights Framework* was announced by the Commonwealth Attorney-General in April 2010, as the government's response to the National Consultation on Rights. The government rejected the proposal for a Commonwealth legislative bill of rights. Instead, the framework comprises a range of lesser initiatives, most of which also were recommended in some form or another by the National Consultation, including the expansion of education about human rights, in the Commonwealth public sector as well as the community at large.

---

[81]   S Gageler SC and H Burmester QC, *In the Matter of Constitutional Issues Concerning a Charter of Rights,* in National Human Rights Consultation, *Report* 2009, Appendix E.
[82]   National Consultation Report n 2, ch.15.

Three proposals are particularly significant for present purposes because they represent an attempt to make good the Australian claim that rights are adequately protected through the parliamentary process. One is a commitment to enact legislation to establish a Parliamentary Joint Committee on Human Rights to scrutinise new and some existing legislation by reference to human rights obligations under the seven international human rights treaties to which Australia is a party. A second would introduce a statutory requirement for a statement of compatibility to accompany all new bills introduced into the Parliament and all subordinate instruments of a legislative character. A third intriguing but underdeveloped proposal would add the President of the Australian Human Rights Commission to the Commonwealth's advisory body on administrative law, the Administrative Review Council, suggesting that the government toyed with, but did not quite adopt, the National Consultation Committee's recommendation that human rights should be a 'relevant consideration' for executive decisions under Commonwealth law. Legislation to give effect to these commitments was introduced into the Parliament in 2010; they had not been enacted when the Parliament was dissolved, but have subsequently been reintroduced.

If these proposals proceed, it remains to be seen whether, and to what extent, they are effective. On the one hand, it is logical to enhance rights protection through the parliamentary process, as one of the principal pillars on which Australian rights protection relies. These proposals also offer an overt commitment to human rights protection, through more systemic and transparent arrangements, which represents a qualitative change from the past. On the other hand, the scheme is both highly ambitious and oddly restrictive. There are at least 126 substantive articles in the seven treaties proposed as rights standards, many of which contain multiple rights commitments. The number of bills and legislative instruments for which statements of compatibility are required, as a basis for parliamentary scrutiny, are very large: in 2009, for example, 248 bills were introduced into the Parliament and thousands of legislative instruments were registered. The inability of a scheme of this kind to assess the compliance of executive action with human rights standards also leaves a gap, rendered all the more significant by the extent of Commonwealth reliance on executive power, not least in the context of intergovernmental arrangements. In the circumstances it is inevitable that, whether the *Framework* is implemented or not, the design of a system for rights protection will remain a live issue.

SELECTED READING

Bailey, P, *The Human Rights Enterprise in Australia and Internationally* (Chatswood, NSW, LexisNexis Butterworths, 2009)

Byrnes, A, Charlesworth, H and McKinnon, G, *Bills of Rights in Australia: History, Politics and Law* (Sydney, NSW, UNSW Press, 2009)

Charlesworth, H, *Writing in Rights* (Sydney, NSW, UNSW Press, 2002)

——, 'Deep Anxieties: Australia and the International Legal Order' (2003) 25 *Sydney Law Review* 423

——, Ciam, M, Howell, D and Williams, G, Evans, C and Evans, S, *Australian Bills of Rights* (Chatswood, NSW, LexisNexis Butterworths, 2008)

National Human Rights Consultation, *Report* 2009

Tate, P, 'Protecting Rights in a Federation' (2007) 33 *Monash University Law Review* 217

Williams, G, *Human Rights under the Australian Constitution* (Melbourne, Vic, OUP, 1999)

Index